The Bauhaus in Calcutta

The Bauhaus in Calcutta: An Encounter of Cosmopolitan Avant-Gardes

Edited by Regina Bittner and Kathrin Rhomberg

Texts by Torsten Blume, Sria Chatterjee, Swati Chattopadhyay, Boris Friedewald, Kris Manjapra, Saloni Mathur, Kobena Mercer, Partha Mitter, and Christoph Wagner. Conversations with Tapati Guha-Thakurta and Sanjukta Sunderason and with R. Siva Kumar.

BAUHAUS EDITION

HATJE CANTZ

FUNDED BY

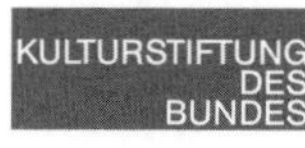

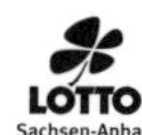

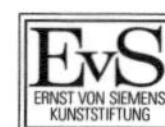

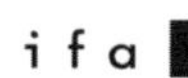

Institut für Auslandsbeziehungen e. V.

Table of Contents

ART HISTORY AFTER GLOBALIZATION

Philipp Oswalt

Foreword

The contemporary perception of the "Bauhaus myth" overlooks the fact that the historic Bauhaus was not a singular phenomenon, but a focal point of the widespread international avant-garde network of its day. Much of what has been attributed to the Bauhaus actually has origins and parallel developments elsewhere; nevertheless, the Bauhaus has also been highly influential. Critical to the success of the Bauhaus was its identity as a melting pot for diverse influences—a platform that brought together representatives of all kinds of backgrounds and directions. The historic Bauhaus network embraced, above all else, the centers of the European avant-garde—whether Moscow, Budapest, or Prague, Zagreb, Vienna, or Zurich, Rotterdam, Paris, or London—yet it also spread beyond Europe to New York and Tokyo, and of course to Calcutta.

In the heroic historiography of the Bauhaus, which often followed the self-stylization of the Bauhauslers themselves, these networks have yet to be sufficiently considered. The Bauhaus Dessau Foundation has therefore recently taken it upon itself to examine these correlations and interactions in exemplary projects. In addition to the exhibition *The Bauhaus in Calcutta,* these include the exhibition *Kibbutz and Bauhaus* (2011–12) and the planned projects on Hannes Meyer's time in the Soviet Union and Mexico, on VChUTEMAS in Moscow, and on the Bauhaus and Japan.

I am most grateful to the editors of this publication, Regina Bittner and Kathrin Rhomberg, and to the entire exhibition team for their committed and skilled development and realization of this exhibition project. Many thanks to the German Federal Cultural Foundation, Lotto-Toto Saxony-Anhalt, the Ernst von Siemens Kunststiftung, and the Institute for Foreign Cultural Relations (ifa), without whose generous support the realization of the project would not have been possible. We are grateful to the Indian partners, especially Professor Rajeev Lochan, Director of the National Gallery of Modern Art, New Delhi, to Reiner Haseloff, Minister President of Saxony-Anhalt, and to Sujatha Singh, Ambassador of India to Germany, for their patronage.

Rajeev Lochan

Introductory Remarks

The Bauhaus exhibition in Calcutta in 1922 marked a milestone in the history of modern art in India. This encounter between the Bauhaus artists—most of whom were already represented in avant-garde exhibitions and galleries internationally—and the modern painters of the Bengal School offers illuminating insights into the reciprocal affinities, progressive intellectual movements, role models, and artistic identities of international modern art.

Here, the paintings entered into an artistic dialogue that also conveys an impression that modernism per se was conceived as a cosmopolitan project, and that artistic innovation and creativity can only evolve when based on exchange and on reciprocal intercultural inspiration. Rabindranath Tagore, whose intellectual authority and international reputation were key to the realization of such an exhibition, perhaps best embodied this global concept. Such a stance was all the more radical and farsighted given the spread of nationalism in late-colonial India. The question to which an answer was sought is one with which we, in today's globalized world of art and culture and beyond, should be familiar: How can a personal, vernacular representation of reality evolve in light of a present in which the dominant aesthetic means of expression stem from sources that bear no relation to the place where their impact is felt?

The principal artists of the Bengal School, whose work is now being exhibited at the Bauhaus in Dessau for the first time, uniquely convey this struggle for a new visual culture in the field of tension generated by cultural differences and global cultural production. The exhibition attests to an autonomous modernism that, in dialogue with the Bauhaus masters, reveals just how much the two parties had in common in the nineteen-twenties.

I am delighted that the National Gallery of Modern Art, New Delhi, has a pivotal role in coordinating this major exhibition. I am pleased to see this artistic dialogue updated in a place which represents European modernism like no other, and which sheds light on the openness that prevailed at the time.

Alexander Farenholtz and Hortensia Völckers

Introductory Remarks of the German Federal Cultural Foundation

When the Bengali life reformer and subsequent recipient of the Nobel Prize in Literature Rabindranath Tagore visited Germany in 1921 during a European tour, the event struck a significant chord with the country's literati. "Perhaps never before have I seen such robust spiritual substance in one man," enthused the philosopher and writer Hermann Graf Keyserling.[1] Even if other contemporaries—Thomas Mann, for instance—derided this Indian's "anemic humanity,"[2] the Tagore cult of the day exemplified the longing for intercultural conciliation and cosmopolitanism, and for the ideal of a harmonious development of personality. For the Bauhaus, the latter represented a thoroughly familiar path to an aesthetic completion of the human being, which embraced cognitive and creative capabilities in equal measure.

Beyond all elective affinities between East and West, it remains astonishing that, just a year after Tagore's visit to Germany, a return visit of sorts to India actually took place. In 1922, it was above all artworks that made the journey to Calcutta: two hundred and fifty graphic works, including thirty-five prints and woodcuts by Lyonel Feininger alone, alongside drawings by Johannes Itten and Wassily Kandinsky and watercolors by Paul Klee. All of which, according to *The Hindu Times*, could be bought for prices ranging from five to fifteen pounds sterling.

Does the Bauhaus project in Calcutta constitute a prototype for the global art fairs of today? Only to a degree, as the present "remake" of the exhibition by the Bauhaus Dessau Foundation shows. As its curators Kathrin Rhomberg, Regina Bittner, and Partha Mitter have discovered, the cultural-historical achievement of the Calcutta exhibition was that it opened up a conclave for a cosmopolitan encounter among artists—promoted by a bold spirit of experimentation and a shared interest in abstraction, cubism, or primitivism.

[1] Hermann Graf Keyserling, *Das Reisetagebuch eines Philosophen*, 5th ed. (St. Goar, 2009), p. 402.

[2] Thomas Mann, *Briefe 1889–1936*, ed. Erika Mann (Frankfurt am Main, 1961), pp. 188–89.

We are still wont to narrate the history of modernism as a European story. This exhibition—for which we thank all those responsible, both in India and in Germany—opens our eyes to the diverse global exchange alliances and intellectual laboratories that resulted in new avant-garde life reforms and in modern art in different locations throughout the world. From Calcutta and from Dessau, these new aspects are now revealed to us in a particularly vivid way.

Captions

1 Title page "Exhibition of Continental Paintings and Graphic Arts," *Catalogue of the Fourteenth Annual Exhibition Indian Society of Oriental Art Samavaya Mansions Calcutta,* December 1922.

2–4 Introductory contribution by Stella Kramrisch to the *Catalogue of the Fourteenth Annual Exhibition Indian Society of Oriental Art Samavaya Mansions Calcutta,* December 1922, pp. 21–23.

Catalogue of
The Fourteenth
Annual Exhibition

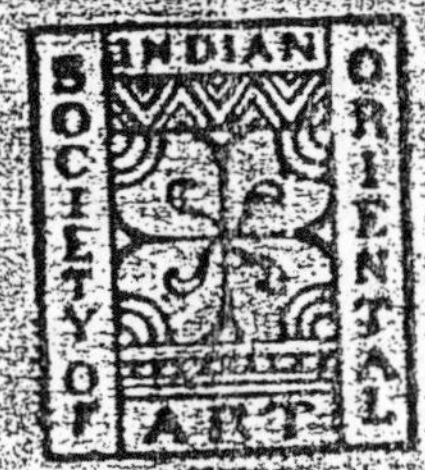

Indian Society of Oriental Art
SUITE 12, SAMAVAYA MANSIONS
December, 1922

EXHIBITION OF CONTINENTAL PAINTINGS AND GRAPHIC ARTS.

It is for the first time that Western Art is represented in India by a number of the most advanced and most sincere works of leading Continental Artists. They do not belong to any school, but come from different parts of Europe, each having his own manner and technique. These Artists met in Weimar and in spite of their variety of form found themselves united in their aim. To realise the eternal truth of all art and to visualise it by the means supplied by the present age, is their creed. They joined hands and became the masters of a State-school of Art, and the method of their teaching is to hold up the example of their own inspired truthfulness and severe discipline. Neither masters nor students are the followers of any "isms" although they are bound to make use of them to a greater or smaller extent. For "Cubism" or "Post-impressionism" are conventions of form, developed out of the need of the moment, and no artist in whom the present is alive can escape their formulae.

Kandinsky, the Russian painter has been for more than ten years the herald of the "Spiritual in Art". His power of abstraction is unswerving, put into action as it is by the fervour of a mysticism which has no other name but that of Russia. He was the first to paint pictures without any subject matter. He avoided all allusions to literature and nature and so made himself free to infuse his inner experience into mere lines and mere colours which are organised into compositions of intoxicating harmony. Kandinsky is *the* "expressionist" among the painters.

Itten, the Swiss Artist is possessed by all the zeal of conviction. He does not stop unless he reaches the very essence of appearance. He visualises, for instance, the scent, freshness and colour of a rose in a few pencil strokes; this utmost economy however is the outcome of numberless experiments as to the structure of a rose, the movement of rose petals, the touch of their cool and smooth surface and the atmosphere in which they breathe. And his sketch confesses that unless you feel your own existence merged into that of the rose and lost in it, you fail to know what a rose means. Itten gains his artistic vocabulary by intuitive abstraction and moulds his compositions by its help and with the logic of a masterbuilder. His method is scientific and serves to express his insight into the rhythm of all visible things, as well as of his own soul. His work has religion.

Feininger, the German, in his constructive aim, ventures on the thorny path of Cubism. He is thorough and infallible, and Cubism with him is an ecstatic though geometrised creed. Order to him is the supreme law imposed on all appearance and each of its paragraphs has the shape of a cube.

Whichever nation and whatever artistic mentality these artists may represent, one feature is common to them and this is their training. All of them were brought up in art-academies, so wellknown all the world over. But every one of them was driven by sheer inner necessity to abandon their lifeless scheme. And so they struggled each in his own way through decoration and symbolism, through impressionism and post-impressionism and all the various artistic currents which have agitated the surface of European art during the last twenty years. Thus they gained a sure footing in the traditions of old, while passing through the multifarious revolutions within their own experience. That gave them broadness and distance to their immediate selves, so that finally they could afford to be only their true selves. For them there is no stop and every year brings a further evolution.

The Exhibition contains water-colour paintings, pencil sketches, etchings and woodcuts. The techniques vary, but in every case an effect is attained peculiar to the material. To these artists, a sound knowledge of the crafts is as essential as the religious devotion with which they work. If the end of civilisation foretold for Europe of the present day is to come true, it must be said that the artists are fighting heroically their last forlorn fight. But all death means resurrection and art in itself is immortal.

The Indian public should study this exhibition for then, they may learn that European Art does not mean 'naturalism' and that the transformation of the forms of nature in the work of an artist is common to ancient and modern India and Europe as an unconscious and therefore inevitable expression of the life of soul and of artistic genius.

St. K.

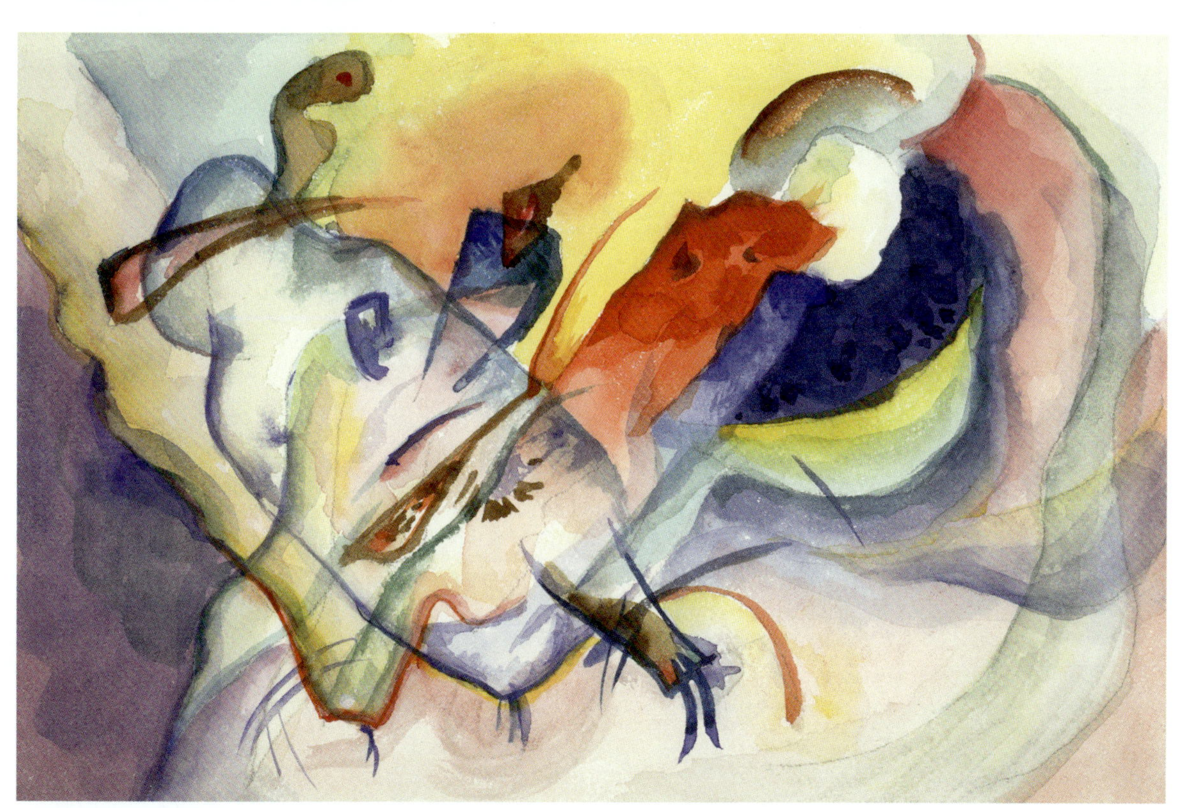

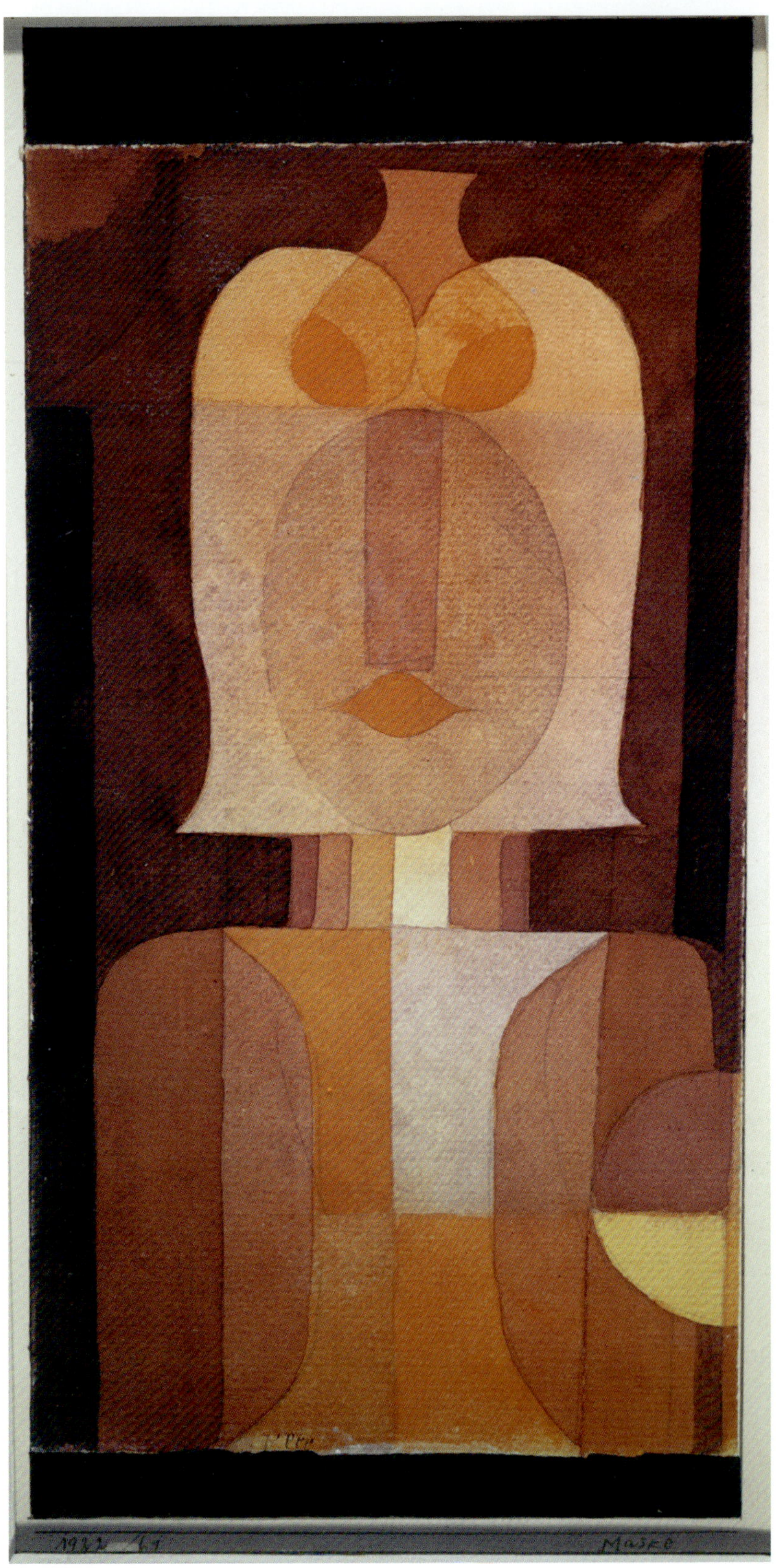
Maske

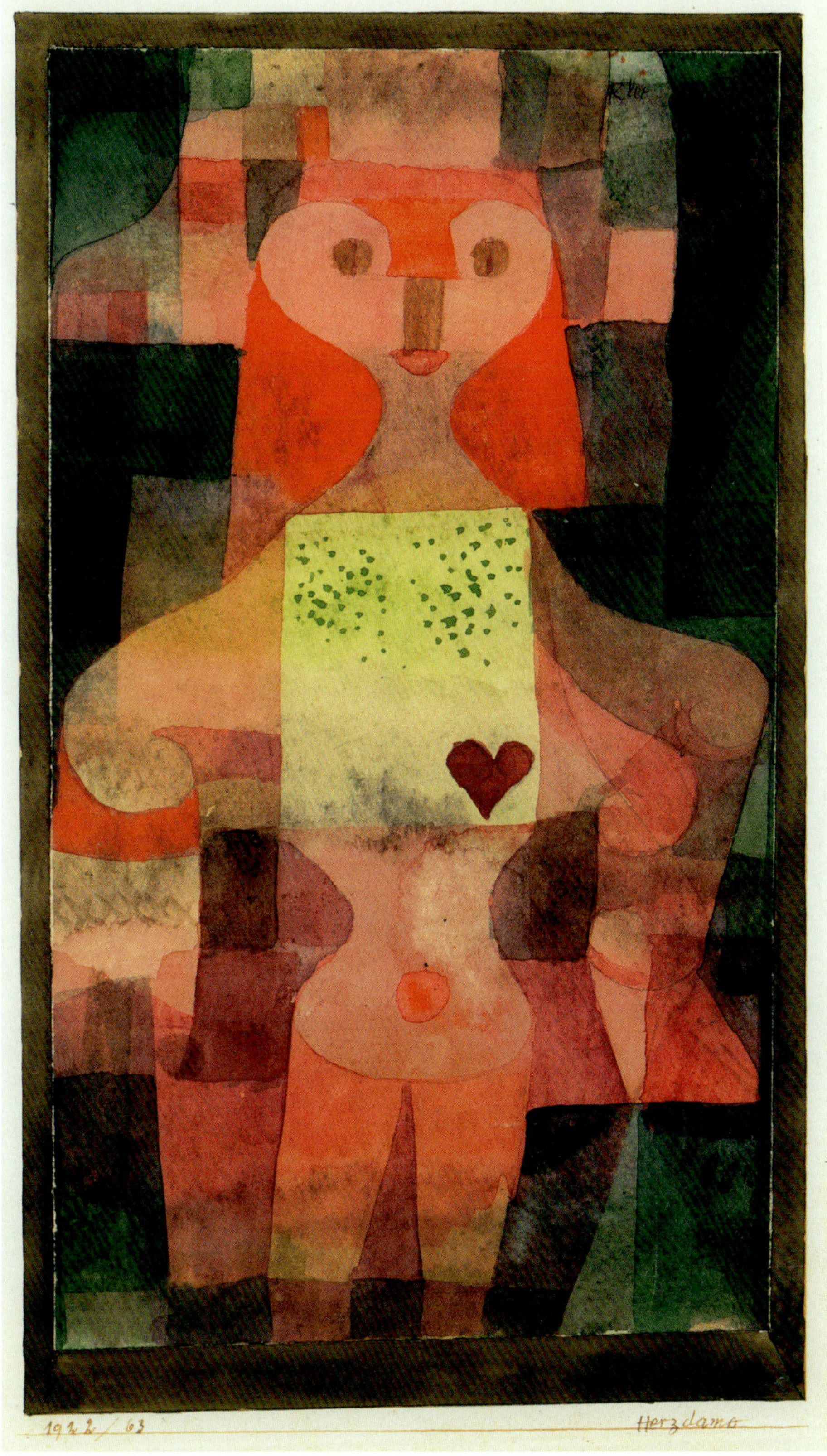
1922 / 63
Herzdame

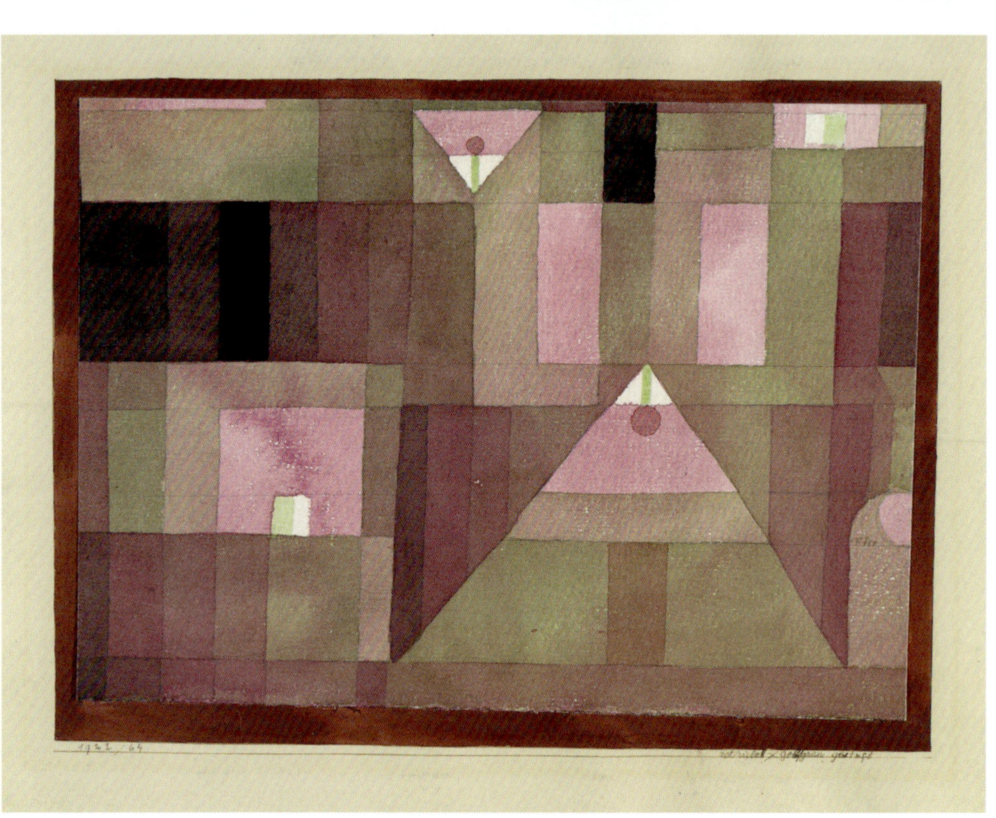

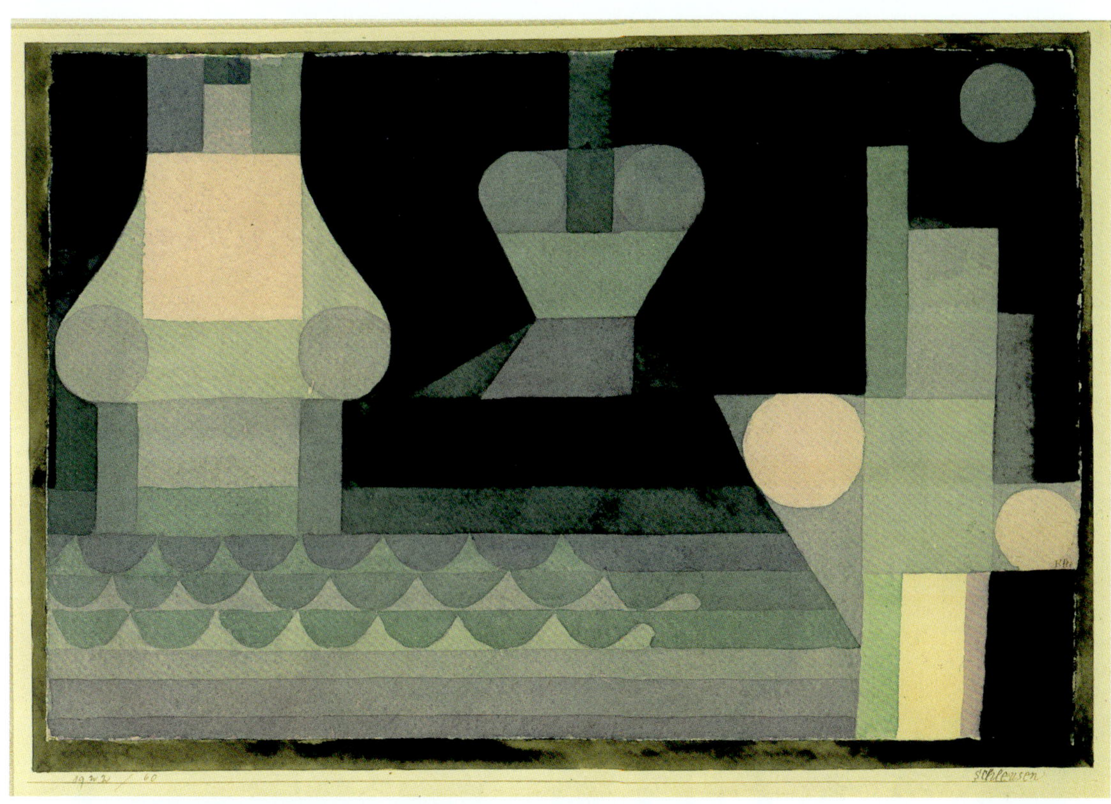

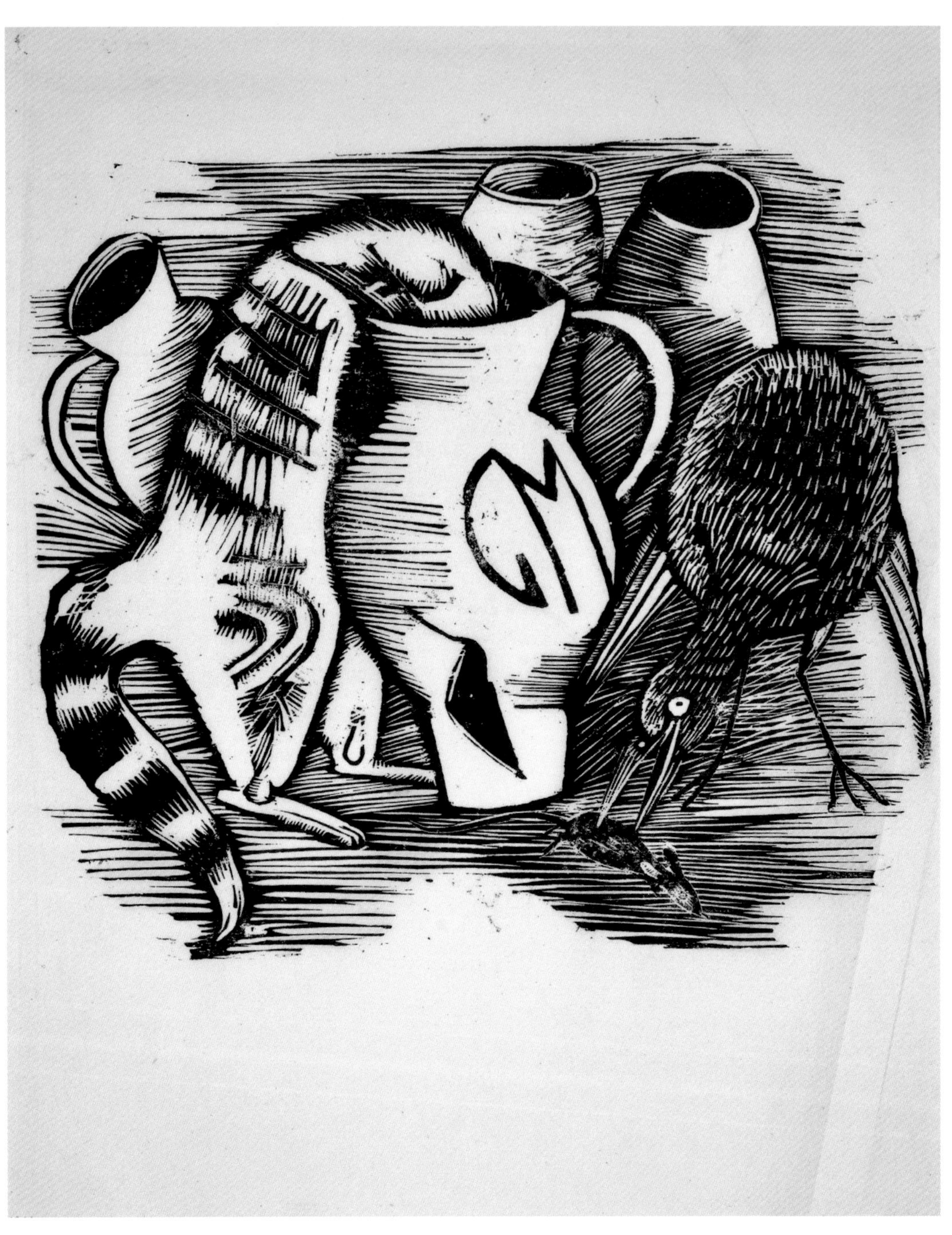

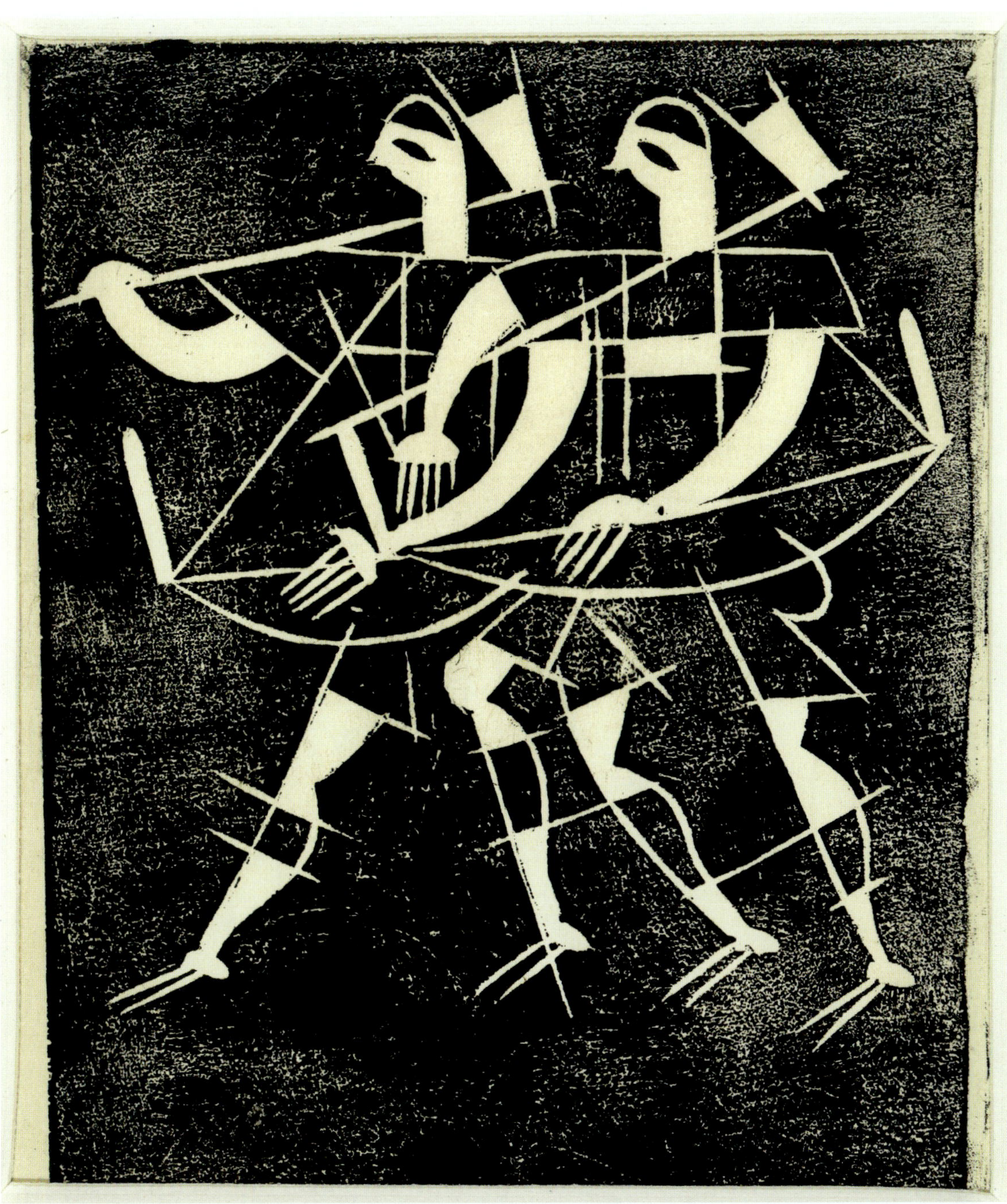

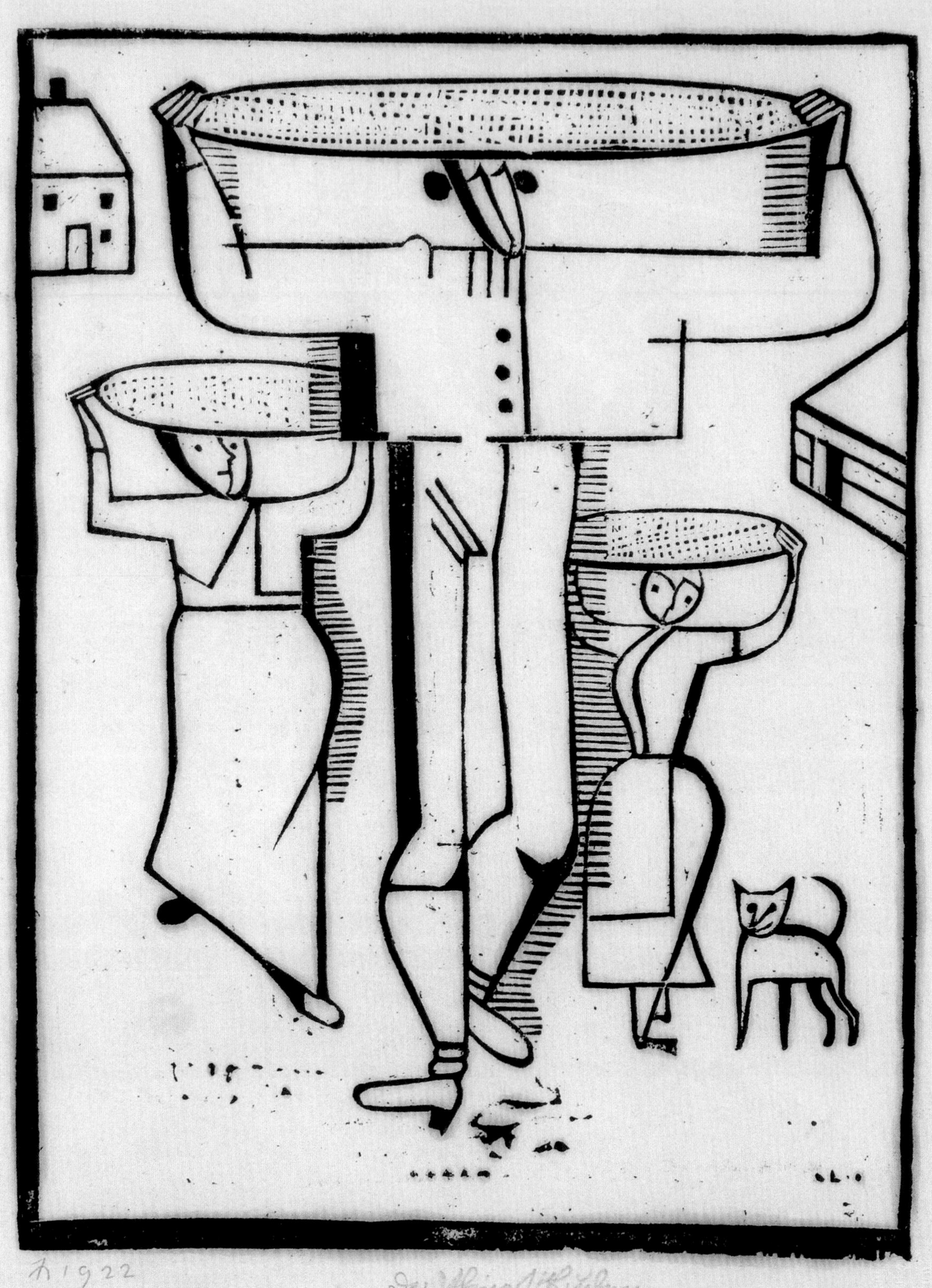
1922

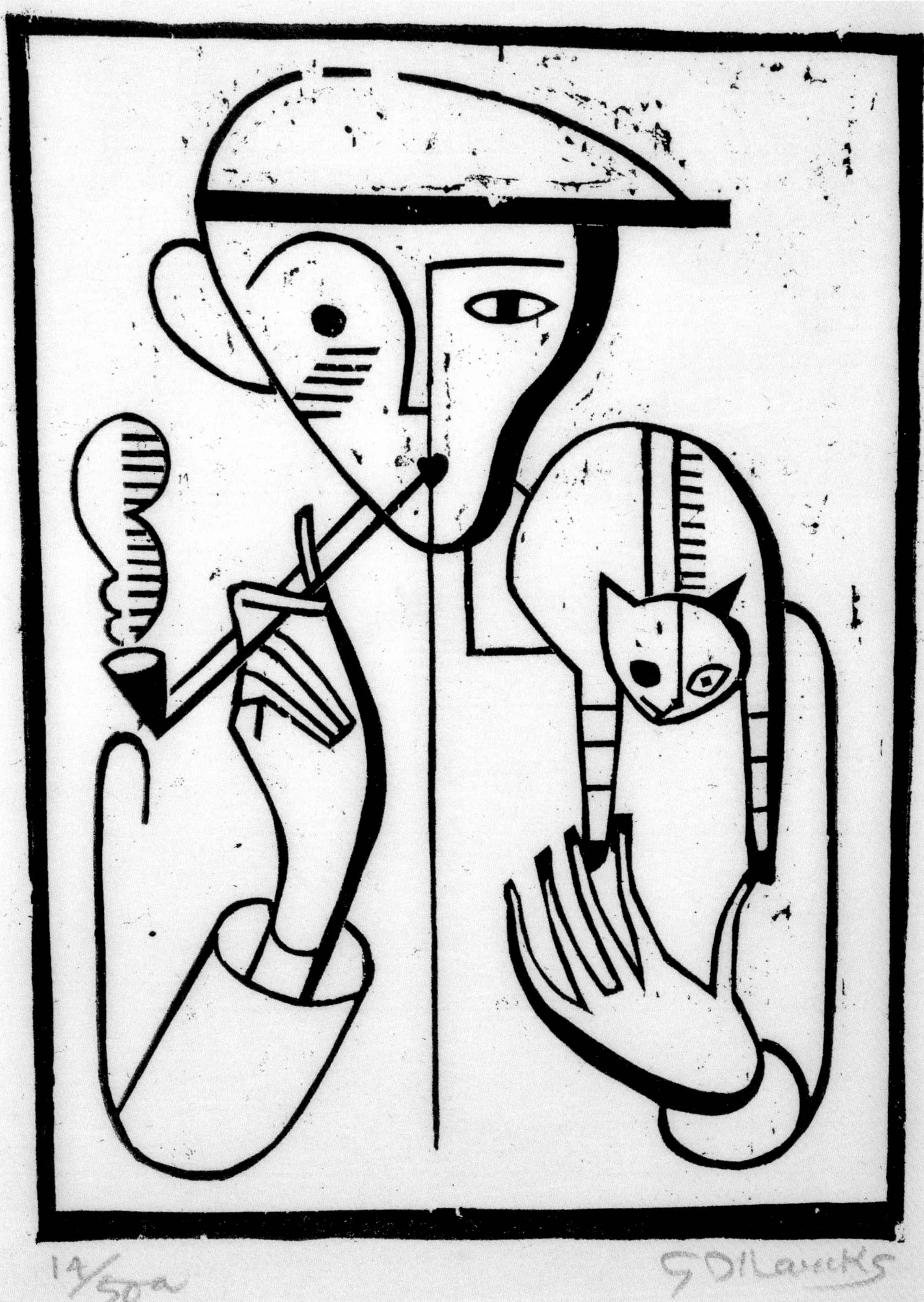

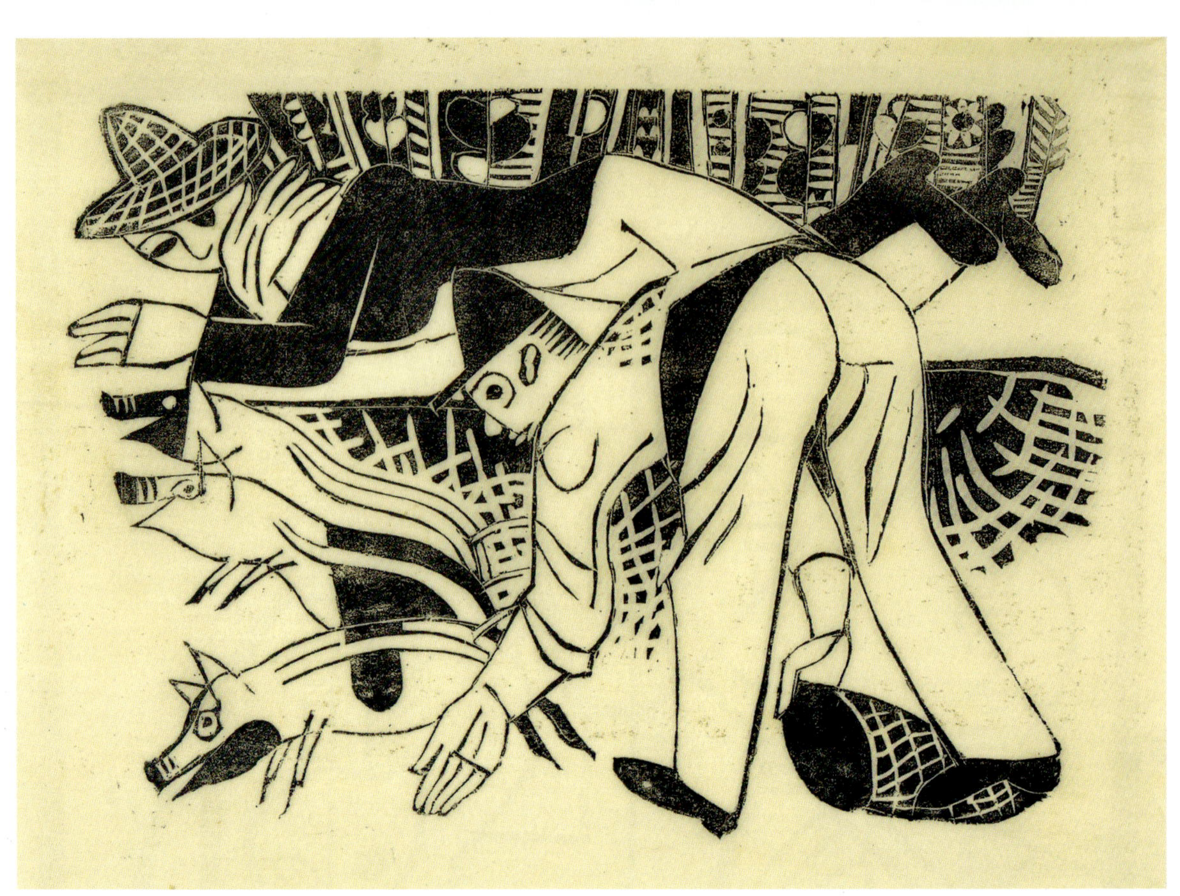

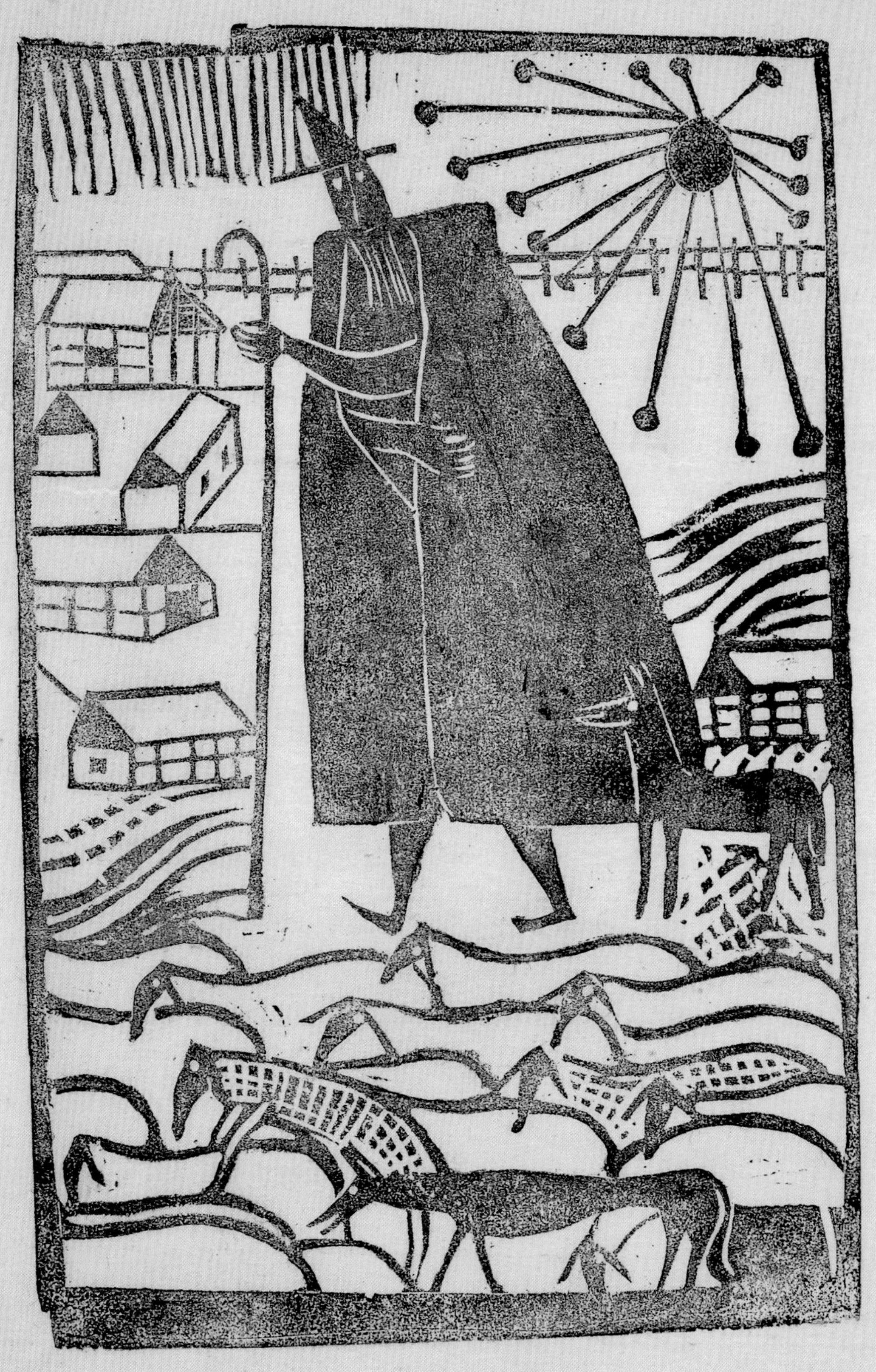

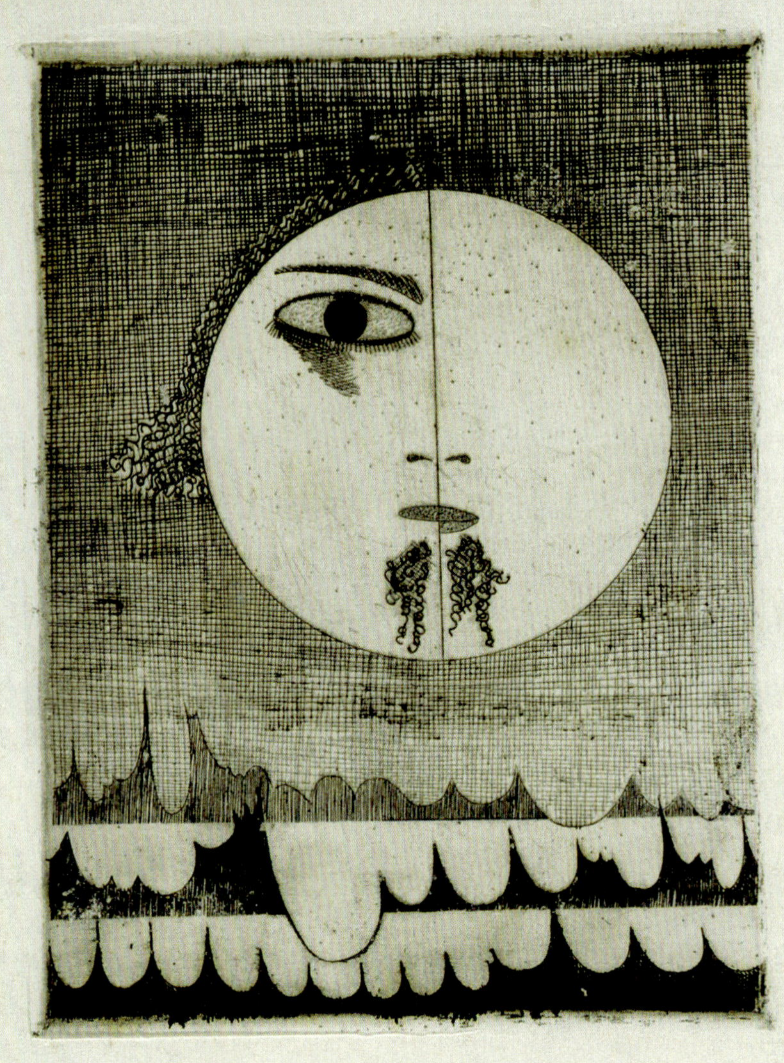
2
Georg Muche
etwa 5 Drucke
Der Mond 1922

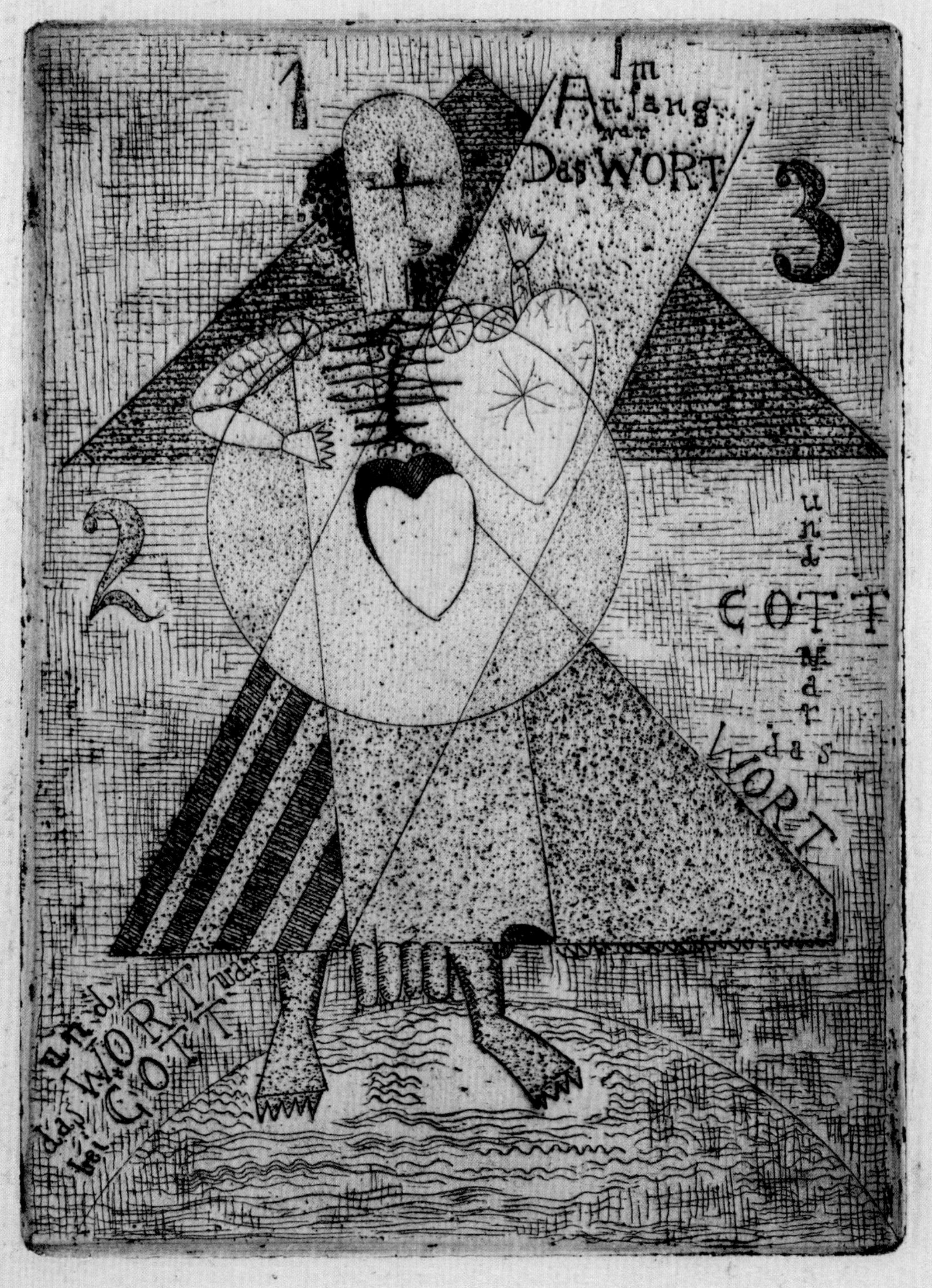
1
Im Anfang war Das WORT
3
2
und GOTT war das WORT
und das WORT war bei GOTT

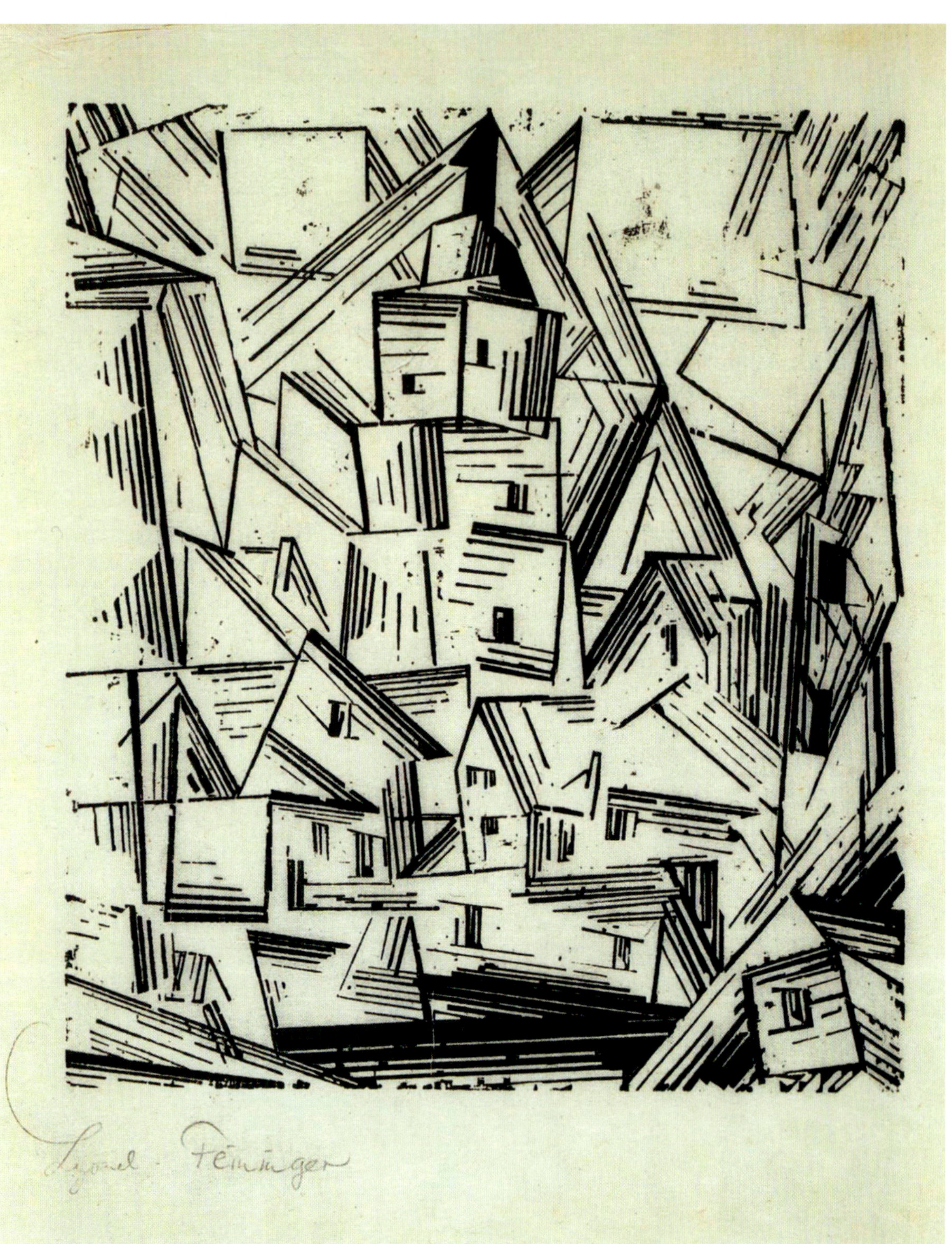
Lyonel Feininger

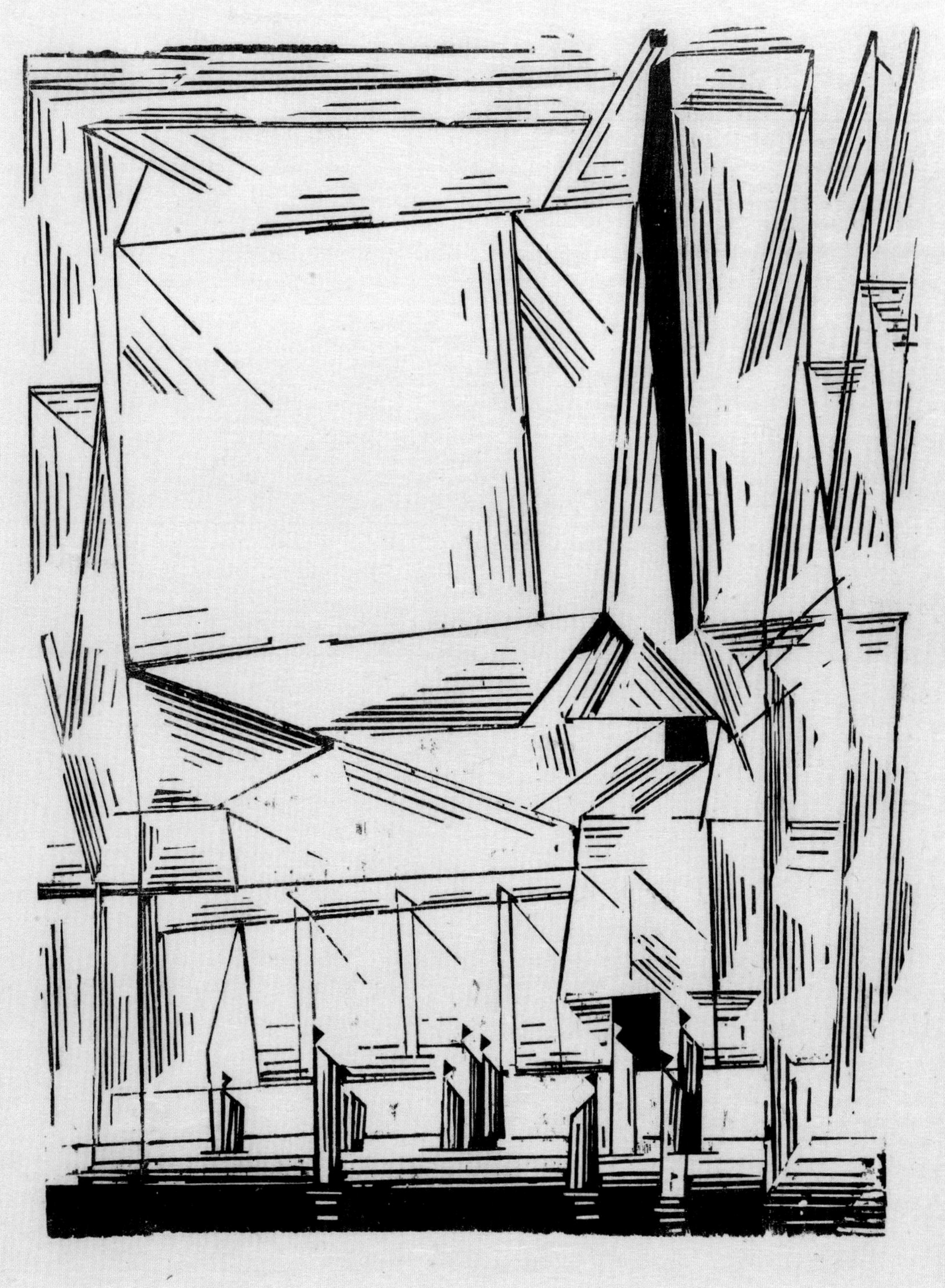

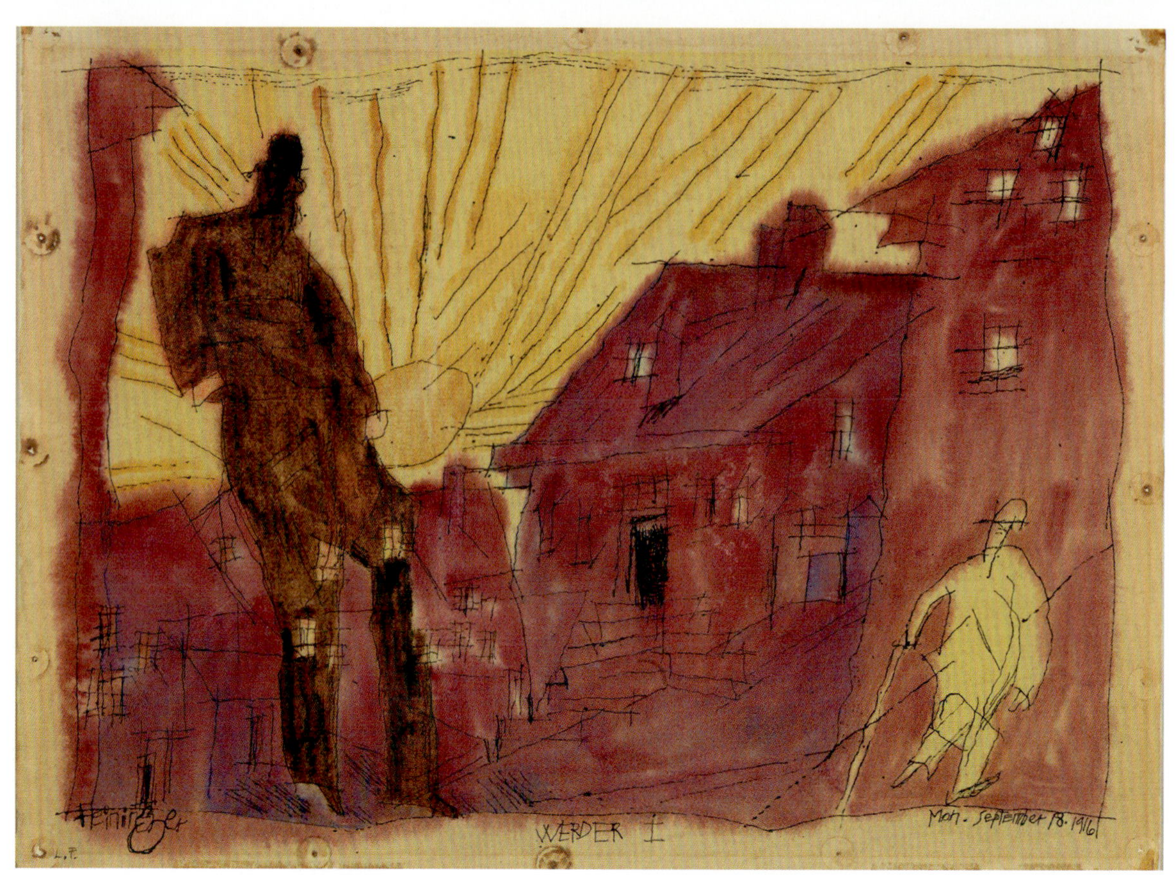
Feininger
WERDER I
Mon. September 18. 1916

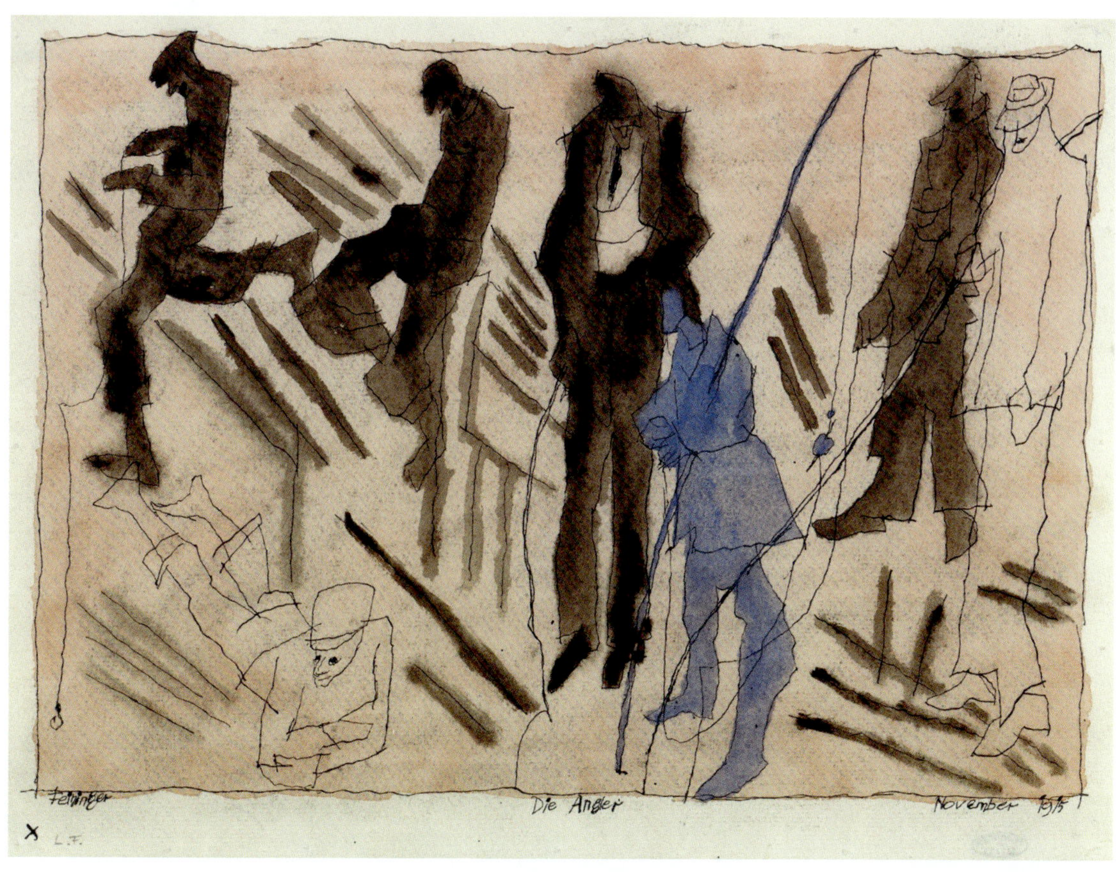
Feininger
Die Angler
November 1915
L.F.

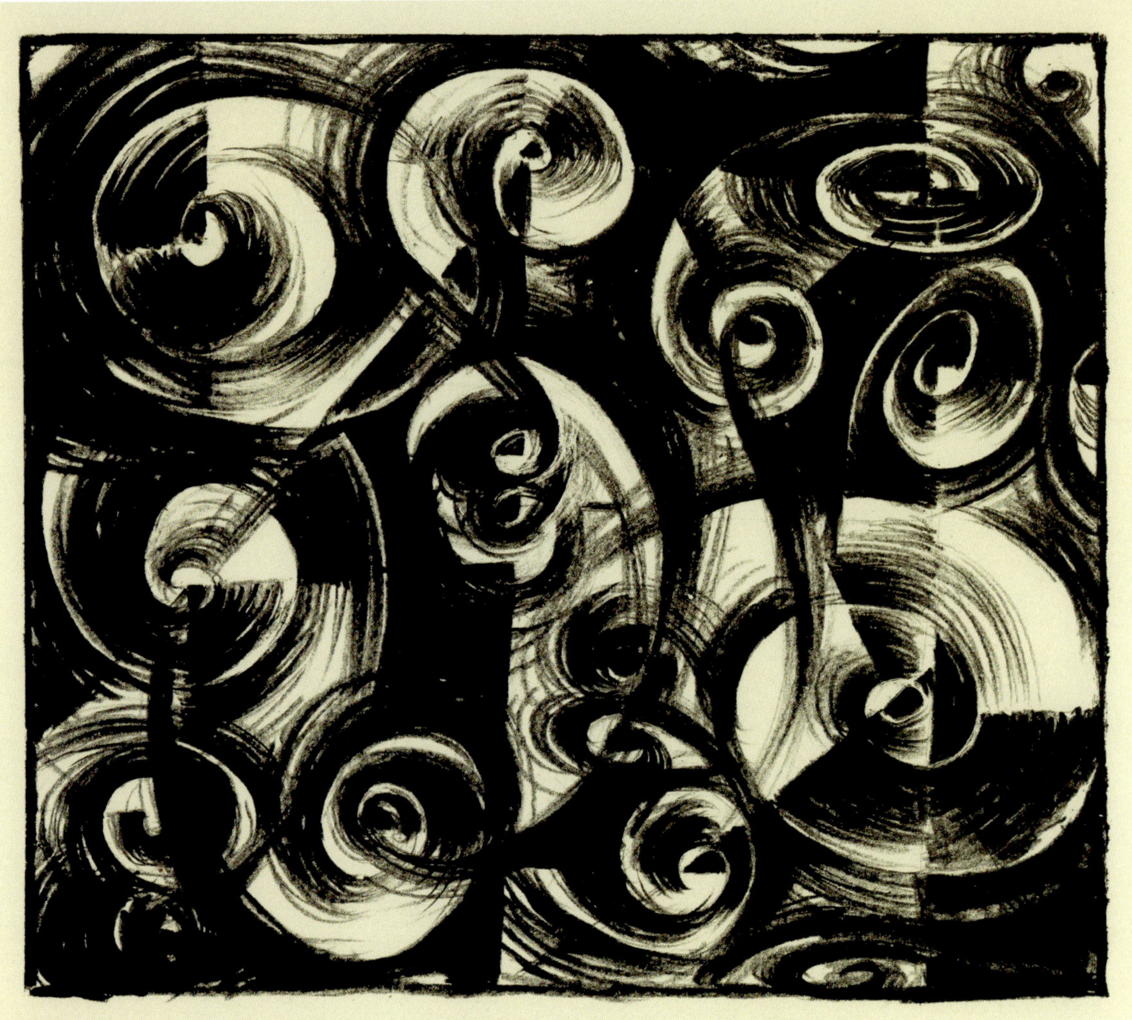

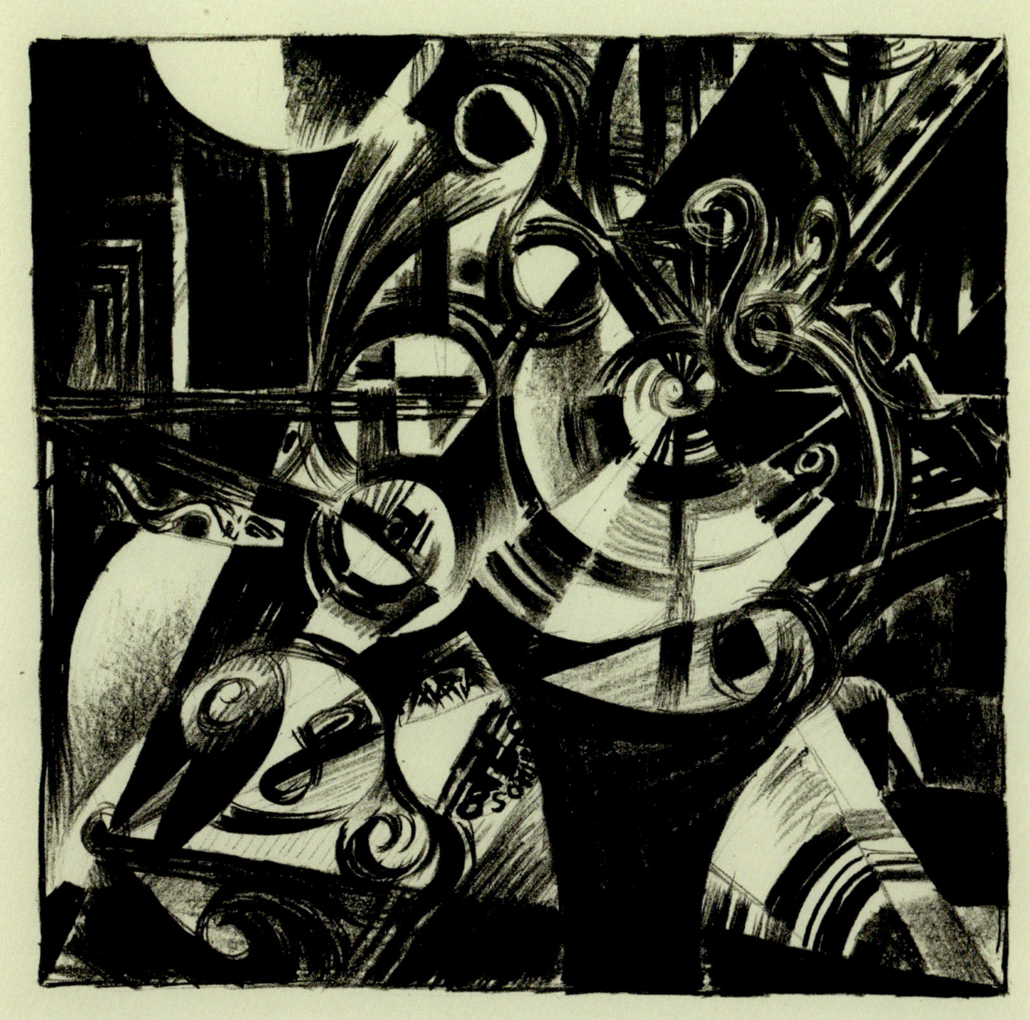

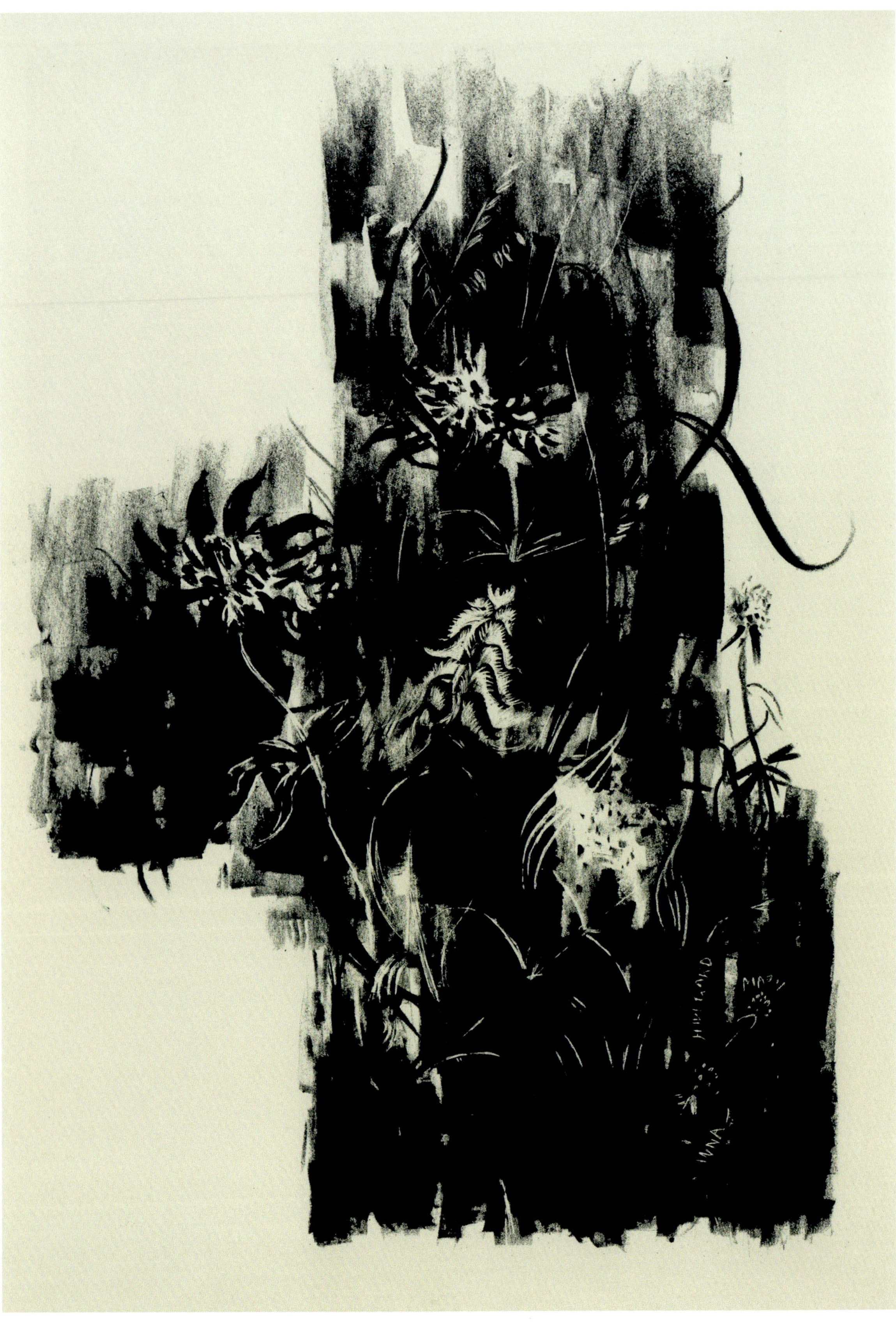

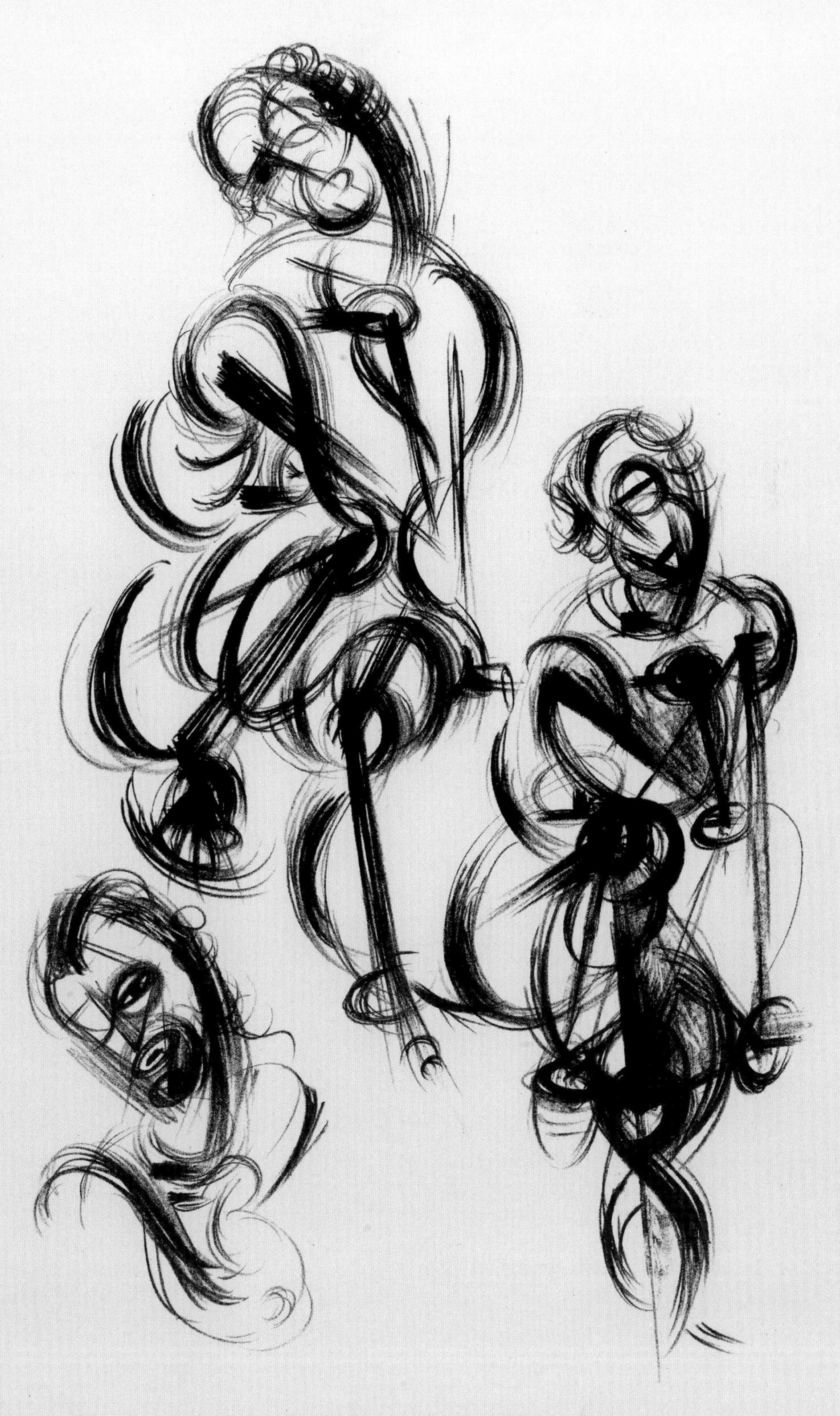

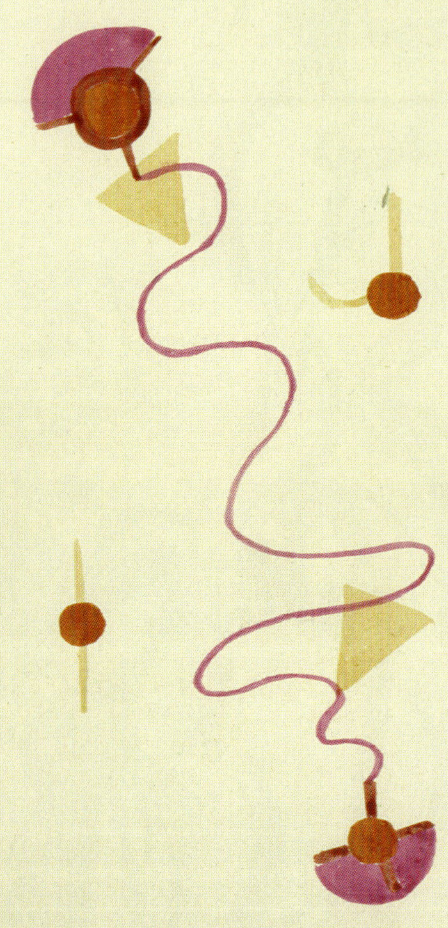

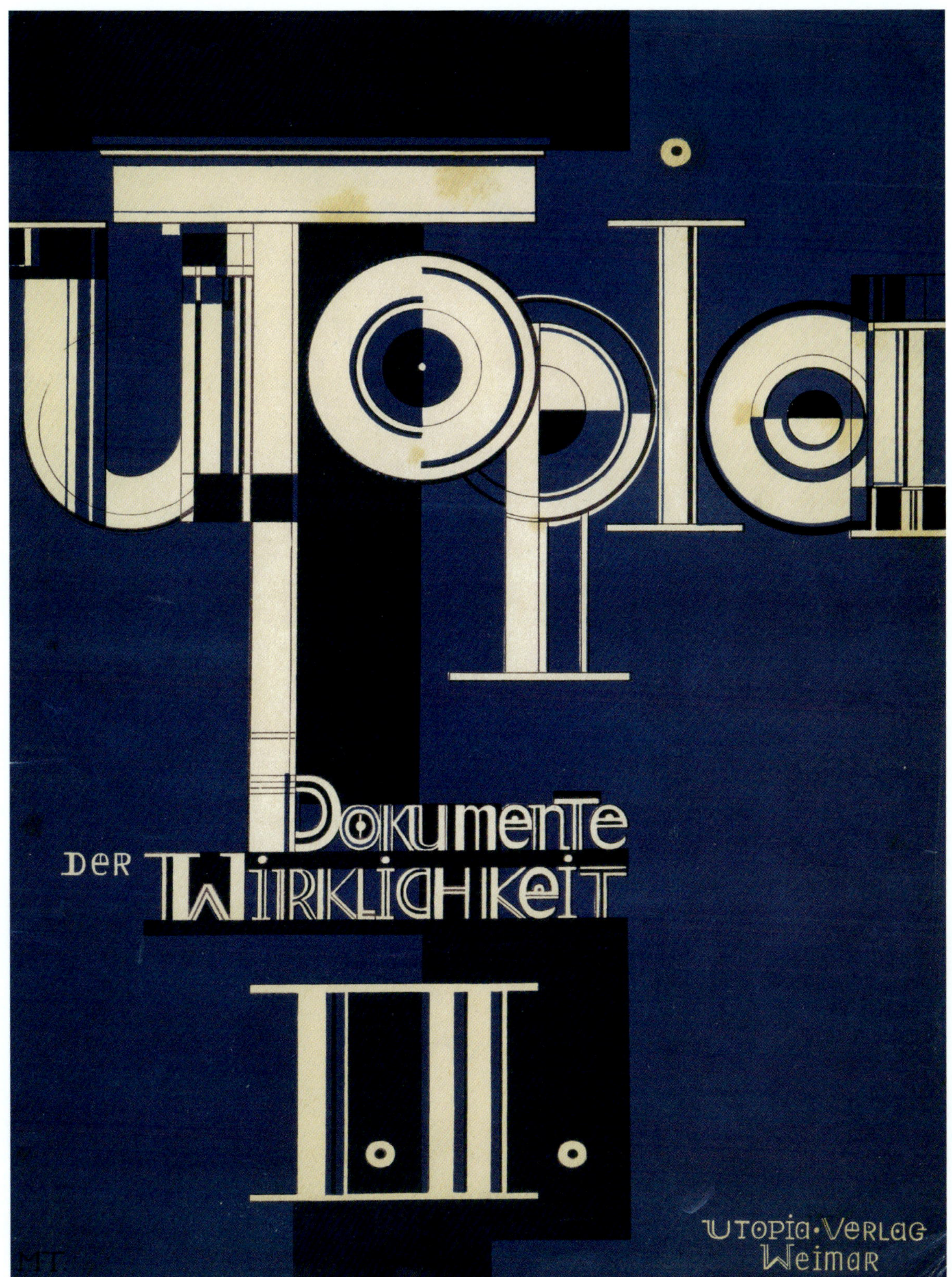
utopia
Dokumente
der Wirklichkeit
UTOPIA·VERLAG
Weimar
MT

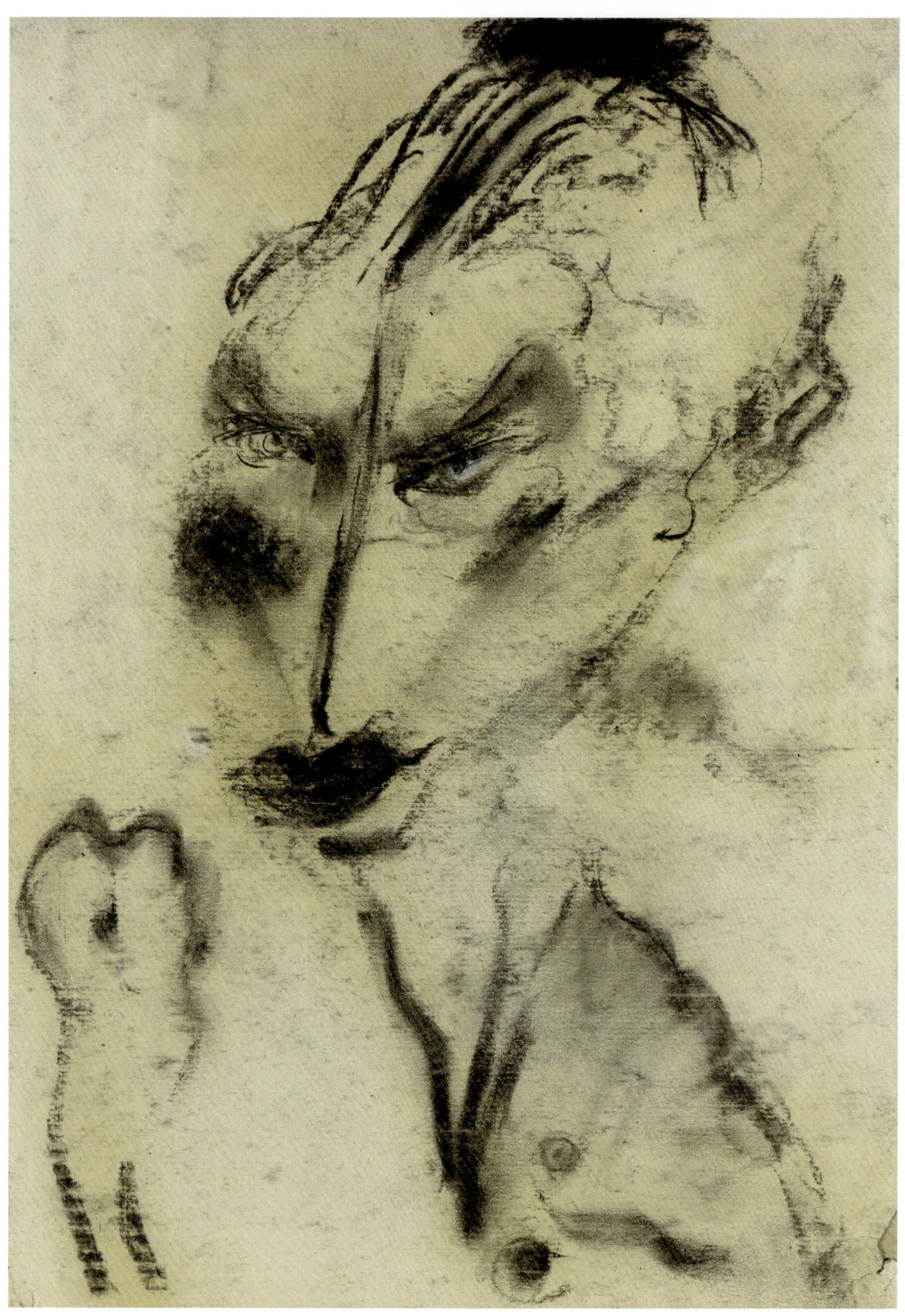

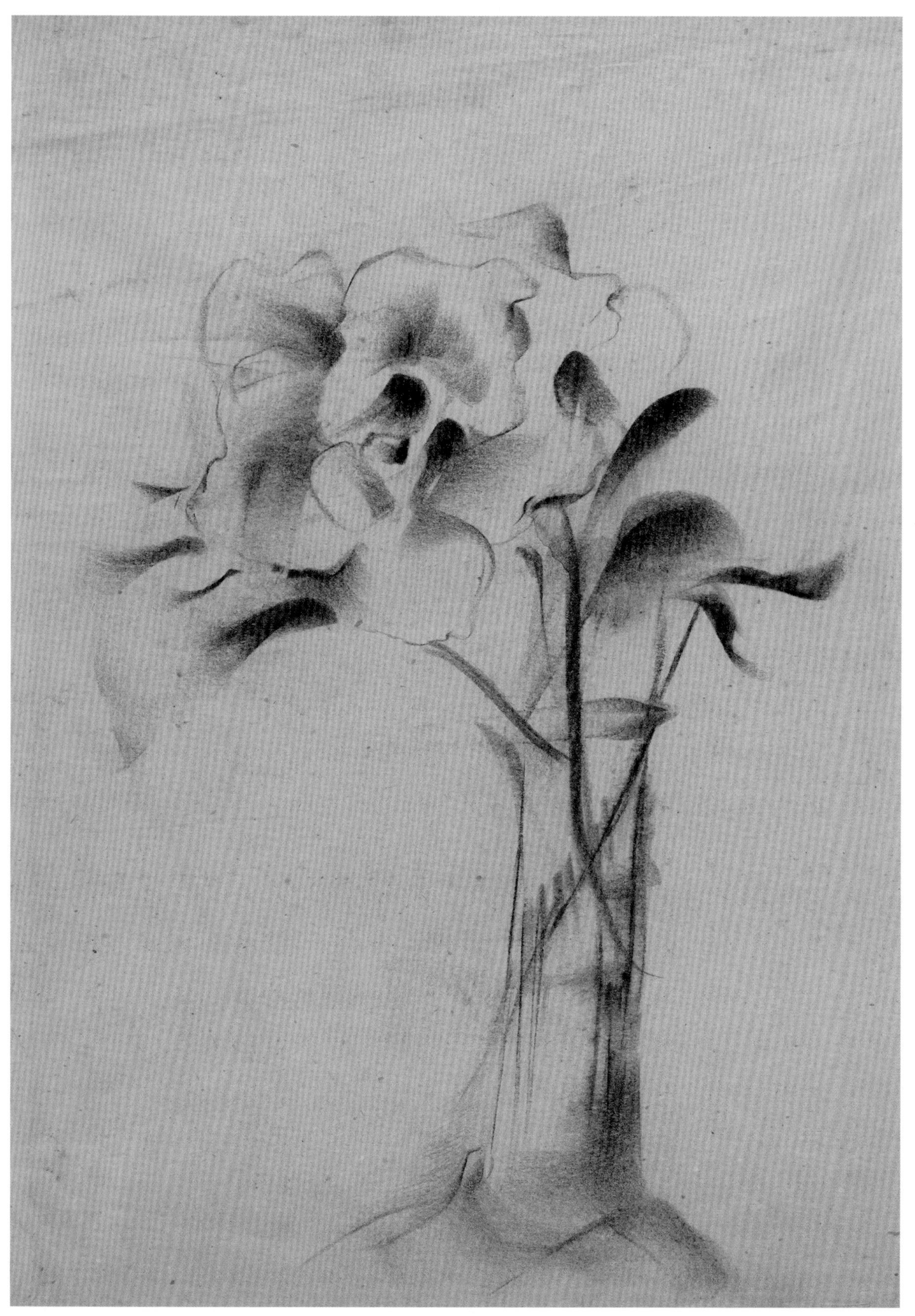

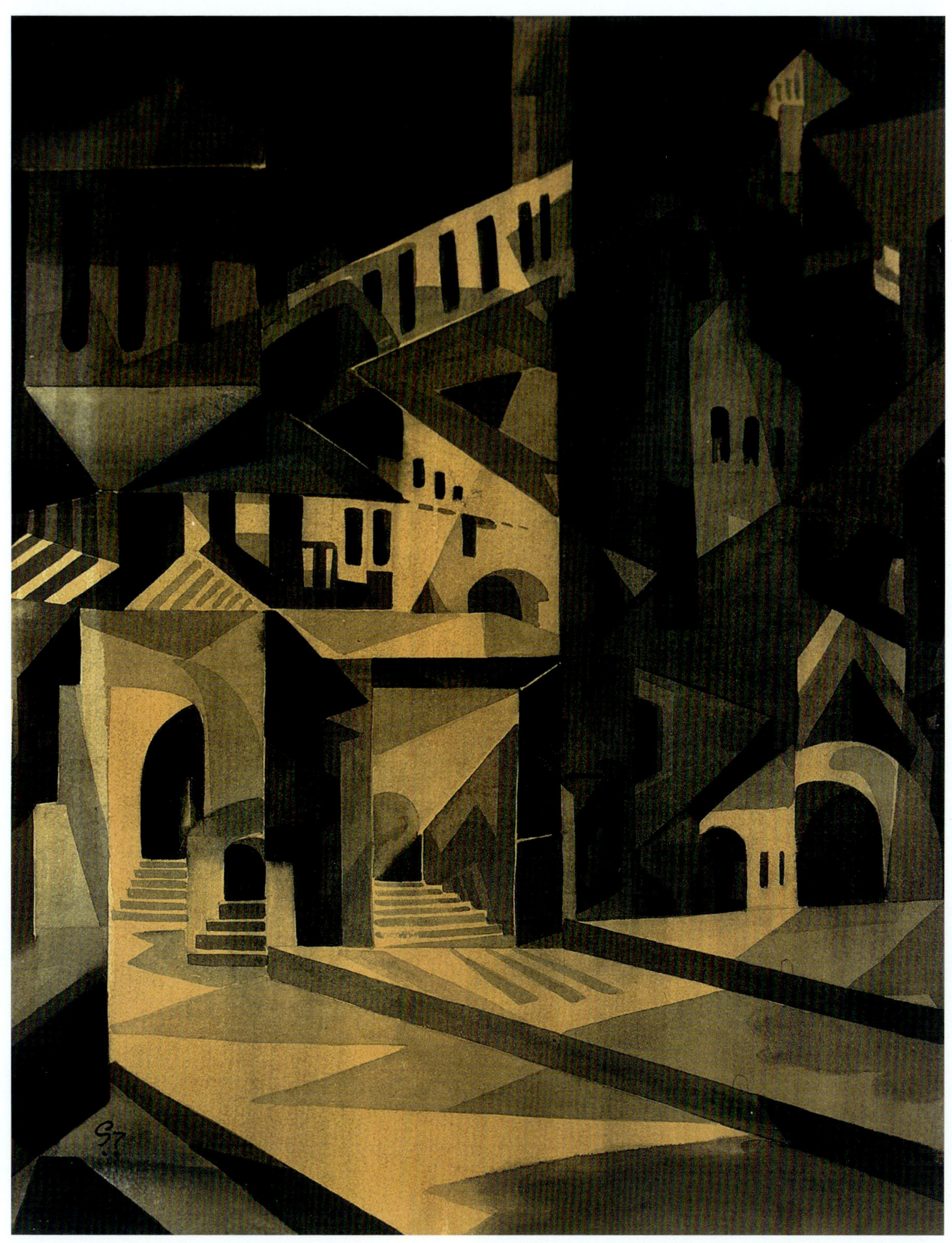

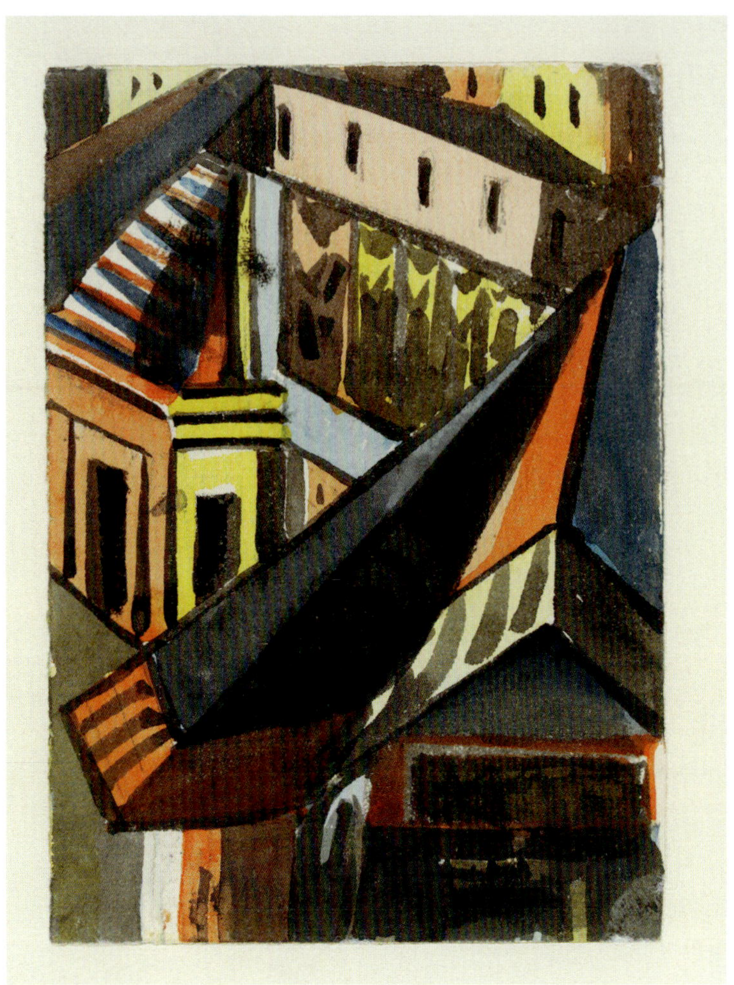

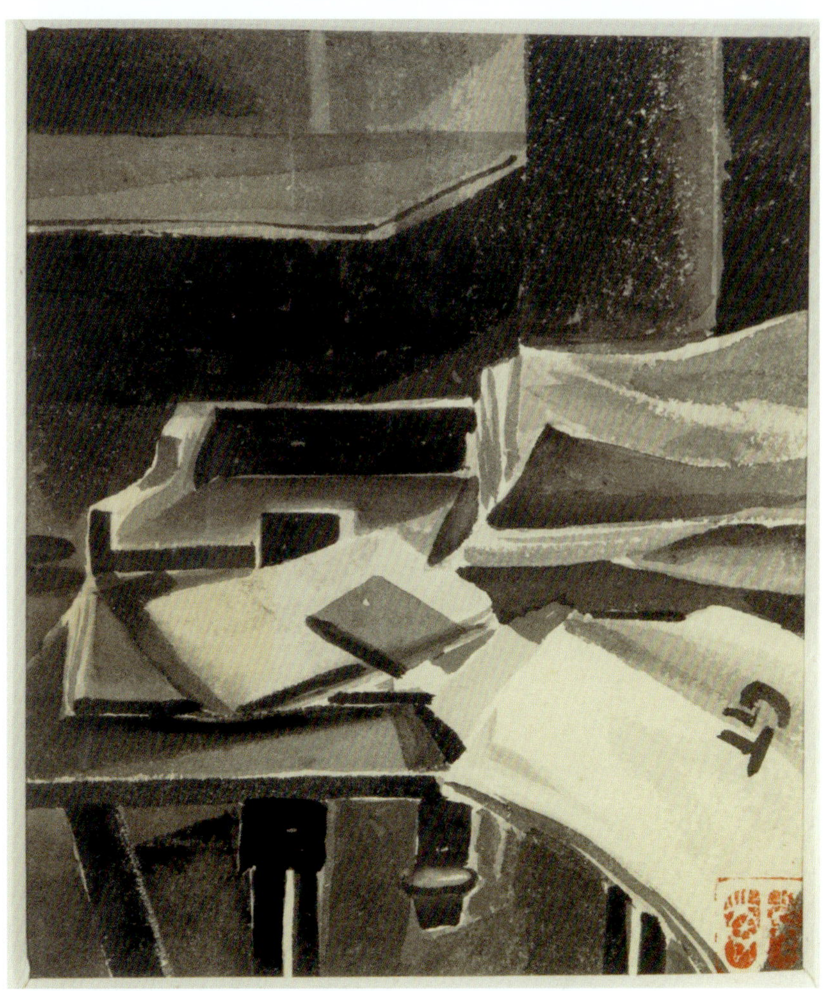

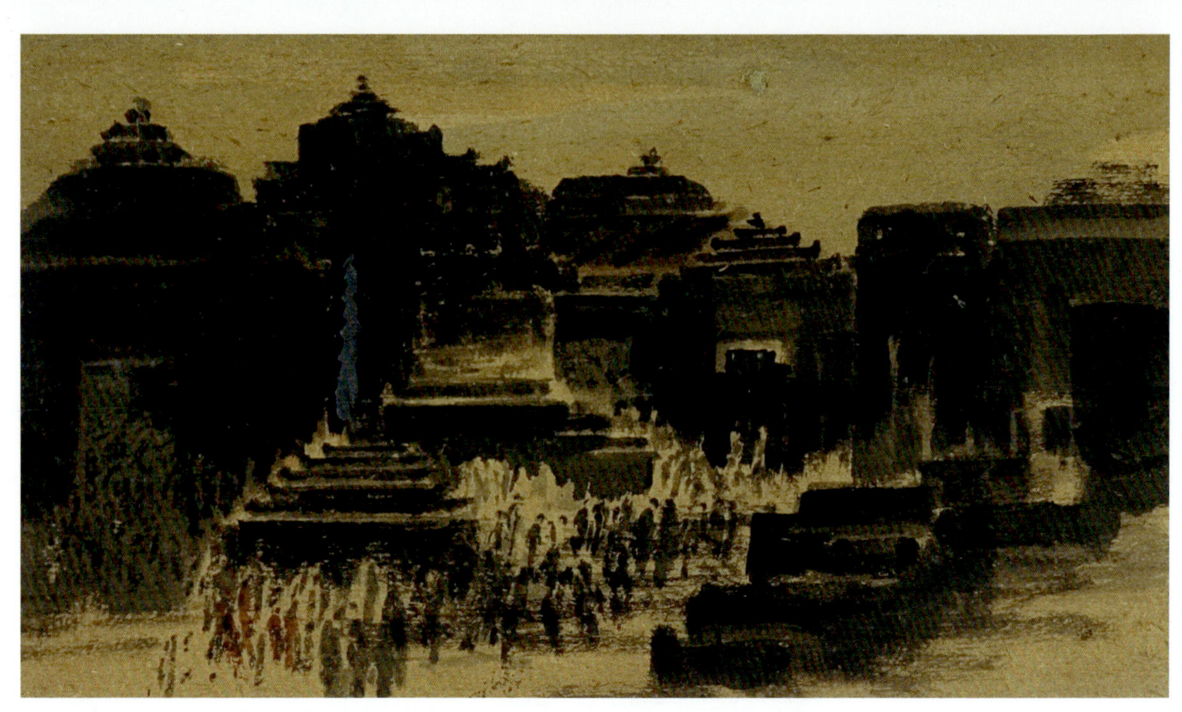

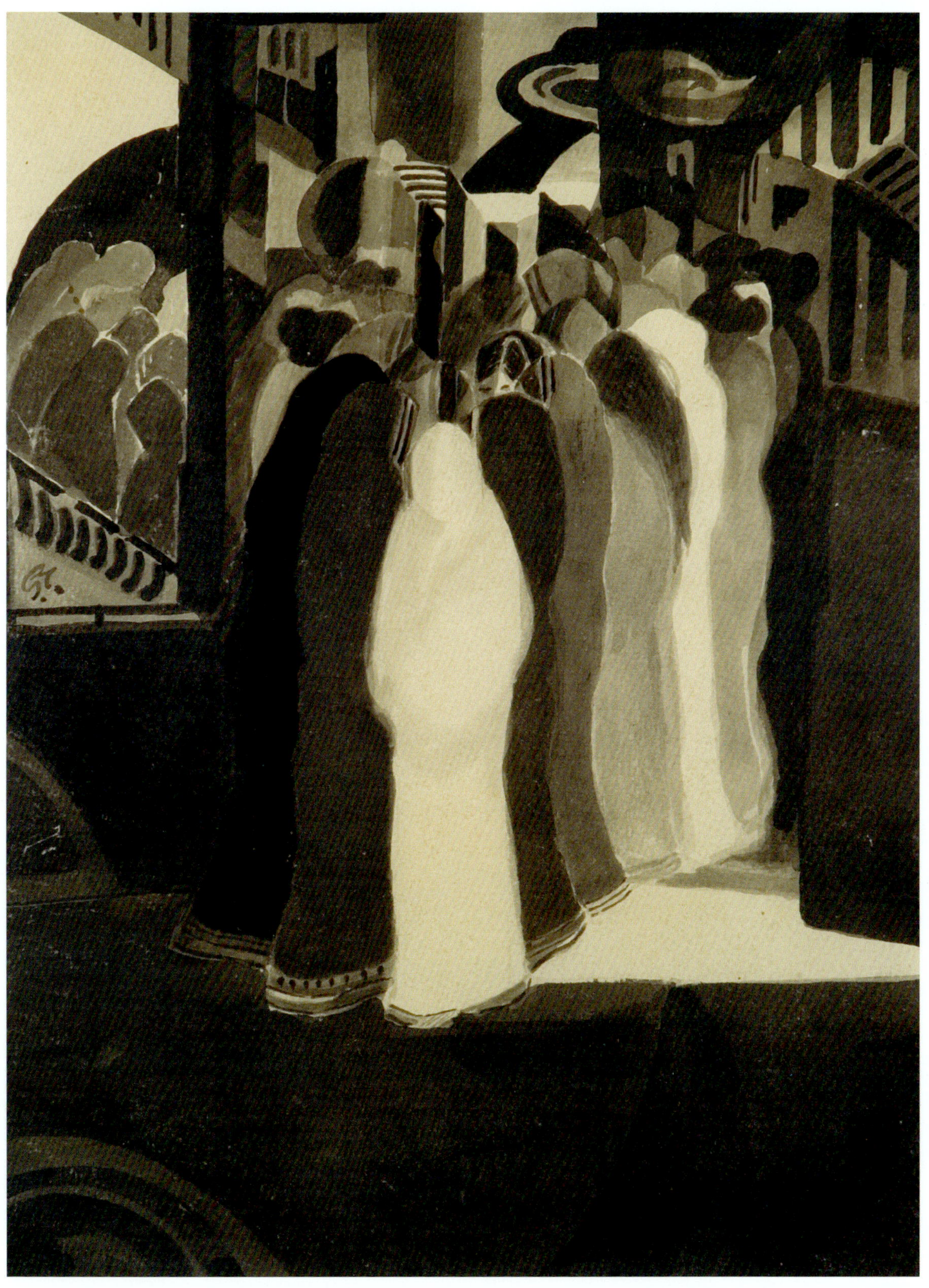

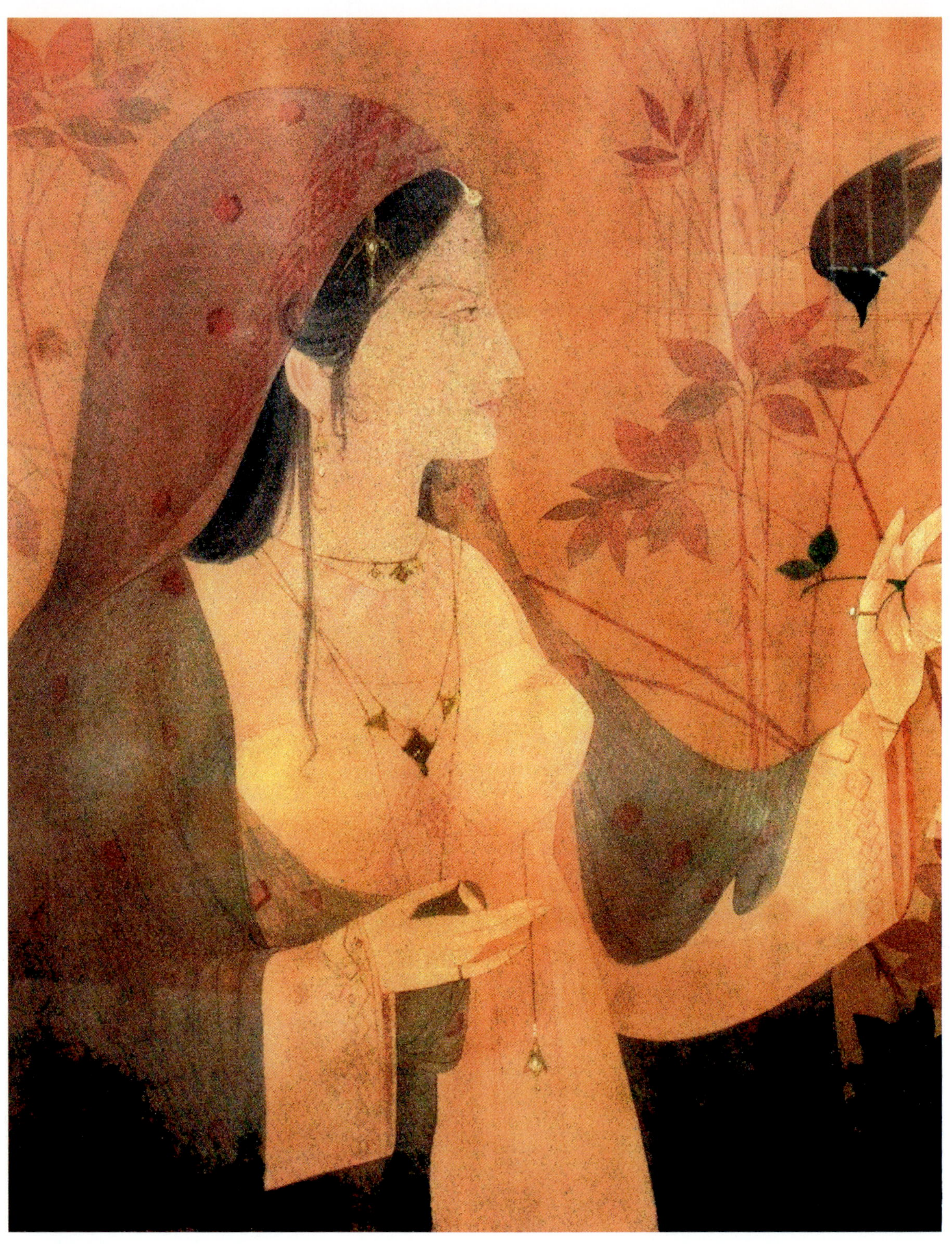

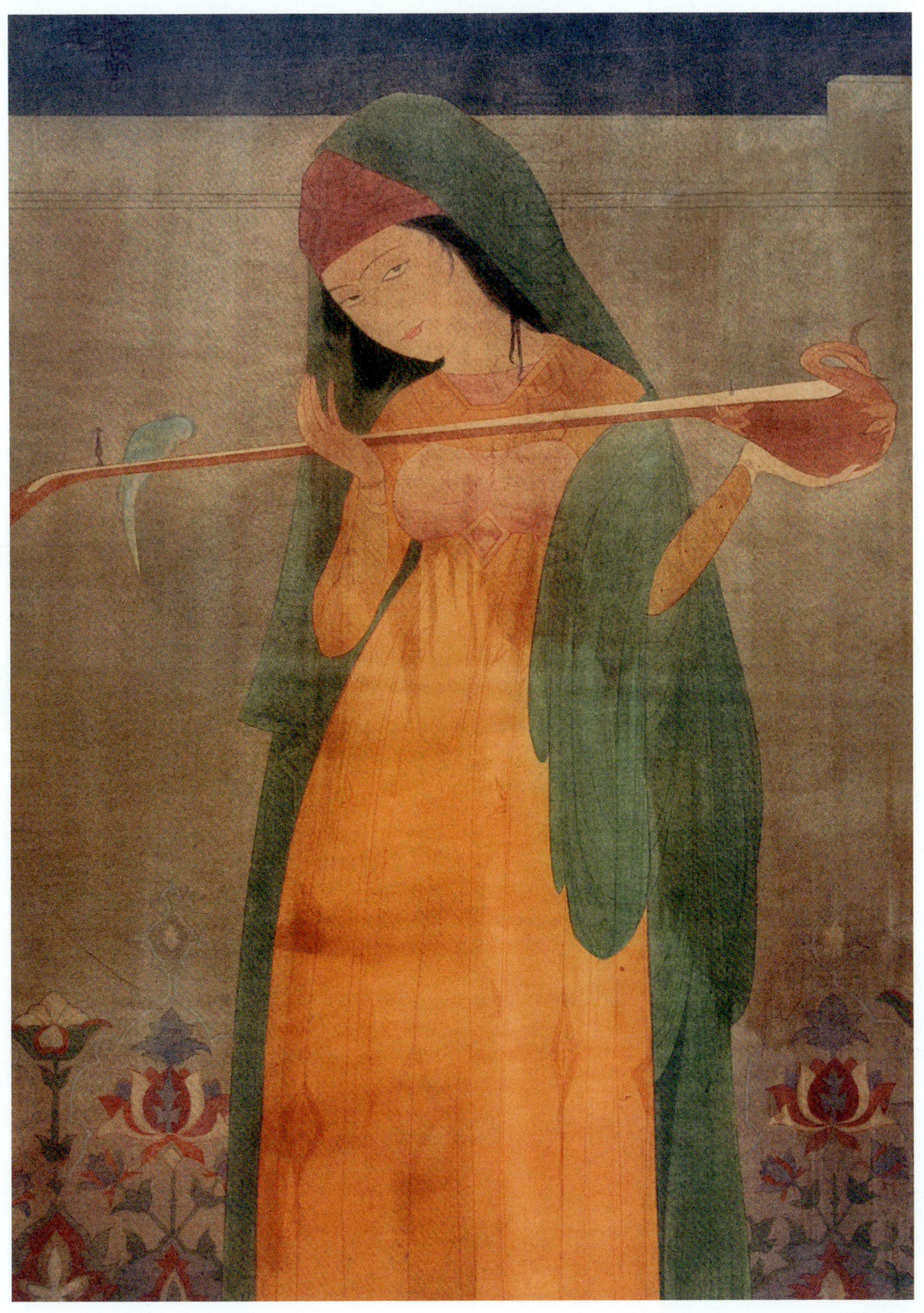

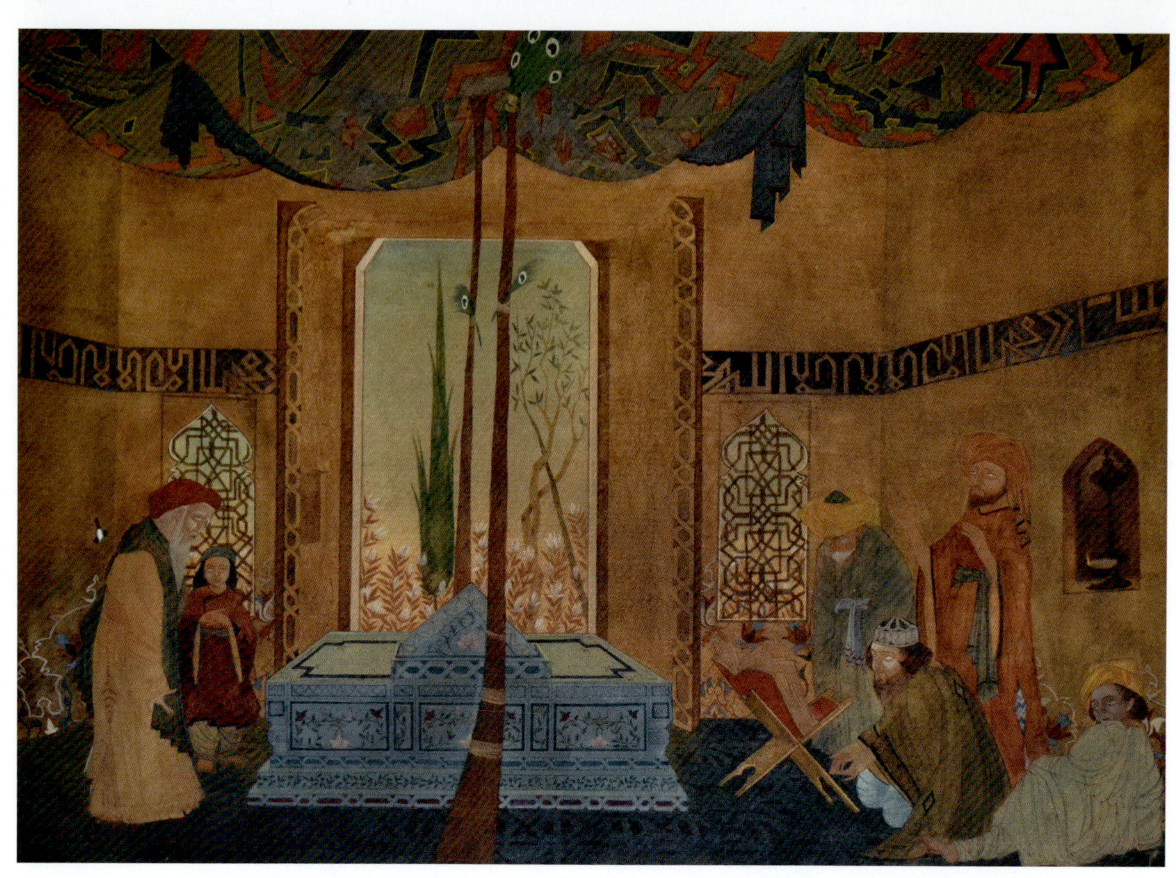

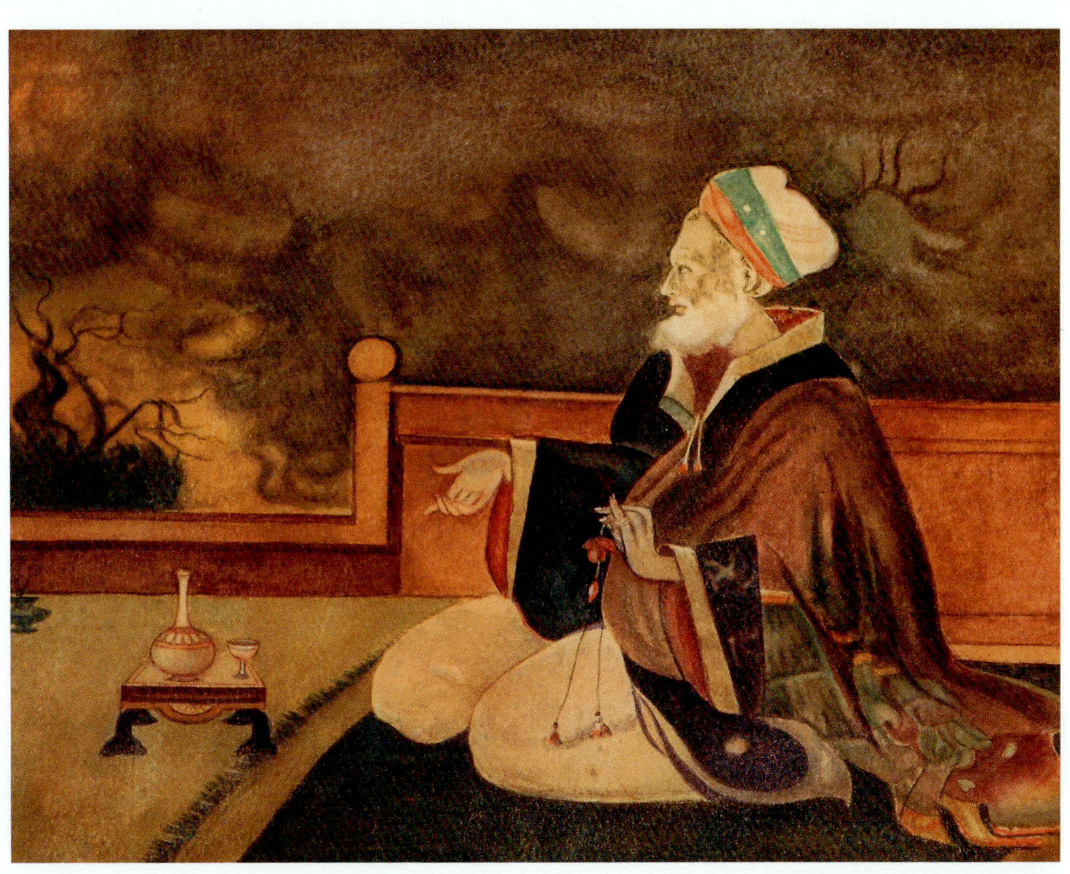

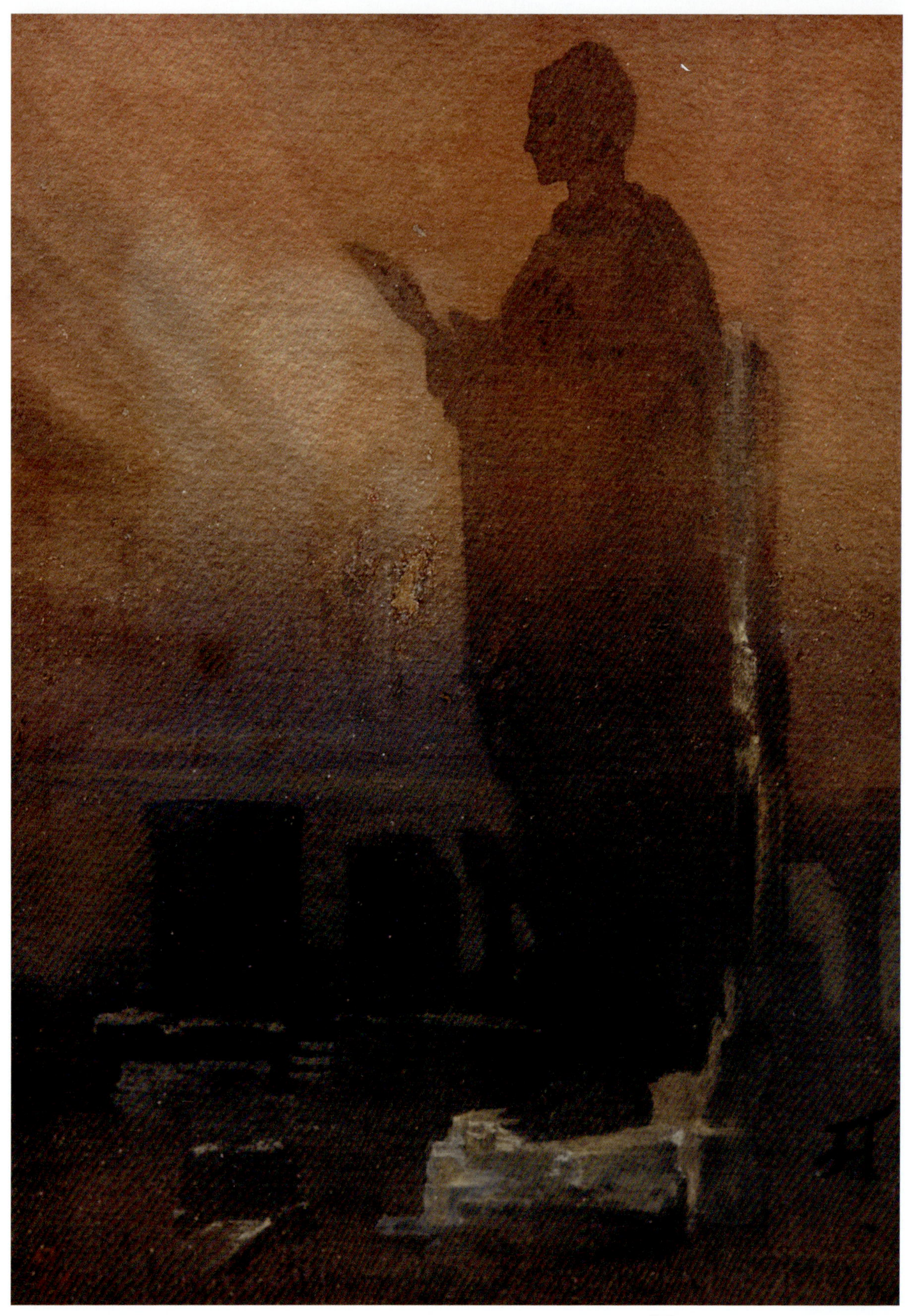

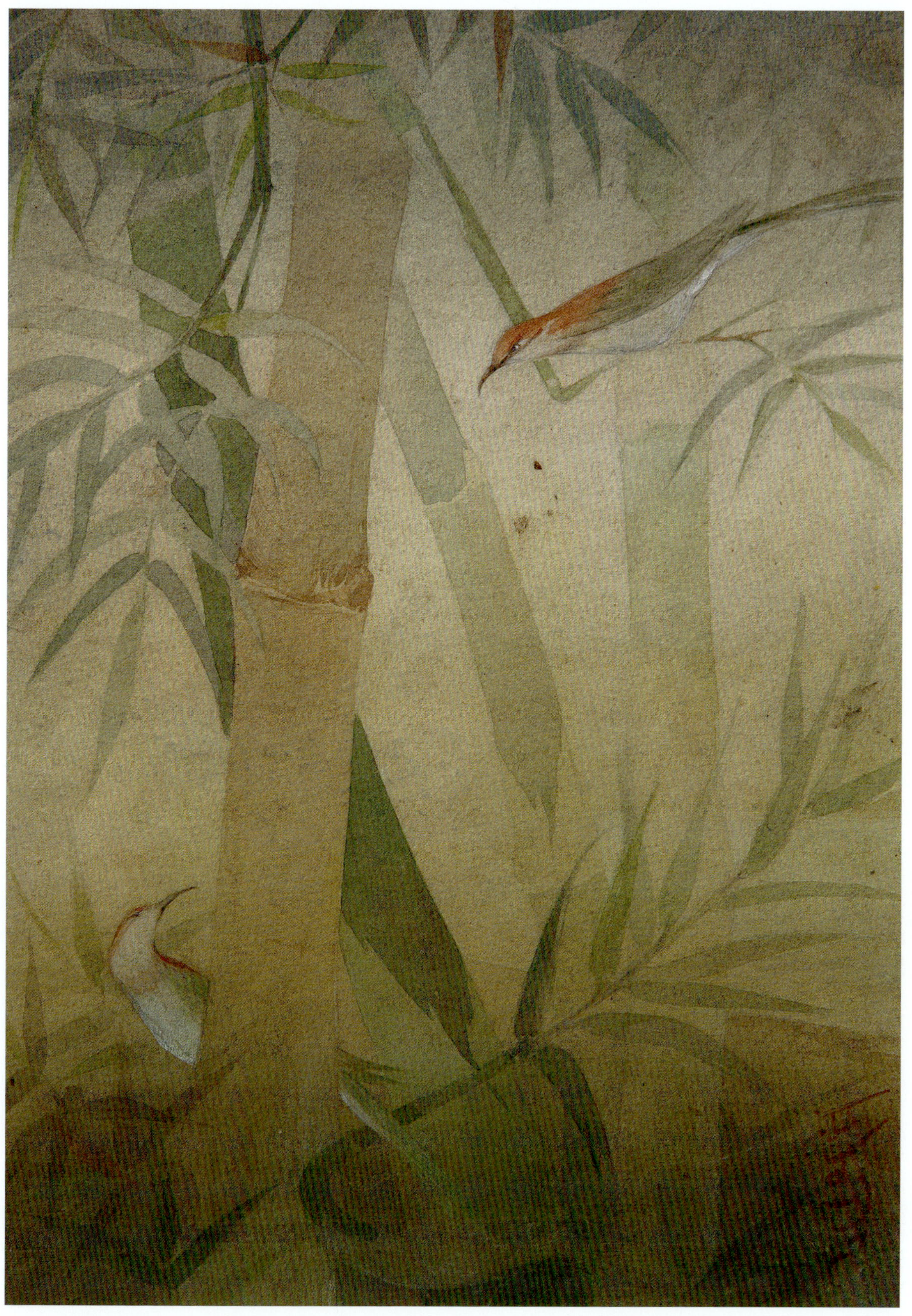

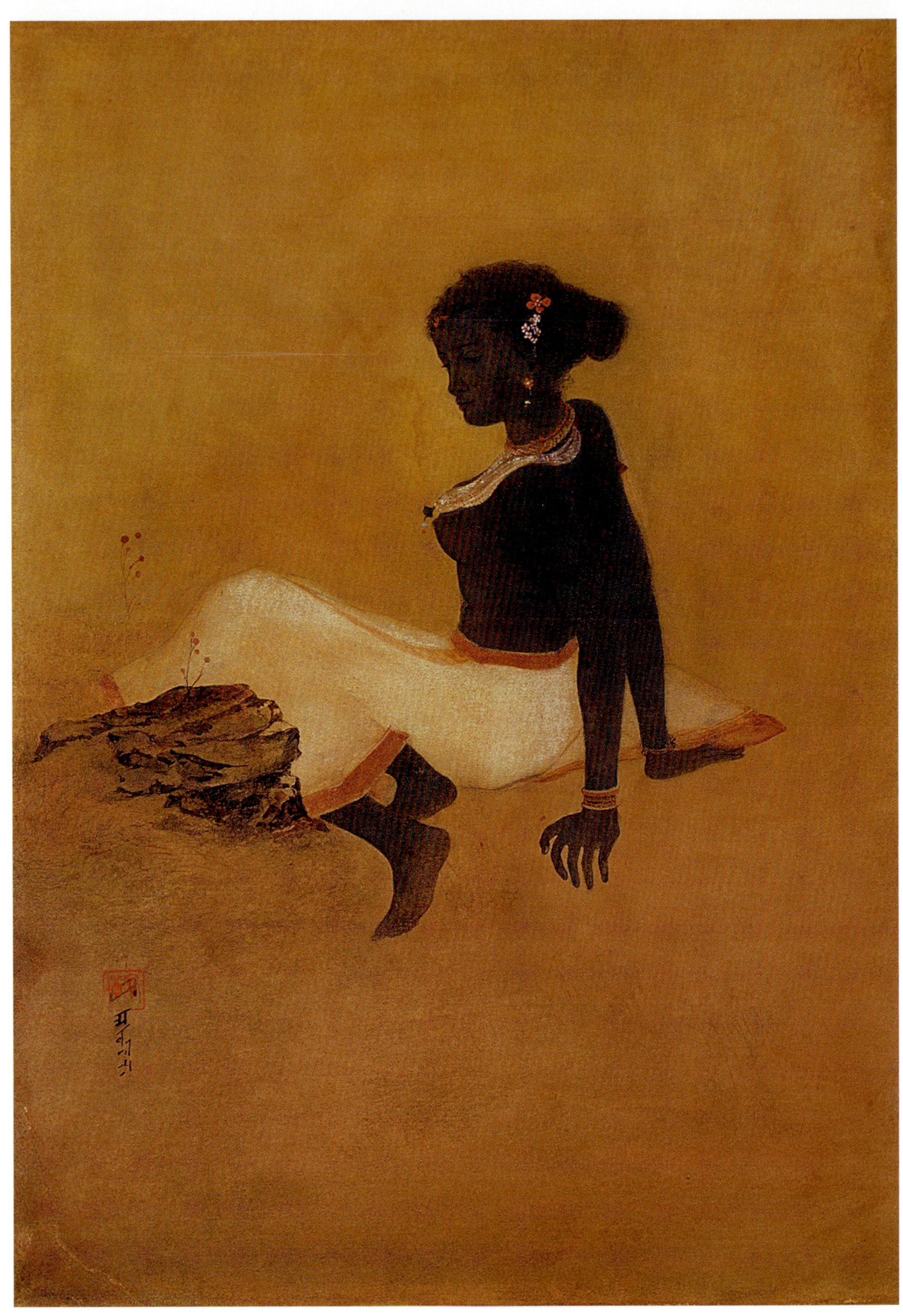

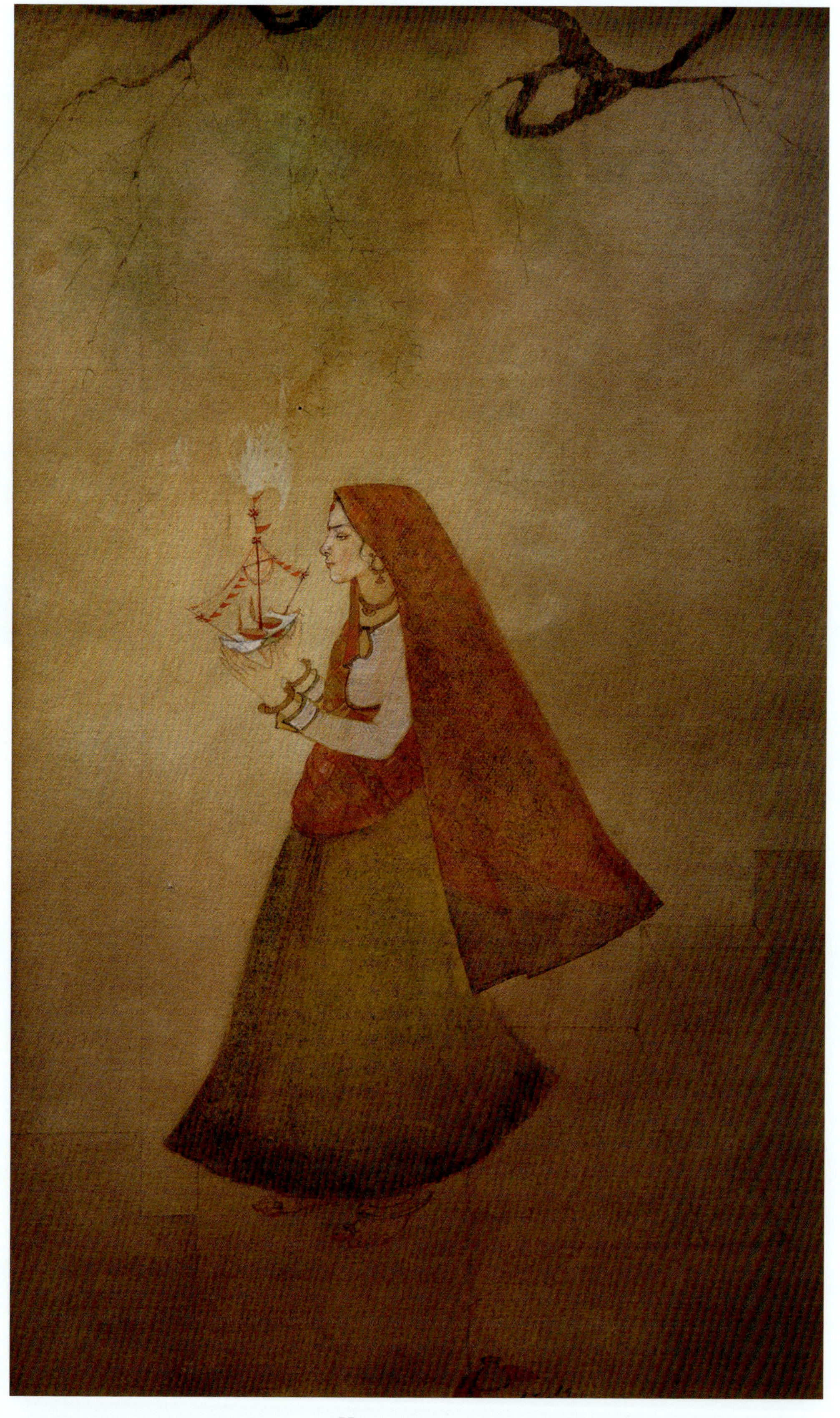

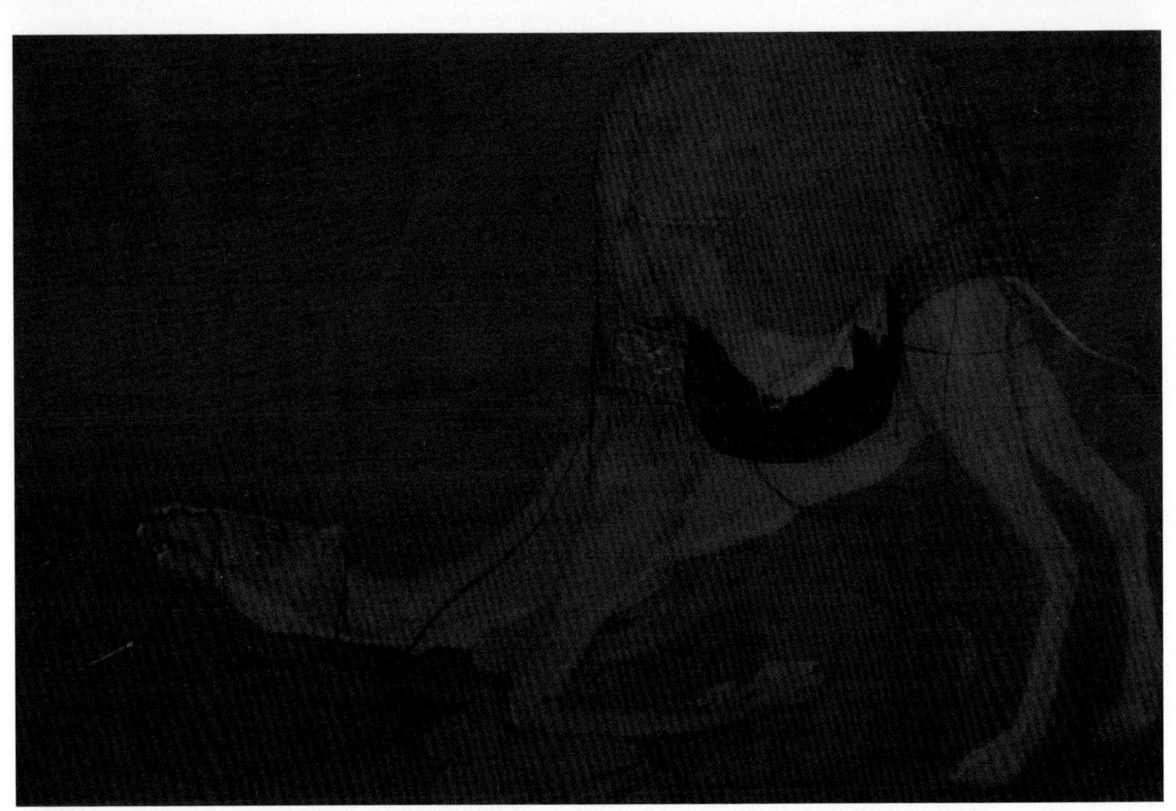

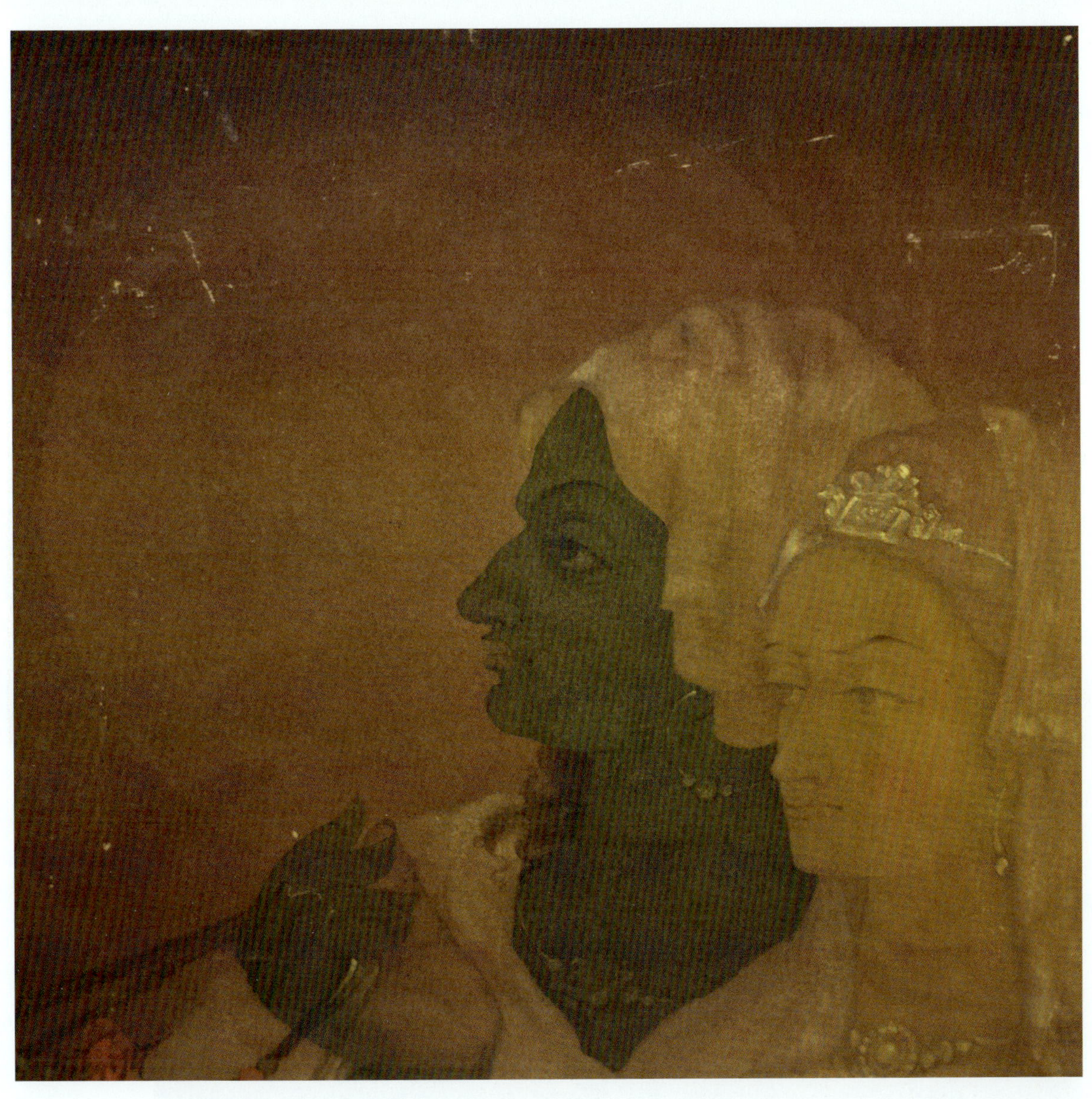

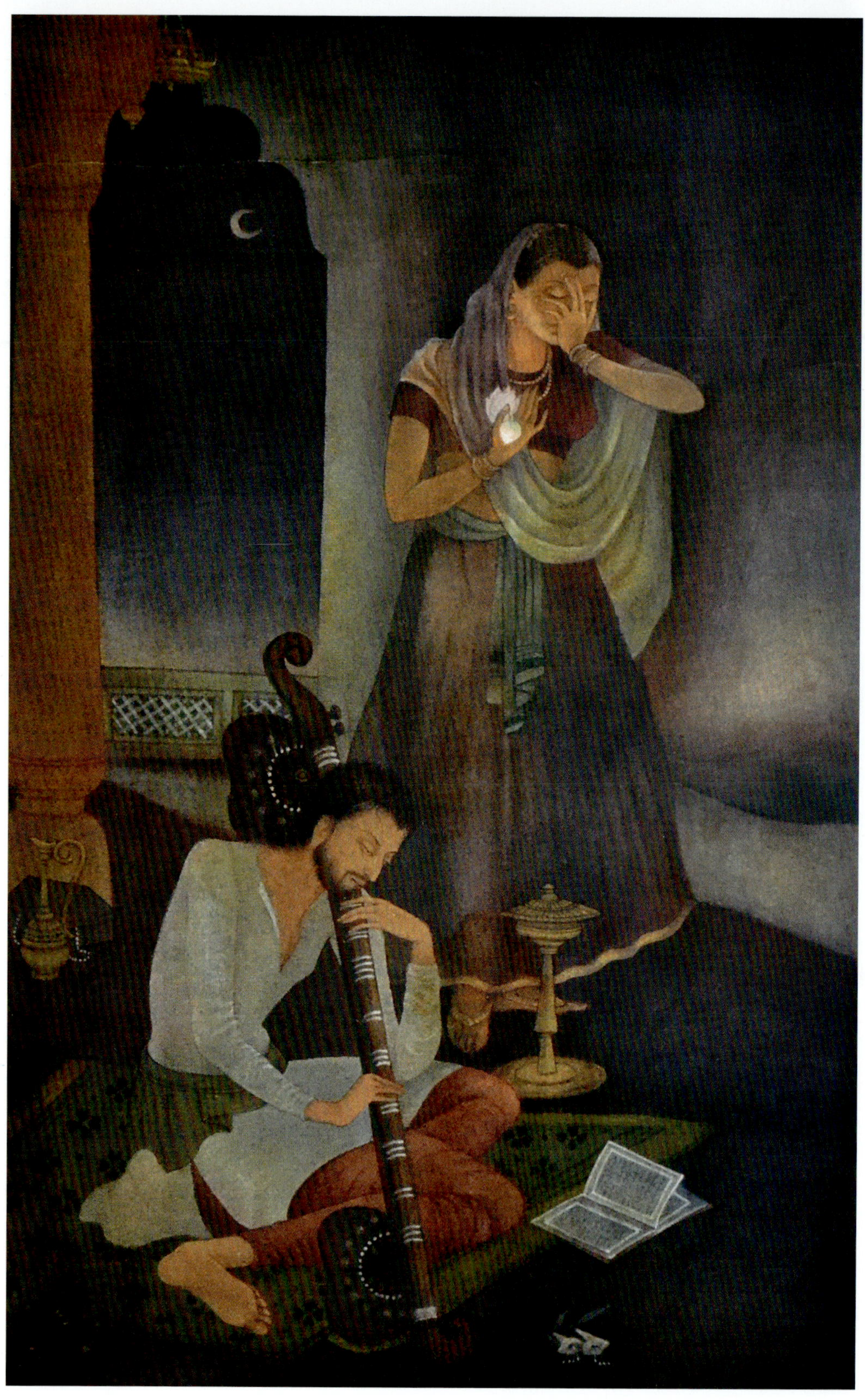

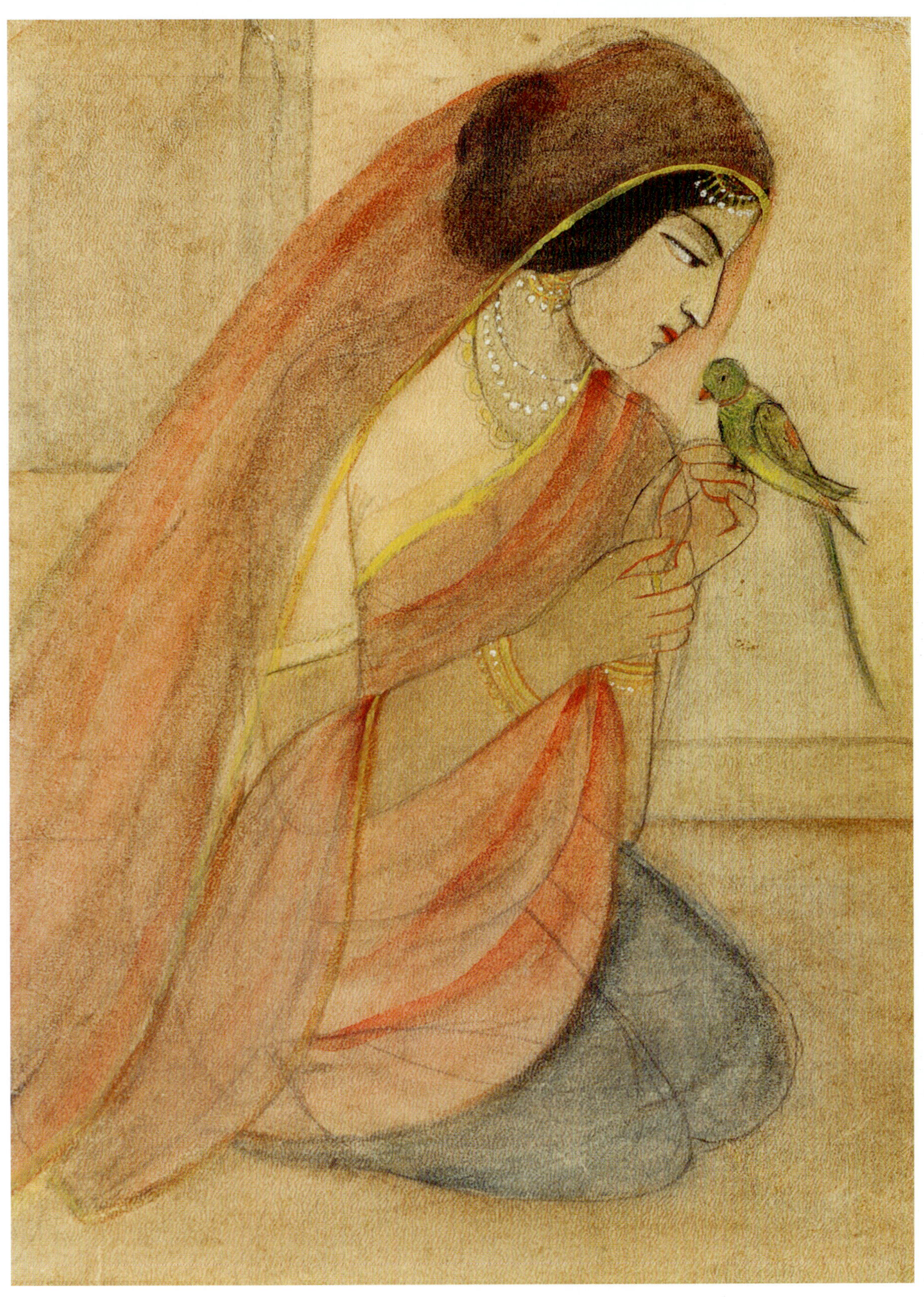

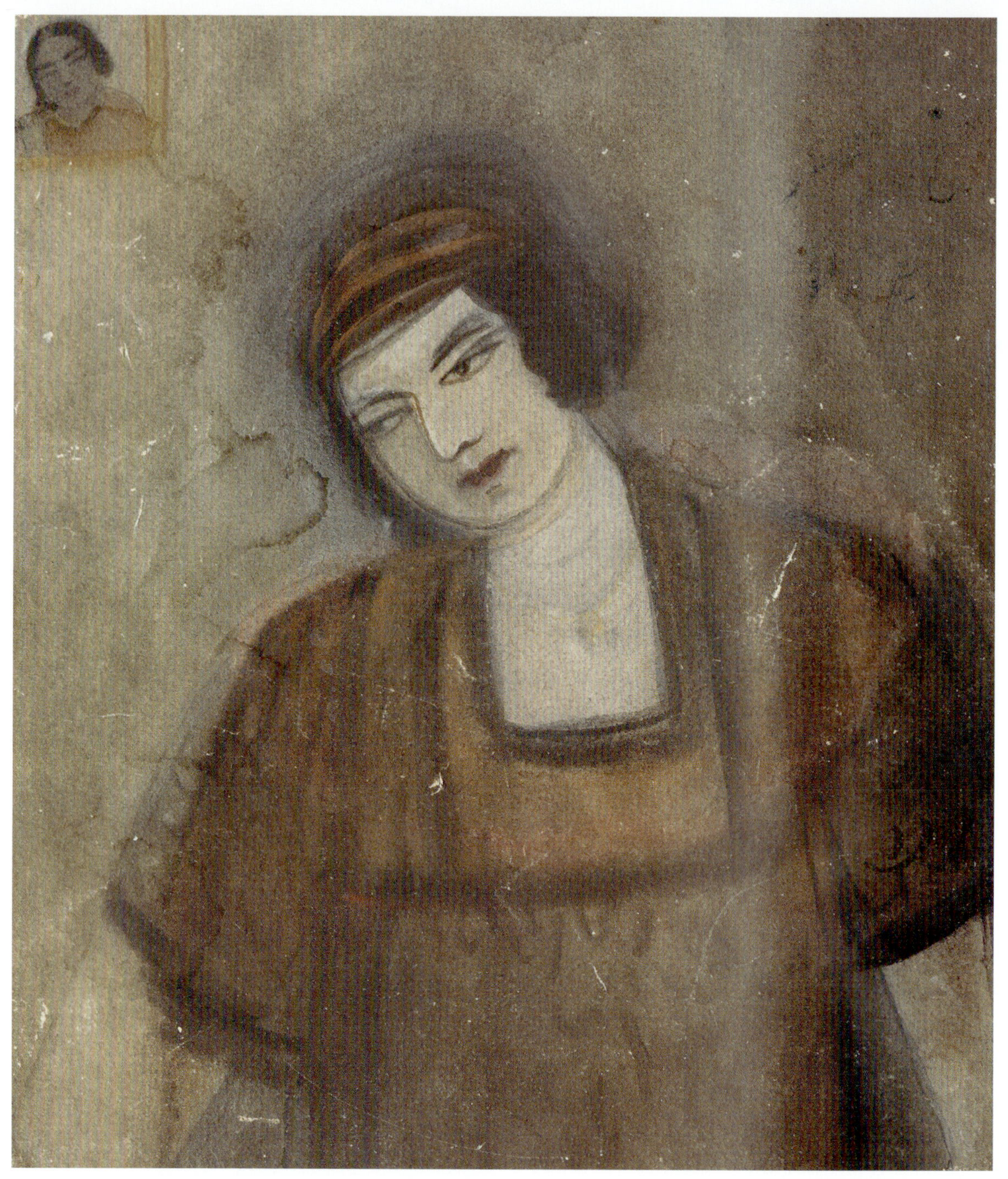

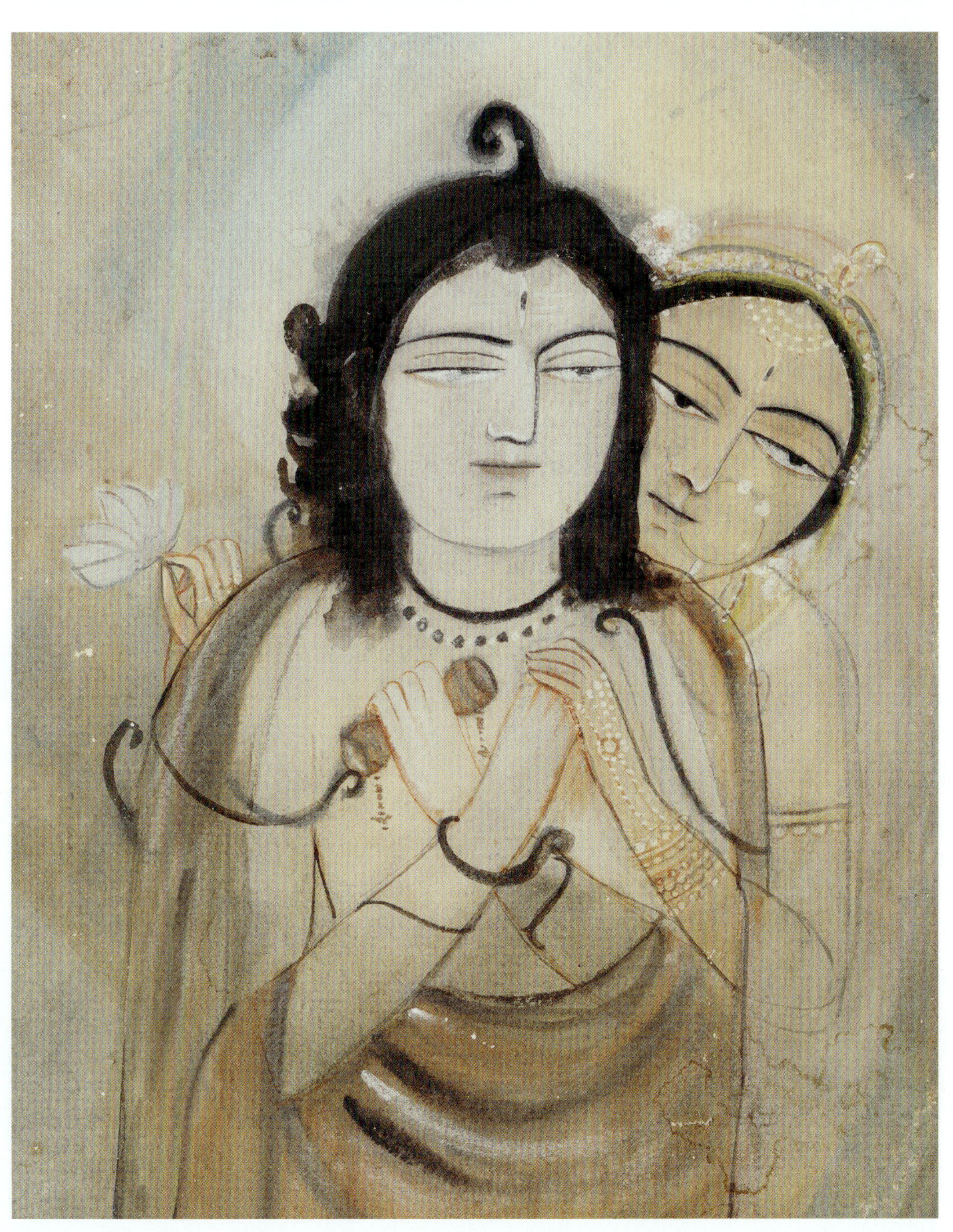

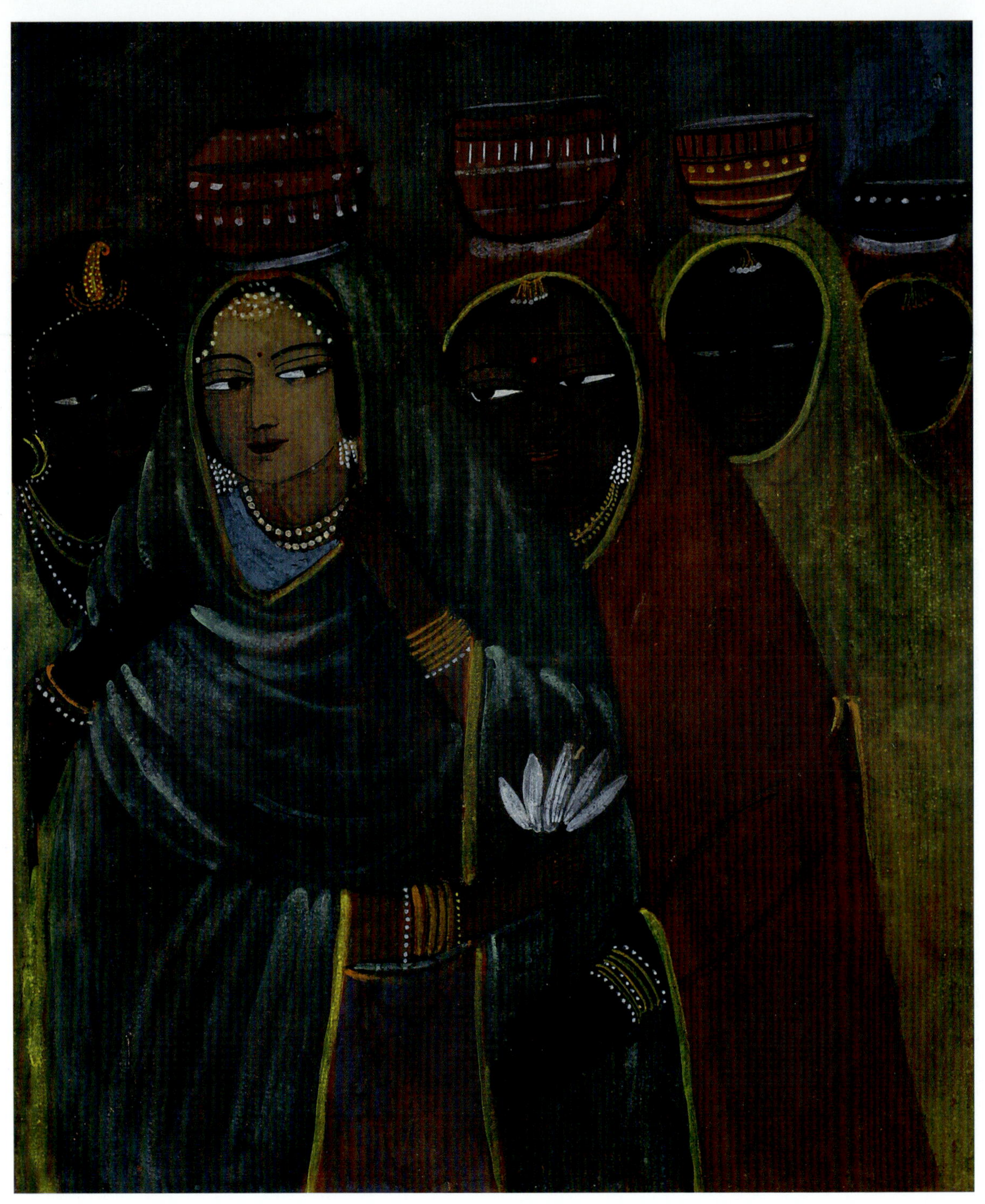

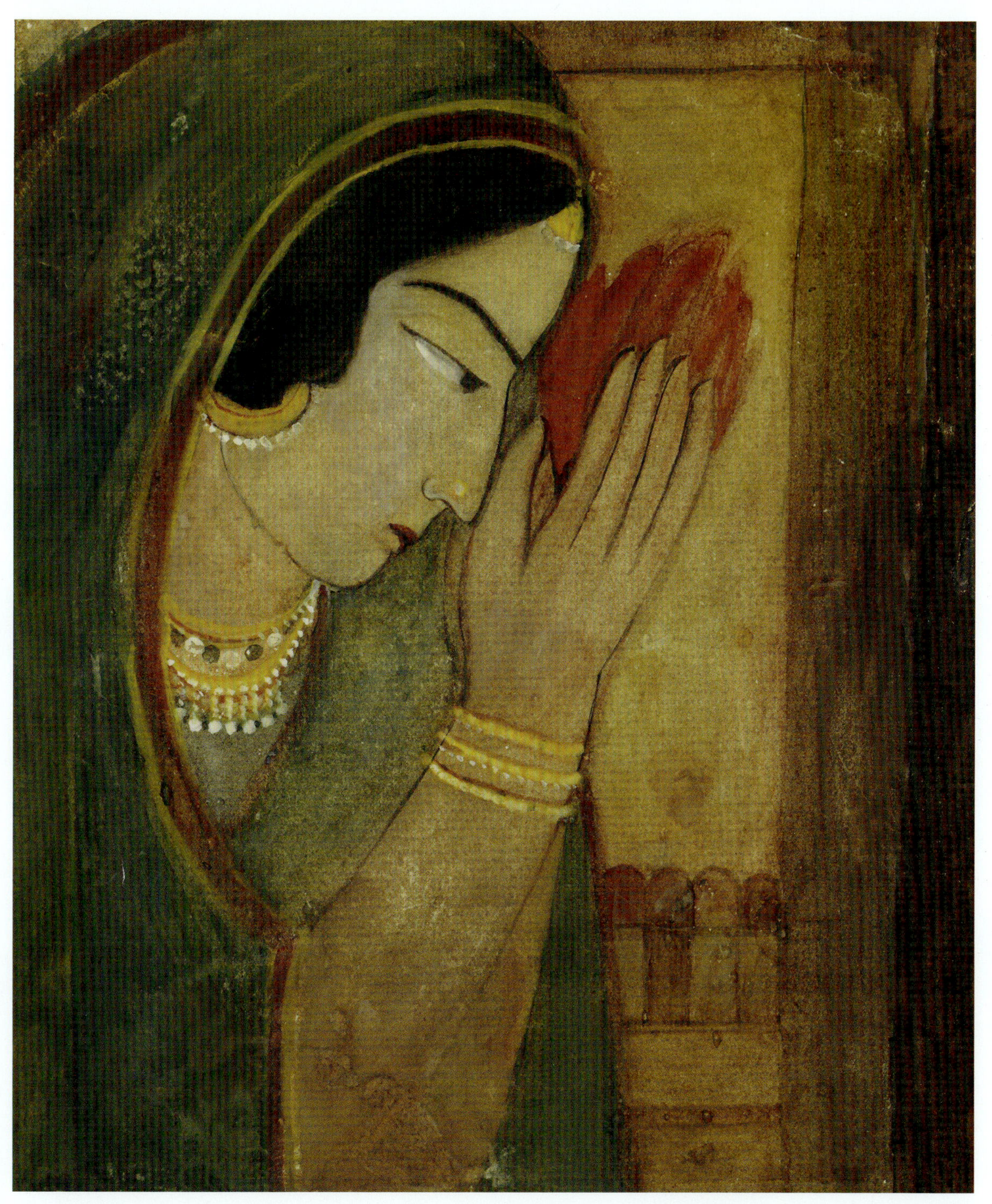

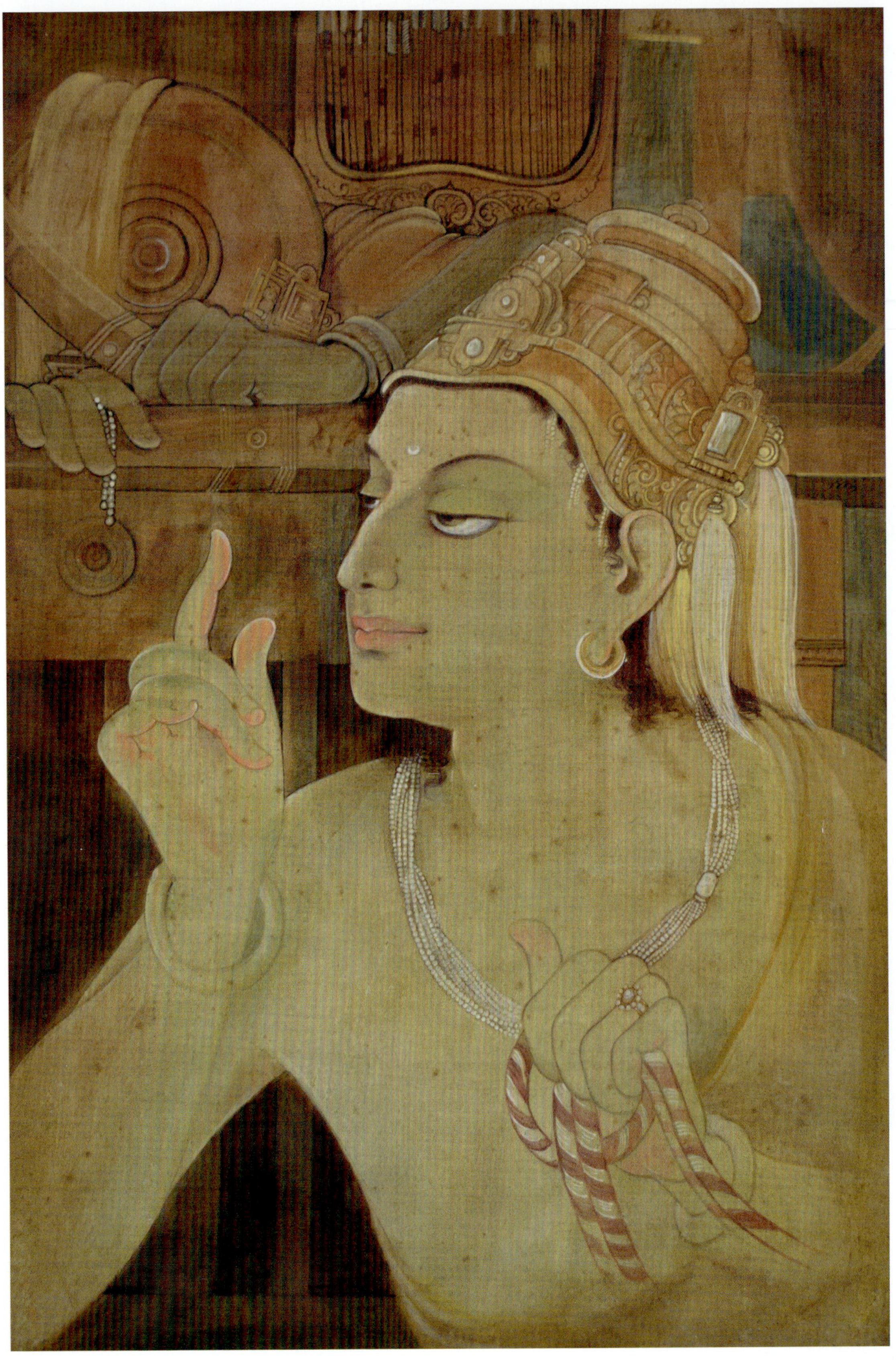

Regina Bittner and Kathrin Rhomberg

The Bauhaus in Calcutta

World Art since 1922: On the Topicality of an Exhibition

The Indian Society of Oriental Art is today based on the fourth floor of Apeejay House in Park Street—one of Calcutta's busiest streets, which, characterized by the morbid charm of its colonial buildings following decades of decline, is now being renovated to make way for international chain stores.

Tejendra Kumar Roy has been attending to the society's heritage for a number of years and knows the legendary history of the 14th Annual Exhibition of 1922, in which works by Bauhaus masters and modern Indian artists were shown side by side in the society's former rooms at the Samavaya Mansions. The Indian Society of Oriental Art works in the field of art education still today. The painting class, which is held three times a week at no charge, is underway next door. Here, sitting in front of easels or resting drawing boards on their knees, young people of all social and ethnic backgrounds learn to draw from a life model. Roy explains that the society still organizes annual exhibitions—although the range and context of its public activities have changed considerably. The society was founded in 1907 as an "Orientalist's Art Club," chiefly by numerous high-ranking representatives of the British colonial government. It was mainly concerned with organizing exhibitions and cultivating the wider public's taste for a new art movement, which developed an independent visual culture based on the local roots, craftsmanship traditions, and pictorial conventions. The enthusiasm for Indian culture expressed by many of the architects of British culture and education thereby revolved around a complex quest for a culture lost in the course of industrialization—a culture as a "homogeneous manifestation of the life of a people,"[1] which centered on craftsmanship and its object culture. If this articulated a criticism of Western modernization processes, then "Orientalism" likewise formed the ideological framework of the British colonial contributors.

Little material evidence remains of the legendary status which this exhibition has gained over ninety-one years of modern, international art historiography. The exhibition building was demolished in the nineteen-forties; possibly the only remaining original exhibition catalogue is now in Lahore,

Pakistan; and photographs of the exhibition are nowhere to be found. There are just two cuttings from the December 15, 1922 issue of *The Englishmen* that report the opening of the exhibition—although the society's own journal *RUPAM* published a lengthy review by the art historian Stella Kramrisch, which placed the exhibition in the context of the Indian artists' search for a cultural identity.

Nevertheless, the sparse material makes one thing clear: the exhibition was a crystallization point for complex cultural departures in late-colonial Calcutta, a metropolis that had a specific presence in the world. The comparatively small community from which the Indian Society of Oriental Art derived its members was part of a wide international network of cultural, political, and intellectual circles and institutions, the activities of which reflected the global nature of the early twentieth century: the First World War, where Indian and British soldiers fought side by side in the trenches, was as global in nature as the desperate struggles for independence that had shaped the political climate on the subcontinent for a decade, reaching a brutal climax in the Amritsar massacre of 1919. The Indian diasporas in Berlin, London, and Paris not only participated in this liberation movement but also formed its intellectual core. This global exchange had gained momentum owing to innovations in communications technologies and transport infrastructures.

At the same time, the exhibition presented a platform for extensive international efforts to redefine the social role of art and, in this context, to reform art education. The painters involved came from educational institutes inspired by a spirit of reform. Wassily Kandinsky, Paul Klee, Johannes Itten, and Lyonel Feininger were among the dominant figures in the council of masters at the helm the Staatliche Bauhaus, which was founded by Walter Gropius in Weimar in 1919. As a product of the Weimar Republic, diverse currents of cultural reform came together here, taking the postwar crisis of meaning and orientation as a starting point for new concepts of the world and doctrines of salvation.

[1] Wolf Gorch Zachriat, *Die Ambivalenz des Fortschritts: Friedrich Nietzsches Kulturkritik* (Berlin, 2002), p. 129.

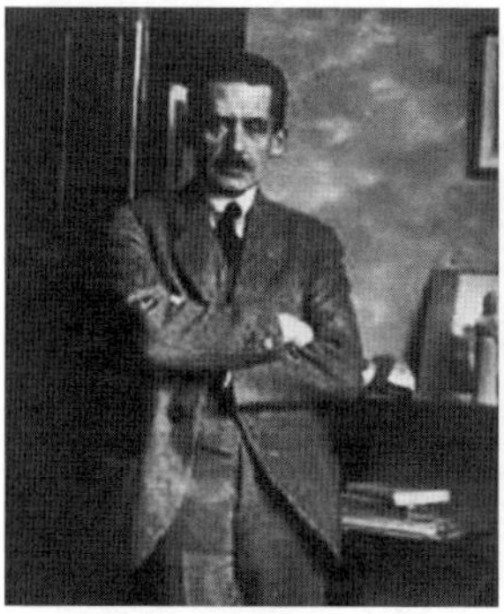

1.1 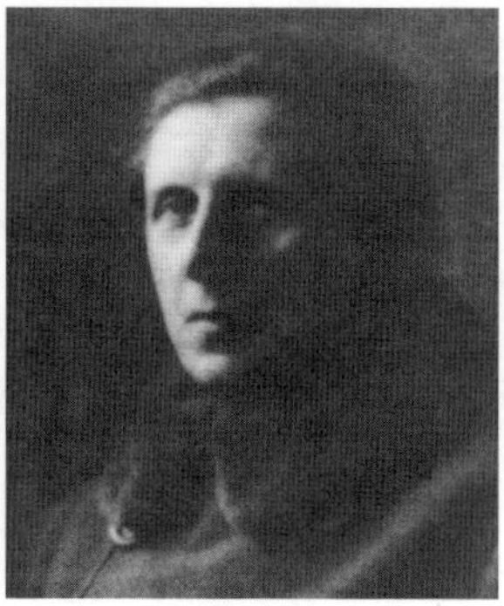 1.2 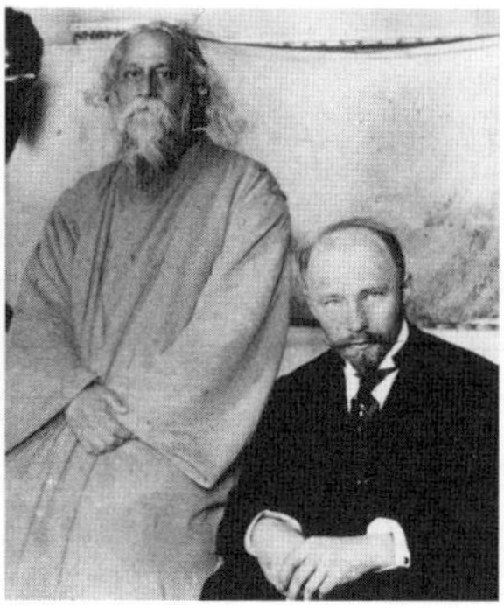 1.3 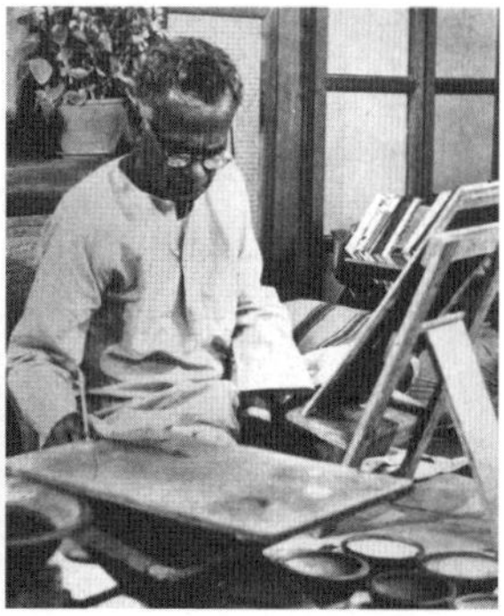 1.4

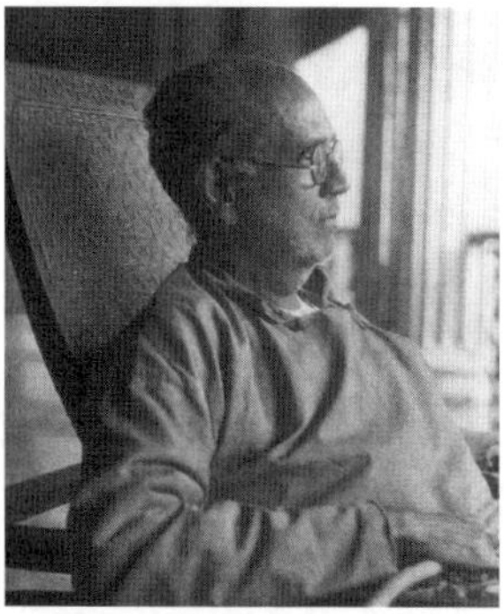

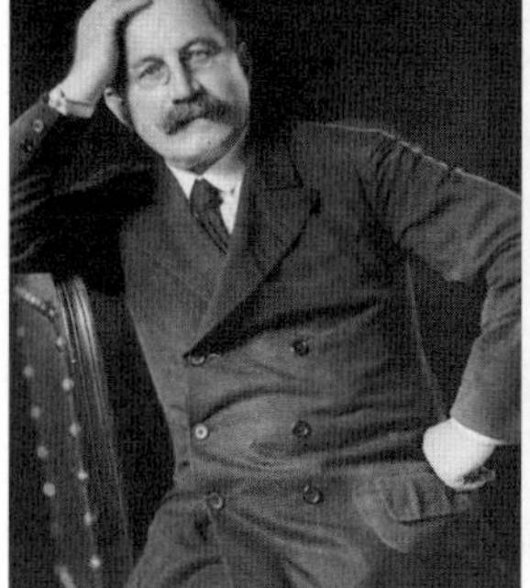
1.5

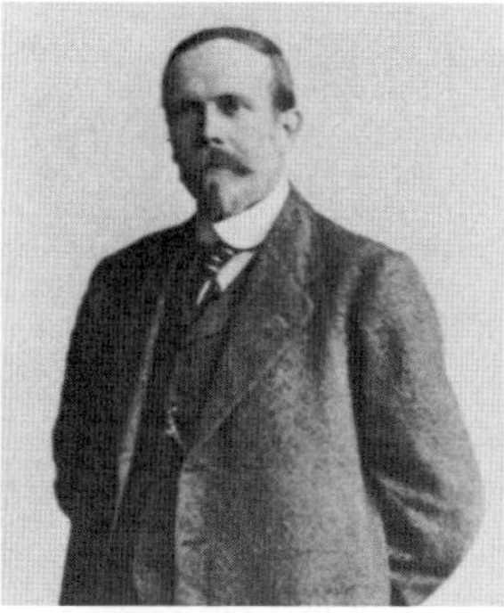

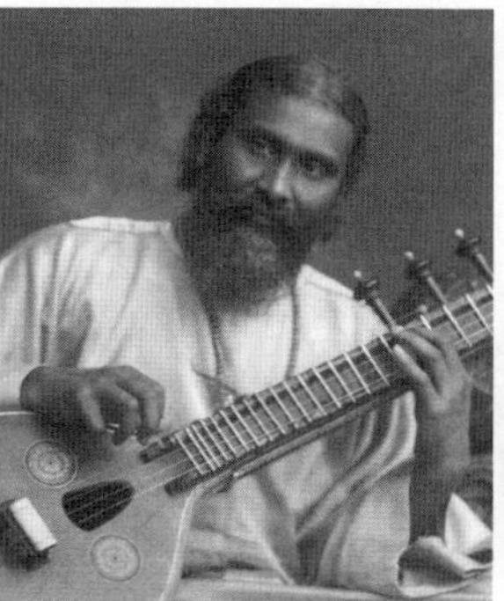
1.6

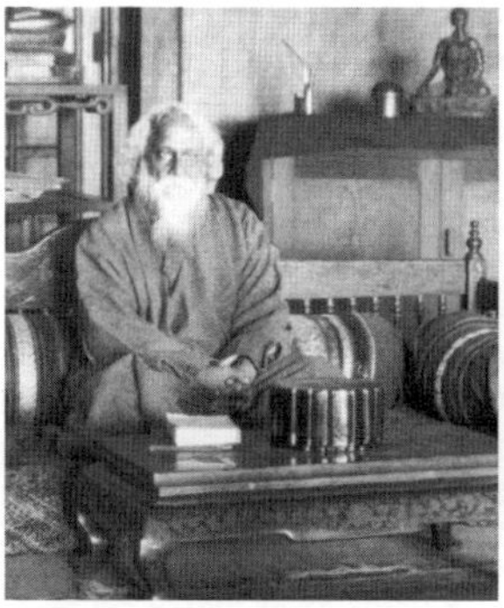

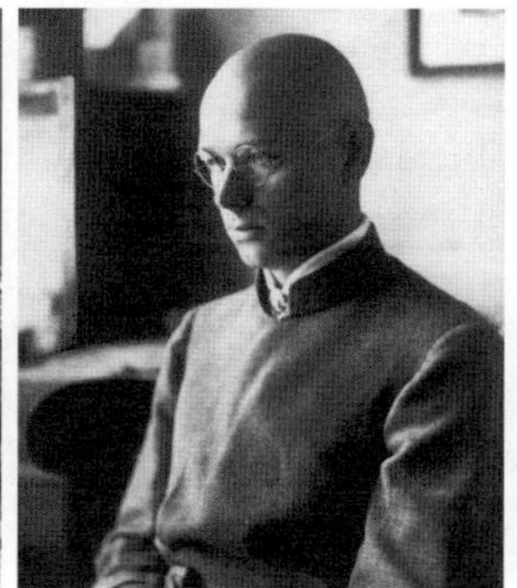
1.7

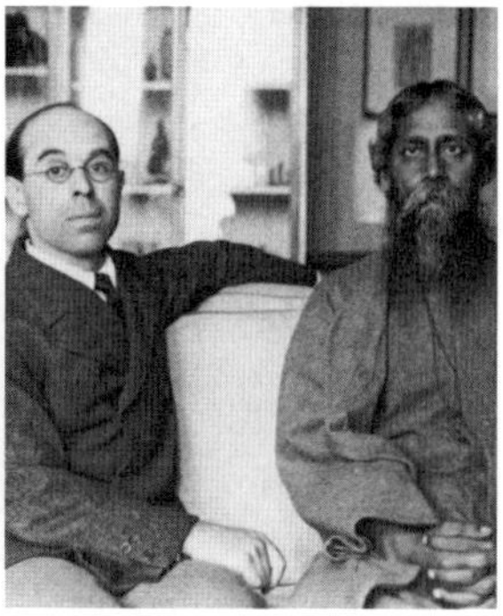

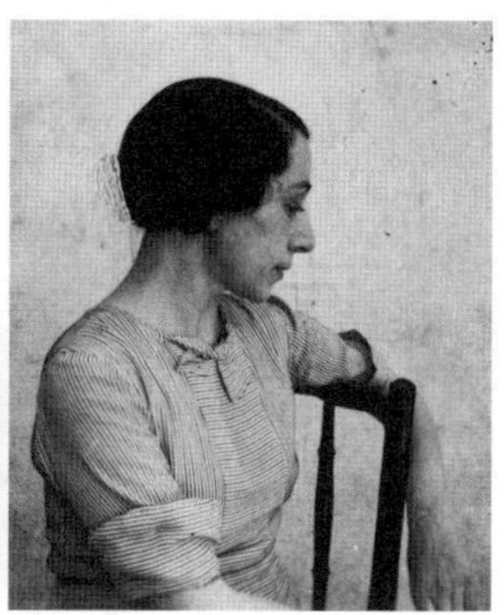
1.8

1.9 1.12

Captions

1.1 Photographer unknown, Walter Gropius at the Bauhaus Weimar, 1920, photograph
1.2 Photographer unknown, Ananda Kentish Coomaraswamy, 1919, photograph
1.3 Photographer unknown, Hermann Graf Keyserling with Rabindranath Tagore, 1921, photograph
1.4 Photographer unknown, Nandalal Bose, n.d., photograph
1.5 E. O. Hoppé, Abanindranath Tagore, 1929, photograph
1.6 Photographer unknown, Ernest B. Havell, n.d., photograph
1.7 E. O. Hoppé, Rabindranath Tagore in his drawing room, Udayan, Shantiniketan, 1929, photograph
1.8 John Trevor, William Rothenstein and Rabindranath Tagore, 1912, photograph
1.9 Photographer unknown, Josef Strzygowski, n.d., photograph
1.10 Photographer unknown, portrait of Hazrat Inayat Khan (Pir-o-Murshid) playing his instrument, n.d., photograph
1.11 Photographer unknown, Johannes Itten at the Bauhaus Weimar, 1920, photograph
1.12 Photographer unknown, Stella Kramrisch, Calcutta (?), ca. 1920, photograph

References to Eastern religion and philosophy manifested in different forms, from theosophy to Mazdaznan: in an intellectual climate that foresaw a "decline of the Western world,"[2] India offered an imaginary space in which the longing for an organic culture, not yet entirely undermined by rationalization and industrialization, took form.

Nandalal Bose, Abanindranath Tagore, and Sunyani Devi were among a generation of artists who studied first at the Government School of Art in Calcutta (now, since 1951, the Government College of Art & Craft) and, from 1919, at the world university Shantiniketan, founded by Rabindranath Tagore. Known as the Bengal School, this movement was based on a rejection of the naturalism taught in the art schools. For Kala Bhavan, the art school in Shantiniketan, India's rural culture presented the framework for an autonomous, independent cultural renewal.

Schools of Departure

In 1921 the London journal *Nation* published a text entitled "A Spiritual Alliance," which stated: "While the whole world is at war, it is some comfort to hear even one voice, however still and small, persistently murmuring of peace. Amid the turmoil and shouting one may still catch the quiet words of an Indian pleading the cause of understanding, friendliness, and forbearance, as though they, and not devastating conflicts, were the most natural things in the world. In such a spirit it is that Rabindranath Tagore has been moving, almost silently, from country to country, and from hemisphere to hemisphere, insinuating his conception of an International university . . . Suspected as a seditious agitator, dogged by Government spies, impugned by official detraction, or, at the best, scornfully tolerated as an impracticable dreamer, he has trodden the well-worn and dolorous path of the spirit."[3]

[2] Oswald Spengler, *Der Untergang des Abendlandes: Umrisse einer Morphologie der Weltgeschichte* (Munich, 2007).
[3] Quoted from Krishna Dutta and Andrew Robinson, *Rabindranath Tagore: The Myriad-Minded Man* (New York, 1995), p. 219.

Captions

2 Photographer unknown, Stella Kramrisch with members of the Indian Society of Oriental Art, n.d., photograph
3–4 Letters from Stella Kramrisch to Johannes Itten, 1922

3

Weimar, den 5. Mai 22.

000001

Sehr geehrter Herr Itten!

Abaundron-nath Pagore und die Society of Oriental Calcutta planen für diesen Herbst eine internationale Ausstellung lebender Kunst, die jedes Land in seiner Kraft und Zukünftigkeit repräsentieren soll. Darf ich Sie bitten, einige Blätterr Zeichnungen, Aquarelle, Lithographien oder auch Holzschnitte zu senden? Transport und Versicherungskosten deckt die Society von vorner herein. Die Verkaufspreise werden in Ruppes festgesetzt, (15 Rupees = 1 englisches Pfund.) Sehr dankbar wären wir, wollten Sie frühere und auch ganz letzte eigene Arbeiten senden und auch solche, die das gesamte Werk des Bauhauses darstellen, vor allem Arbeiten von Herrn Klee. Auch gute Schülerarbeiten wären sehr willkommen.

Bitte um bald möglichste Antwort, ob Sie geneigt sind unsere Einladung anzunehmen, wieviel Blätter ungefähr wir erwarten dürfen und wie hoch Porto und Versicherungskosten kommen werden. Nach erfolgter Ausstellung werden die unverkauften Arbeiten selbstredend umgehend zurückgestellt.

Mit den besten Empfehlungen

Stelle Kramrisch,
Santiniketran, International University,
Bengal, India.

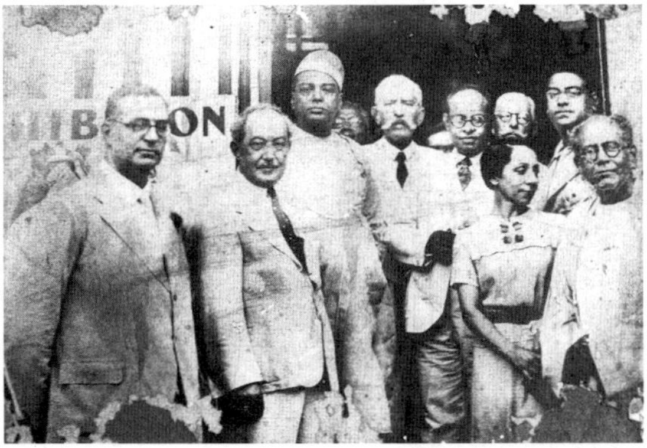

2

000002

Santiniketan 12.VI.22

Sehr geehrter Herr Itten,

Vielen Dank für Ihre Zusage die Ausstellung in Calcutta betreffend.
– Da Sie nicht erwähnten wie hoch Porto und Versicherungsspesen kommen würden, schickt die Society eine Anweisung für Pfund 2.–. Es ist schwer von hier deutsche Postgebühren zu berechnen. Im Fall einer Mehrausgabe kann diese mit der Society verrechnet werden. Die Kosten der Rücksendung trägt selbstredend die Society.

Die Ausstellung soll am 1.

000003

Oktober eröffnet werden Dauer 1 Monat. Vom Verkauf eines jeden Bildes werden 20 % abgezogen. Die Verkaufspreise für original aquarelle, Zeichnungen etc. bewegen sich zwischen 5 bis 15 Pfund.

Es wäre gut die Bilder wenn möglich ungerahmt und unverglast zu senden. Beides wird hier vor der Ausstellung besorgt werden. Glas und Rahmen sind schwer zu packen und könnten während der Reise die Arbeiten beschädigen.

Schülerarbeiten sind uns sehr erwünscht. Wäre es möglich eine größere Zahl zu senden? Mit der Liste der Arbeiten der Meister ist die Society vollkommen einverstanden, doch hätten wir gerne, wenn möglich

000004

mehr gesehen. Bitte senden Sie auch Photos Ihrer großen Arbeiten.

Es wäre gut wenn die Bilder vor Mitte September hier ankämen, das heißt sie müssen Mitte August aufgegeben werden. (spätestens in der 3. ten August woche).

Die Adresse der Society ist:

Dr. Abanindranath Tagore
„Indian Society of Oriental Art"
5, Dwarkanath Tagore Street
Calcutta, India.

Mit den besten Empfehlungen

Dr. Stella Kramrisch
International University
Santiniketan
Bengal

4

Rabindranath Tagore's travels through Europe and the USA in the second decade of the twentieth century were primarily motivated by the search for patrons for his international university, which he wished to establish 150 kilometers north of Calcutta in Shantiniketan. He had already opened a school here at the beginning of the century—a school defined by a progressive education system that departed from the Western canon and focused on more playful and natural teaching methods. Dance and drama classes, for instance, were therefore taught in direct contact with the rural population in their natural environment. Primary-level education thereby formed a cornerstone of Tagore's efforts to reform the education system.

In 1919 Rabindranath Tagore established the world university Visva-Bharati, a Sanskrit name that, roughly speaking, means "the universal presence in one place." The title was programmatic: Tagore's aim was to bring the world's most compelling thinkers together here and to initiate cultural change from this reciprocal inspiration: the encounter between East and West. The choice of location was also programmatic, for rural India harbored the cultural traditions that in turn formed the basis for a new national identity. The school was made up of three closely interlinked institutes: a progressive art school (Kala Bhavan), a school of music and performance arts, and an Indology department, where most of the international academics, including Stella Kramrisch, worked. Sriniketan, located a kilometer away from Kala Bhavan, was an important part of Tagore's program, which also championed agricultural reform: given the fact that the majority of the Indian population lived rurally, the regeneration of the rural economy and the improvement of village life was a priority. In the process, the project's objective of revitalizing rural craftsmanship traditions was to be met not only by teacher-centered instruction, but also through practical experience. Here at Sriniketan, work focused not only on the cultivation of the land, but also on traditional crafts such as weaving and pottery. Hence there was a lively exchange between Shantiniketan and Sriniketan.

Captions

5 List of artworks for the exhibition of the Indian Society of Oriental Art in Calcutta: Lyonel Feininger, 1922, manuscript

6 List of artworks for the exhibition of the Indian Society of Oriental Art in Calcutta: Paul Klee, 1922, manuscript

7 Shambu Shaha Vasatotsav, students from Sangit-Bhavana in the foreground, 1939, photograph

8 Photographer unknown, Tagore's villa in Jorasanko, n.d., photograph

Ausstellung Calcutta, Oktober 1922

Zeichnungen und Aquarelle.

000064

				£
1.	On the Quay	Feder Zeichn.	1911	15.–
2.	The Estuary	" "	1911	15.–
3.	Ships in the Offing	" "	1911	15.–
4.	Sunrise	Gouache	1911	15.–
5.	The Village	Feder Zeichn.	1911	15.–
6.	The Disparagers	Feder – Aquarell	1911	15.–
7.	Fellow	Feder Zeichn.	1913	15.–
8.	The Anglers	" "	1914	15.–
9.	Die Angler	Aquarell	1915	15.–
10.	Strasse in Arcueil	"	1915	15.–
11.	Karneval	"	1915	15.–
12.	Werder I	"	1916	15.–
13.	Der Mann m. d. Rad	"	1916	15.–
14.	Ehringsdorf	"	1918	15.–
15.	Gabendorf	"	1918	15.–
16.	Fischerflotte	"	1921	15.–
17.	Marine	"	1921	15.–
18.	Gutshof I.	Feder Zeichn.	1922	15.–
19.	Gutshof II	" "	1922	15.–

Holzschnitte.

1.	Windmühle	1967	Holzschnitt.	5.–
2.	Kirche	2033	"	5.–
3.	Kirche	2103	"	3.–
4.	Marine	2104	"	3.–
5.	Marine	1939	"	3.–
6.	Dorf	2039	"	5.–
7.	Mellingen	1965	"	5.–
8.	Vollersroda	1968	"	5.–
9.	Schiffe	1930	"	5.–
10.	Kreuzende Schiffe	1955.	Holzschnitt	5.–
11.	Gelmeroda	2045	"	5.–
12.	Pariser Häuser	2006	"	5.–
13.	Marine	1895.	"	5.–
14.	Schlachtflotte		"	7.–
15.	Das Tor	2035	"	7.–
16.	Railroad Bridge	1919	"	5.–

Die Preise sind in englischen Pfund angegeben
Lyonel Feininger

5

Klee Bauhaus Weimar

000067

Lieber Herr ...!
wollen Sie diese Bilder ins Gesamtverzeichnis der Bilder für die Tagoregesellschaft aufnehmen ...

Nr	Bezeichnung	Titel	Gattung	Verkaufspreis*
1	1922/64	rotviolett/gelbgrüne Stufung	Aquarell	zehn engl. Pfund
2	1922/66	Zwei Kioske	"	zehn " "
3	1922/63	Herzdame	"	fünfzehn " "
4	1922/61	Maske	"	zehn " "
5	1922/60	Schleusen	"	zehn " "
6	1922/58	Gestirne über dem Tempel	"	fünfzehn " "
7	1922/57	Gedicht einer Blüte	"	fünfzehn " "
8	1922/62	Abendsonne	"	zehn " "
9	1922/65	Palast	"	zehn " "

Klee

6

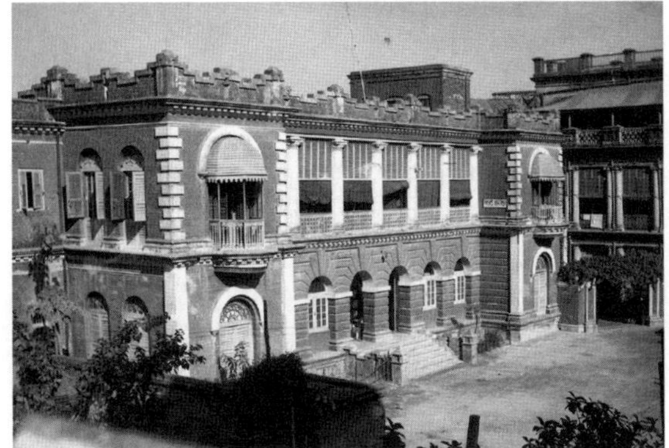

8

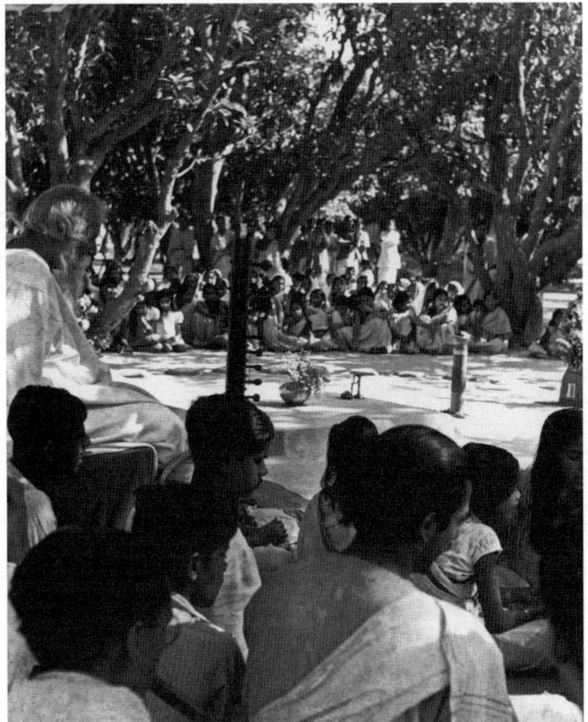

7

The educational reform pursued in Shantiniketan was directly associated with the Indian independence movement. Yet Tagore's international efforts to find funding for this project were certainly also motivated by the idea of independence from British dominance. This comes clearly to the fore in the correspondence between William Rothenstein, a leading advocate of "Orientalism" in London, and Rabindranath Tagore, his longtime friend.

Education as a Colonial Project

Education was central to the colonial project which, rooted in a fin-de-siècle "civilizing mission," was to replace the policy of exploiting resources and workforces. This policy was based on the conviction that non-Westerners had neither education nor culture and therefore first had to be civilized. In this context, the development of the art schools was awarded greater importance. However, the educational concepts that were applied were based on those of the British art schools. Parallel to this shift in colonial policy, in Britain the criticism of industrialization and its implications for society had led to the rise of a new interest in non-European cultures, particularly in Indian culture. William Morris and John Ruskin were among the group of social reformers and cultural critics who, in view of the fragmentation and alienation caused by industrial production, advised a return to craftsmanship as a model for a harmonious integration of lifestyle and production methods. Interestingly, this anti-industrial cultural criticism applied not only to premodern societies, but also to a revaluation of Indian culture.[4] It is only in this context that the debate following a lecture given in London in January 1910 by Ernest Binfield Havell, Director of the Government School of Art in Calcutta from 1896 to 1906, may be understood. Influenced by the spirit of British social reform, Havell publicly criticized the Empire's education policy in the Indian art schools. This, he maintained, was influenced by the prejudice that Indian culture was of no value, meaning that Indian artists were forced to adopt the norms and concepts of Western art. This attitude was manifested most clearly in the divide between the applied and fine arts.

[4] Christian Kravanga, "Im Schatten großer Mangobäume: Kunsterziehung und transkulturelle Moderne im Kontext der indischen Unabhängigkeitsbewegung," in *Das Erziehnungsbild: Zur Visuellen Kultur des Pädagogischen*, ed. Marion von Osten and Tom Holert (Vienna, 2010), p. 108.

[5] Quoted from Mary M. Lago, ed., *Imperfect Encounter: Letters of William Rothenstein and Rabindranath Tagore* (New York, 1972), p. 5.

[6] Swati Chattopadhyay, *Representing Calcutta: Modernity, Nationalism and the Colonial Uncanny* (London and New York, 2005), p. 132.

[7] See Tapati Guha-Thakurta, *The Making of a New "Indian" Art: Artists, Aesthetics and Nationalism in Bengal, c. 1850–1920* (Cambridge, 1992), p. 276.

Havell then presented as an example the Government School of Art, where the orientation toward the Indian tradition in painting, sculpture, and crafts had resulted in something completely new. Havell's lecture was heavily criticized by panel member Sir George Birdwood: in his view, Indian art was only about objects of applied art, not about fine art. William Rothenstein, an artist and statesman of the arts who headed the Royal College of Art in London from 1920 to 1935, vehemently defended Havell and stated: "If artists had only realized earlier in their Western art the value of Eastern ideas, . . . Western art would have had an entirely different character."[5] This controversy rumbled on in the international and British press where, under the heading *Art in India,* the debate on the value of artistic forms of expression in the West and East continued. In Calcutta, too, there was a prompt response to Havell's statement. Abanindranath Tagore—co-director of the Government School of Art along with Havell and its first Indian director after his departure in 1906—welcomed this step forward, and Rothenstein's letter to *The Times* was published in one of Calcutta's most important art journals, *The Modern Review.* The founding of London's India Society, which soon became a center for the enlightened "Orientalist" doyens of culture and education, may also be traced back to this debate. The London-based controversy therefore provides specific insights into the transcultural network of actors and institutions that, from London to Calcutta, played a part in the reorientation of India's art schools and its culture and education policy in general.

World Cities

In the context of the independence movement, Calcutta therefore provided a starting point for this cultural renewal—for Calcutta was the capital of British India until 1911 and served as an urban epicenter for negotiations between the colonialist demands for power and control and the Bengali urban-middle-class struggles for emancipation. This, too, is where the British Empire set a "global modernity" in motion as early as the nineteenth century with the founding of museums, art schools, galleries, and theaters. At the same time, the Bengali middle class set up a complex institutional network of newspapers, magazines, publishers, literary societies, and art associations that provided public platforms for an independent intellectual Bengali culture.[6] At its heart was the Tagore family, whose home in the Jorasanko district was a meeting place for the protagonists of the new art movement in Calcutta. Salons were held regularly here, and the Bichitra Club emerged from these. Here, prominent Bengali literati, artists, and intellectuals came together for evenings of readings, performances, and music.[7] But it was the Indian Society of Oriental Art, rather than the salons, that provided the institutional basis for the new art movement. The exhibitions that it organized helped raise public awareness of the "new school of painting" which had taken shape at the Government School of Art under the leadership of Havell and Abanindranath Tagore. Havell shared the conviction that art, and art alone, was in the position to establish a bridge to the intellectual and spiritual dimension.[8] The involvement of Abanindranath Tagore, nephew of the winner of the Nobel Prize in Literature, was a serendipitous event in art history. With his revival of traditional Indian painting techniques and pictorial concepts, as well as his familiarity with Japanese painting and Western art movements, he had initiated a transformation of visual culture where local and global elements were uniquely intertwined. In an essay published in the nineteen-forties, Stella Kramrisch describes him as the first modern Indian artist and also sketches the huge field of tension generated by the imported Western culture, and the emerging nationalism that characterized the cultural and intellectual climate in Calcutta. "This is the situation. A modern town, an incoherent population, an imported British civilization, on Indian soil . . . Calcutta is in India but far from being wholly of India, it is an international and commercial settlement. The people of India and Bengal who live in it had to unlearn much of their Indian and Bengali ways to keep themselves alive in it. Now they slowly try to remember. They are helped by the paintings of Abanindranath Tagore, the first Indian painter brought up in an international and modern town who painted in 'Indian Style.' "[9]

The art movement—later known as the Bengal School—that was initiated at the Government School of Art in Calcutta and advanced thereafter at Kala Bhavan in Shantiniketan is a manifestation of the Indian artists' complex exploration of the conditions of cultural colonialism. The Indian "modernists" thereby combined local, indigenous traditions with global elements to shape a cosmopolitanism that subverted the binary logic of imperialism and nationalism.[10]

[8] Kravagna "Im Schatten großer Mangobäume," in Osten and Holert 2010 (see note 4).

[9] Stella Kramrisch, "The Genius of Abanindranath Tagore," *The Visva-Bharati Quarterly* (May–October 1942), pp. 66–67.

[10] See Partha Mitter, "Reflections on Modern Art and National Identity in Colonial India," in *An Interview: Cosmopolitan Modernism*, ed. Kobena Mercer (Cambridge, MA, and London, 2005), p. 42.

Captions

9 Photographer unknown, Government School of Art (students in class), n.d., photograph

10 Letter from Stella Kramrisch to Josef Strzygowski, November 22, 1920

9

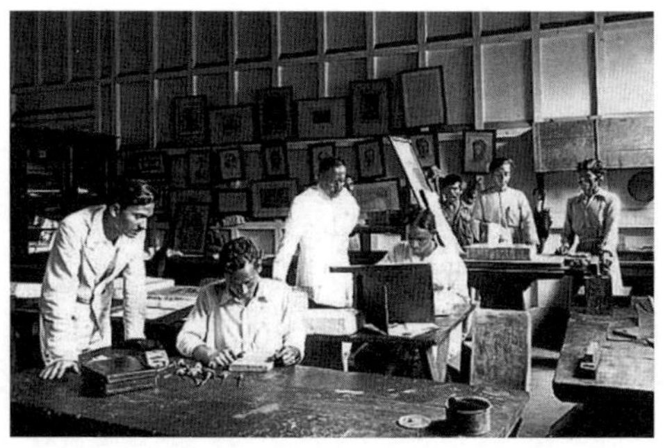

22. XI. 20.

Verehrter Herr Hofrat!

Vielen Dank für die Einführung bei Professor Rothenstein.

Hier hat man die unbeschränkte Möglichkeit zu arbeiten und ich konnte „das Wesen der altindischen Kunst" erweitern und umarbeiten. Mr. Rollestone von der „India Society" hat das deutsche Manuskript gelesen und interessiert sich dafür. Auf Wunsch Prof. Rothensteins habe ich einen Teil ins Englische übersetzt. Es hängt von ihm ab, ob die India Society (Oxford-Presse) es veröffentlichen wird.

Jetzt arbeite ich über „die Schule von Sarnath", die wie mir scheint, den Mittelpunkt der künstlerischen Bewegung von 102 v. – 600 n. chr. gebildet hat.

Das Tanzen habe ich vollkommen aufgegeben, nicht allein meines Versprechens halber, sondern aus der Einsicht, daß man sich für ein Ding und zwar für das wesentliche entscheiden muß, um etwas zu leisten.

Die 'Royal Asiatic Society' hat mich aufgefordert einen Vortrag zu halten. Ich werde über das Verhältnis von Ikonographie und künstlerischem Problem, wie es sich in Indien gestaltet, sprechen.

Das ist alles, was ich bis jetzt erreichen konnte. Sehr wenig. Für die nächste Zukunft will ich trachten, so schwer es auch geht, mich über Wasser zu halten! Ich möchte hier bleiben und weiter arbeiten, um dann vielleicht nach Indien zu kommen.

Bitte es nicht als Zudringlichkeit zu betrachten, wenn ich meinen Vater wieder ins Institut schicke, für den Fall, daß Herrn Hofrat eine Rücksprache mit ihm erwünscht ist.

Ihre dankbare

Stella Kramrisch.

10

Group Photo with a Lady

There is a dusty photo of the Austrian art historian Stella Kramrisch with members of the Indian Society of Oriental Art, which was probably taken at the entrance to the 14th Annual Exhibition at the Samavaya Mansions. Kramrisch had advised the chairman of the Indian Society of Oriental Art, Abanindranath Tagore, to contact Johannes Itten in Weimar in order to request works by Bauhaus artists for the society's 14th Annual Exhibition. By all accounts, Kramrisch knew Itten from Vienna. Here, she had cultivated her interest in India with the support of her professor, Josef Strzygowski, who was one of the first to push to have Western art history opened up to the study of non-European art and culture. Strzygowski was a member of the "Kreis der Freunde des Bauhauses" (Friends of the Bauhaus) and had also lectured on their behalf. He was also in contact with Rothenstein and the India Society in London. Kramrisch had already drafted a dissertation on early Buddhist monuments when, in view of the dire situation in postwar Vienna, she decided in 1919 to travel to Britain on a scholarship to study at the University of Oxford. Here, she met William Rothenstein, Director of the Royal Academy of Art, who attended one of her lectures. Her meeting with Rabindranath Tagore must have come about in England, too: either by chance in the British Museum, or at Rothenstein's home. Tagore's invitation to Shantiniketan dates back to this possible meeting.

Caption

11 Letter from Stella Kramrisch to Josef Strzygowski, August 23, 1921, p. 1.

52 Blenheim Terrace
London NW8
23. VIII. 21.

Verehrter Herr Hofrat,

Mit gleicher Post sende ich 17 Reproduktionen indischer Miniaturen und Zeichnungen. Photos aus dem British Museum, South Kensington und Privatsammlungen (Thakur Seesodia und Col. Hendley) sind mir für nächste Woche versprochen worden.

Tagore schreibt mir aus Santiniketan daß er mich, sobald ich den Paß bekomme, erwartet. Ich bin Herrn

At the time, Europeans found it exceptionally difficult to get a visa to India. In the early twentieth century, the people of India protested against their colonial rulers by means of the non-cooperation movement and its boycott of British products; the political climate between British India and the Empire was fraught with conflict. William Rothenstein's letter to Rabindranath Tagore, which describes meeting Stella Kramrisch, makes this situation clear.

From 1921 to 1923, Kramrisch taught Indian and European art history at Shantiniketan. In 1923, she accepted a lectureship at the University of Calcutta. Here, she was not only the first European academic to teach Indian art history, but also the first woman in her faculty. Although Kramrisch played a part in the intellectual life of Calcutta—this included her membership in the Indian Society of Oriental Art—what we know of her situation as a migrant and the first European academic in Calcutta remains rather contradictory. So while her journey to India may have been motivated by enthusiasm for the country, which was especially prevalent in Vienna (Alma Mahler also intended to travel there), it is equally true that the economic and political situation in postwar Austria offered few perspectives for young academics, and that the search for employment opportunities abroad was therefore advisable. Moreover, after the outbreak of the Second World War, the European route was generally closed to Kramrisch, who was of Jewish descent.

Although she specialized in early Indian art relatively early on in her career, she also acted, at least in Calcutta, as a mediator between Indian and Western modernism. In her essay in the catalogue for the exhibition of 1922, she pointed out the importance of this encounter between European and Indian art. In the same text, she highlighted a unique attribute of the Bauhaus Weimar, where artists from all over Europe were united, not by the pursuit of any of the numerous fashionable –isms, but by the desire to realize the "eternal truth of all art" and to portray this with the means available at the time.[11] Here, Kramrisch was certainly referring to Walter Gropius's Bauhaus manifesto. However, she was less interested in the programmatic objectives of the dogmatically designed building than in the spiritual dimension, which is associated with creative activity.

[11] Stella Kramrisch, "Exhibition of Continental Paintings and Graphic Arts," *Catalogue of the Fourteenth Annual Exhibition Indian Society of Oriental Art Samavaya Mansions Calcutta* (December 1922), p. 23.

Caption

11.1 Letter from Stella Kramrisch to Josef Strzygowski, August 23, 1921, pp. 2–3.

Hofrat unendlich dankbar. Nicht nur für die Unterredung mit Tagore sondern daß ich überhaupt das Glück hatte Ihre Schülerin zu sein.

Meine Arbeit habe ich zwei mal umgeschrieben und hoffe, daß sie im Herbst erscheint. Ich bin eben dabei eine größere Arbeit über Rythmus und Raum in der Kunst des Ostens niederzuschreiben und habe eine vergleichende Studie über Puppenspiele, ausgehend vom Wajang vollendet.

Da das Verhältnis Indiens zur Regierung sehr kritisch ist und eine Verordnung die Einreise von 'ex-enemies' nach Indien für 5 Jahre nach dem Waffen-

stillstand verbietet, ist es fraglich ob Ausnahmen gemacht werden. Sollte ich im Herbst fahren können, so würde ich mich in Wien aufhalten und mit Freude im Institut mitarbeiten.

Ist Herrn Hofrat das Werk von François Valentyn – bekannt: Oud en Nieuw Oost-Indiën..... (Dordrecht–Amsterdam 1724). Dort sind in Deel 4, Stuk 2 Kupferstiche nach Mogul-Miniaturen. Die meisten Gestalten und ihre Gruppierung originalgetreu indisch, vor einem perspektivischen Hintergrund mit "Chinoiserien".

Immer Ihre

aufrichtig ergebene

Stella Kramrisch.

11.1

Wassily Kandinsky's art theoretical discourse *Concerning the Spiritual in Art,* which Kramrisch had already absorbed in Vienna, presented the foundation for an understanding of art, the objective of which expressly did not lie in the representation of reality, but in the expression of an underlying mental-spiritual state. In an essay about the relationship between Indian and European art, which appeared in the magazine *RUPAM* in July 1922, she exposes these reciprocal cultural affinities: "Not only Indian Art, but first of all the Indian outlook, has a deep effect on modern spirituality, while at the same time the East accepts European civilization. Whatever the result may be this exchange means movement. Movement is a sign of life and life is productive, whether it is in the purposed sense or by contradiction and reaction, makes no difference."[12]

India at the Bauhaus

Many of the Bauhaus artists who had exhibited at the Samavaya Mansions—Paul Klee, Wassily Kandinsky, Johannes Itten, Margit Téry-Adler, and Sophie Korner—believed in different ways that emotion might be viewed as a unifying force against the art world's entrenched academicism. In the early twentieth century, many artists and intellectuals were confronted with what they saw as a deep-seated crisis in perception. How might one shed light on and find metaphors for the fragmented, dynamic, and rationalized present? And was it not the role of art to counter the dictates of rationality, to reveal buried layers of truth and knowledge from a new perspective? Furthermore, new technologies had radically changed the means of image and perception. In the quest for a new, socially pertinent artistic agenda, the avant-garde was also susceptible to esoteric doctrines. The avant-garde in Europe had absorbed both the theosophical theory of Helena Blavatsky

[12] Stella Kramrisch, "Indian Art and Europe," *RUPAM: An Illustrated Quarterly Journal of Oriental Art* 11, ed. Ordhendra C. Gangoly (July 1922), p. 86.

Captions

12 Eugen Stolzner and Stella Kramrisch, *1. Tanzabend des Anbruch, 9. Mai, Mittlerer Konzerthaussaal* (1st Dance Night of New Beginnings, May 9, Middle Concert Hall), 1910–19, print (poster)

13 Letter from Josef Strzygowski to Walter Gropius, 1919

14 Paula Stockmar, portrait of Johannes Itten in Bauhaus garb, ca. 1921, photograph

15 Louis Held, Grand Ducal Saxon School of Arts and Crafts, Weimar, ca. 1905–08, photograph

13

76

Verehrter Herr Gropius ! Mit wahrer Befriedigung lese ich das Programm(Arbeitsplan !) des staatlichen Bauhauses. Schade dass ich nicht in Jena sitze und mithelfen kann. Die Abteilung "Kunstgeschichte" könnte ich machen, das würde mich mehr befriedigen als die Arbeit hier an der Universität. Ich hätte an Ihrer Stelle überhaupt nicht von Kunstgeschichte, sondern in erster Linie von Kunstbetrachtung und Wesen gesprochen. Die leidige Geschichte liefert ja nur den Stoff, ist an sich tot.

Ich habe meine orientalischen Arbeiten aufgegeben und arbeite ausschliesslich und planmässig über Wesen der bildenden Kunst. Wir müssen von der Aesthetik loskommen und unsere künstlerische Einsicht ausschliesslich auf dem Leben und seinen Urkunden aufbauen.

Herzliche Grüsse und Glückauf ! Strzygowski

14

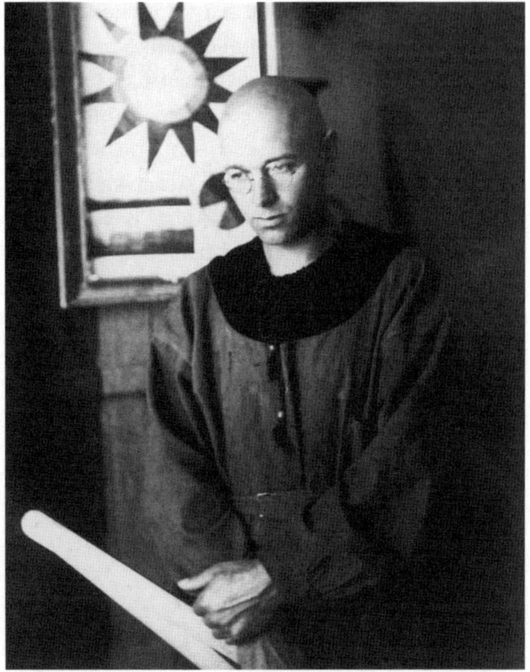

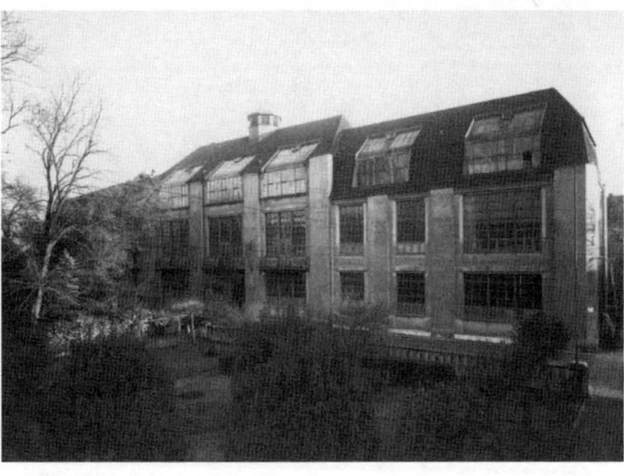

12

and the anthroposophy of Rudolf Steiner. Many artists made art as a means to greater knowledge and understanding—a means that allows access to deeper layers of consciousness and existence and can bring the intuitive and pure to the fore. At the Staatliche Bauhaus in Weimar the advocates of these positions encountered another offshoot of the European avant-garde which, likewise searching for new modes of plausible aesthetic action in the modern industrial age, adopted a rationalistic, constructivist position. The artist Gerhard Marcks, who was likewise represented in the exhibition in Calcutta, had turned away from the controversy between the "pure artists" and the "utility functionalists" in Weimar. At the Bauhaus, there were two conflicting principles at stake: the "Americanism of rationality and technology and the reform obscurantism of emotion that integrated a convoluted mix of an infatuation with India, the nature movement, the settlers' movement, vegetarianism and Tolstoyism."[13]

While Kandinsky's discourse *Concerning the Spiritual in Art* was for many artists and intellectuals a programmatic text of sorts that symbolized a "spiritual shift" with regard to the rejection of the representation of nature, his theory nevertheless oscillated between rational science and esoteric doctrines. Johannes Itten, on the other hand—whom Walter Gropius had met in Vienna through Alma Mahler—had become interested in theosophy and anthroposophy at an early stage. His devotion to the Mazdaznan doctrine, having evolved from the study of theosophy, had an influence on his pedagogical approaches at the early Bauhaus. This was a religion that combined both Christian and Hindu concepts, a vegetarian diet, and breathing and yoga exercises, which Itten also practiced at the Bauhaus in Weimar.[14]

[13] Klaus von Beyme, "Esoterik am Bauhaus," in *Esoterik am Bauhaus: Eine Revision der Moderne*, ed. Christoph Wagner (Regensburg, 2009), p. 27.

[14] See Christoph Wagner, "Johannes Itten und die Esoterik: Ein Schlüssel zum frühen Bauhaus?," in Wagner 2009 (see note 13), p. 119.

[15] Partha Mitter, *The Triumph of Modernism: India's Artists and the Avant-garde, 1922–1947* (London, 2007).

Laboratory of Transcultural Modernism

What makes the exhibition in Calcutta a fascinating early example of the globalized production of art and culture is the fact that the European and Indian avant-gardes, in the rejection of the bourgeois painting tradition of the art academies and in the complex language of abstraction, found a common projection screen for a criticism of the industrial modern age, which prevailed in both the East and the West. If, for Western artists confronted by the crisis inherent to industrial rationality, this was the search for spiritual alternatives in the spiritual spaces and images of India, for Indian artists the culture of traditional rural India became a point of departure for the development of a new visual culture, by means of which they emancipated themselves from the largely urban-influenced colonial value system of the British Empire. The exhibition of the Indian Society of Oriental Art, which established a dialogue between Bauhaus artists and modern Indian artists, thereby represented the crystallization point of an avant-garde movement that, from the very beginning, was set up and understood as a cosmopolitan project. Here, the diverse interconnections between European and non-European modernizations in the context of asymmetrical global circumstances were suddenly revealed.

The artists were united by the belief that artistic production should contrive to make a critical contribution to the dilemmas and predicaments of everyday life under the conditions of industrial modernization. In this way, art was to intervene in everyday life. The unification of art and life, whether as a specific form that acknowledged the underlying truth of an image or as a temporary reality in the actions of communities, was an avant-garde agenda that bridged the continental divide.

As the crystallization point of a transcultural avant-garde, this exhibition also simultaneously challenged an art historiography that attempted to use the concept of influence to explain the relationships between European and Eastern cultural modernisms. The Bauhaus artists' affinity with Eastern doctrines has also been described with such historiographic narratives. The imaginary place, the basis for the concept of influence that Europe invariably formalizes as the starting point of modernism, has been subject to critical revision by postcolonial theorists. Concepts of export and straightforward adoption have been replaced by those of interpretation and negotiation.[15] Here, the transmission of "center" into "periphery" is of less interest than the complex relationships and interconnections between different global spaces. This new way of thinking is, however, reflected in debates about "world art" or "global art" in academic discourse and research projects. Yet this attempt to overcome art history's now more widely acknowledged Eurocentric stance has not come about overnight. It is, rather, a consequence of the radical political, cultural, and economic shifts that occurred after the end of the Cold War. Since then, in the field of art—as the Indian art historian and curator Nancy Adajania has noted—cultural geographies have been gradually redefined, based not on the reversal of the old center-periphery model, but on a new cartography founded on commonalities, reciprocal ties, and diversity.

Nevertheless, this new way of thinking does not yet appear to affect the criteria for the collections of major museums of modern art. Whether in London, New York, or Berlin, now as in the past, there is no place in avant-garde collections for non-European art or even Eastern European art. Modern non-European works are at best devalued as experiments in the sense of "trying to be Picasso."[16] In disputes such as these, as under colonial conditions, the artists are denied the power to take control and to develop their own artistic positions. The history of this exhibition is therefore hugely topical. Its story is now being told in that temple of modernism, the Bauhaus in Dessau, by means of a complex transcultural network of cities, people, histories, images, ideas, and institutions, and it lays out the panorama of an early twentieth-century globality, permeated by hierarchies and made up of travel movements, international correspondence, political upheavals, demarcations, and emancipation movements. From Calcutta, this unique exhibition about the international avant-garde therefore reveals Europe's modernism from a fresh perspective.

[16] Monica Juneja and Franziska Koch, "Multicentred Modernisms: Reconfiguring Asian Art of the Twentieth and Twenty-First Centuries," http://archiv.ub.uni-heidelberg.de/ojs/index.php/transcultural/article/view/6181/1764 (accessed January 2013).

Partha Mitter

Modernity, Art, and National Identity in India

Background to the Bauhaus Exhibition in Calcutta, 1922

When I started documenting the exhibition of Bauhaus artists held in Calcutta in 1922, I had not drawn out fully its transcultural implications for our century. Since then, the conference *bauhaus global* held in Berlin in 2008, not to mention my involvement in this particular show, has given me the opportunity to think afresh about the wider implications of the exhibition.[1] Such a transcultural event was possible only because the Bauhaus avant-garde artists had much in common with the Bengali artists who were similarly concerned with resisting academic naturalism. Germans and Indians came together in mutual sympathy born of perceived oppression. Defeat in the Great War of 1914–18 and the harsh terms of the Versailles Treaty made the Germans sympathetic to the anticolonial struggle. Likewise, Bengali intellectuals, including Rabindranath Tagore, were attracted to German culture because of its distance from the British Empire.[2] The critic Max Osborn describes the works of the nationalist Bengal School of Painting shown in Berlin in 1923 as expressing India's quest for cultural regeneration, which he compares with the search for the validation of the German soul.[3]

The dramatic transformation of the material conditions in traditional societies such as India was accomplished through Western science and technology. Indians were deeply impressed with "modern" values and the ideology of progress. Unlike the impact of technology, however, the reception of Western academic naturalism was more uneven and problematic. How can one make sense of the complex Indian responses to colonial art, the tensions, contradictions, and deep ambivalences embedded within the Westernization process?

Art history has been obsessed with drawing up genealogies of stylistic influences. However, such an approach leaves much to be desired because it remains limited to external considerations: for instance, to what extent were Indian artists successful in emulating their European sources? By this token, Gaganendranath Tagore (1867–1938), as an example, is seen merely as "Picasso manqué."[4] But the moment one goes beyond the question of cultural borrowings, other more interesting questions come into focus.

Conventional art history simply does not take into account the cultural contexts that led these artists to respond to Western art, completely ignoring the "agency" of these artists, their conscious choice. In this complex period of Indian history, artists were engaged in creating a language of resistance to colonial rule through their critical interpretations of the visual language of Western academic art. Thus the story is one of complex and conflicting crosscurrents of institutions, ideologies, and artistic agency.[5]

Indeed, the West had provided a powerful impetus to artistic flowering in modern India. However, this was part of a wider global development. Transport and communication revolutions—railways, steamships, and the telegraph—which enabled colonial empires such as Britain to secure global dominance, also had a contradictory global effect; it created the ideal conditions for communications across the globe. Print capitalism[6] and hegemonic languages, notably English, French, and Spanish, encouraged a worldwide circulation of ideas and artistic styles, creating what I have called a "virtual cosmopolis."[7] Indians, including artists, shared in this worldwide print culture, generating new forms of modernity. In fact, such global circulation of ideas also affected the West when artists around the globe became "armchair

[1] Partha Mitter, *The Triumph of Modernism: India's Artists and the Avant-Garde, 1922–1947* (London, 2007); Partha Mitter, "Bauhaus in Kalkutta," in *bauhaus global: Gesammelte Beiträge der Konferenz bauhaus global vom 21. bis 26. September 2009* (Berlin, 2011), pp. 149–58.

[2] Kris Manjapra's forthcoming work deals with the history of the intersection of German and Bengali intellectuals.

[3] Max Osborn, *RUPAM: An Illustrated Quarterly Journal of Oriental Art* 15–16 (1923), p. 74; Mitter 2007 (see note 1), pp. 27 and 68.

[4] Partha Mitter, "Decentering Modernism: Art History and Avant-Garde Art from the Periphery," *Art Bulletin* 10, no. 1 (December 2008), pp. 531–74.

[5] Partha Mitter, *Art and Nationalism in Colonial India 1850–1922* (Cambridge, 1994), pp. 3–12.

[6] The American scientist Benedict Anderson uses the expression "print capitalism" to describe how, starting in the sixteenth century, publishers printed books in the languages of the people instead of the elitist Latin, driven by a desire to increase book sales. This resulted in "imagined communities" that initially shared a common language. See Benedict Anderson, *Imagined Communities: Reflections on the Origin and Spread of Nationalism* (1983; repr., London and New York, 2006).

[7] See Mitter 2007 (see note 1), pp. 11–12 and 100.

[8] Mikhail Bakhtin, *The Dialogic Imagination: Four Essays,* ed. Michael Holquist, trans. Caryl Emerson and Michael Holquist (Austin, 1981); Michael Holquist, *Dialogism: Bakhtin and His World* (London, 2002).

[9] For a study of this artist, see Mitter 1994 (see note 5), pp. 179–218.

[10] Partha Mitter, "Mechanical Reproduction and the World of the Colonial Artist," in *Beyond Appearances? Visual Practices and Ideologies in Modern India,* ed. Sumathi Ramaswamy (Delhi, 2003), pp. 1–32.

[11] Partha Mitter, "Frameworks for Considering Cultural Exchange: The Case of India and America," in *East-West Interchanges in American Art: A Long and Tumultuous Relationship,* ed. Cynthia Mills et al. (Washington, DC, 2012), pp. 20–37.

travelers," ransacking all periods and cultures for inspiration. Let us not forget the role of Africa and the so-called "primitive" peoples in the rise of the avant-garde art of Picasso and other modernists. We may understand such global flows of ideas not as a linear process but as a dialogic one. Formulated by Mikhail Bakhtin, the dialogic process describes a continuous dialogue with other works of art and literature. The process appropriates the "texts" of others and transforms them according to one's creative intentions.[8]

Art in colonial India was informed by the interaction—often in an agonistic mode—between the received Western visual language and the construction of nationalist resistance in art. The background to the rise of nationalist art in India is the consolidation of British rule in the eighteen-fifties that brought about a transformation of art practices, institutions, and artistic outlook. Impersonal colonial art schools replaced the traditional workshop and the personal master-apprentice relationship. Art exhibitions and art societies created an art-conscious public that took over from aristocratic patronage. Artists themselves gained independence and high social status as gentlemen artists, though they lost the security of court patronage. The arrival of academic naturalism in India was part of global Westernization, and by the end of the nineteenth century Indian taste was thoroughly Victorian. The first nationalist stirrings thus addressed the visual language of Victorian art, as epitomized by the most famous academic artist of colonial India, Raja Ravi Varma (1848–1906). Varma's celebrated history paintings used the grammar of academic naturalism, but reinvented by him to imagine India's literary and epic past. The sentimentality of his themes from Sanskrit classics went hand in hand with the new image of voluptuous women, a blend of Kerala and Guercino.[9] Finally, the diffusion of academic naturalism in the construction of national self-definition was consolidated by the processes of mechanical reproduction. Again, it was Varma's oleographs of Indian gods and goddesses that adorned the princely palaces as much as they lit up humble dwellings.[10]

Varma died in the knowledge that he had become a nationalist icon. And yet, it all went wrong within a year of his death. His works in the Victorian mode were dismissed by the younger generation as a hybrid product of colonial art teaching. The earlier optimism regarding Western knowledge and technology was beginning to be challenged in both the East and the West, as diverse thinkers such as John Ruskin, William Morris, and Karl Marx began expatiating on the crisis of European capitalism. The Bengali savant Swami Vivekananda's rapturous ovation at the World Congress of Religions in Chicago in 1893 marked a turning point in the Western response to Indian spirituality as an alternative to urban capitalist materialism.[11] An international network of Europeans disillusioned with the technological materialism of the West joined forces with Indian nationalists to forge a new ideology. This was one of the reasons that lay behind the fact that several

Europeans participated in the creation of the first nationalist art movement in India. Vivekananda's foremost disciple, the erstwhile Irish nationalist Margaret Noble, joined the Indian nationalist movement, inspiring the artists of Bengal to create historic murals in the service of the nation.[12]

However, the most direct influence on nationalist art was Ernest Binfield Havell, the English head of the colonial art school in Calcutta, who was inspired by William Morris's Art and Crafts Movement and its repudiation of Renaissance naturalism. Havell identified the spirituality of Indian art with its "decorative" quality that was not tainted by naturalism. Havell's first attempts at replacing European art instruction with an Indian one did not meet with success. He needed an Indian ally who could implement his new Indian teaching methods. His meeting with Rabindranath Tagore's young nephew, the painter Abanindranath Tagore (1871–1951), changed the course of Indian art. Abanindranth had made some experiments in indigenous miniature style in his series on the medieval poet Jayadeva's mystical poem "Gita Govinda." He joined the art school at Havell's invitation and began to develop in earnest a nationalist alternative to Varma's art. At the school, Abanindranath discovered the rich heritage of Mughal art. The young artist began to gather a group of sympathetic students at the school: Nandalal Bose, Surendranath Ganguly, K. Venkatappa, Asit Haldar, and Kshitindranath Majumdar, the most talented ones, engaged with him in the solemn task of "recovering the lost language of Indian art."[13]

Abanindranath Tagore received his first public recognition at the grand Imperial Durbar of 1903. The oil painting, *The Last Moments of Shah Jahan* (referencing the builder of the Taj Mahal), was a veritable manifesto in its self-conscious "archaeology," especially its meticulous rendition of the Mughal *pietre dure* marble, as well as its flat treatment emulating Mughal miniatures. The melancholy spirit of the work was, however, essentially Victorian. Indeed, the leader of the Bengal School set the scene for a nostalgic evocation of history, namely, the dying moments of the emperor prefiguring the passing of the Mughal Empire.

In addition to local publicity, Havell used his connections with the London art world to build up Abanindranath Tagore's reputation abroad.[14] Despite the success of *The Last Moments of Shah Jahan,* Abanindranath had misgivings about oil painting and the luminosity of Mughal miniatures as

[12] Mitter 1994 (see note 5), pp. 254–49.

[13] Ibid., pp. 279–94.

[14] Ernest Binfield Havell, "Some Notes on Indian Pictorial Art," *The Studio* 27 (1903), pp. 25–33.

[15] Mitter 1994 (see note 5), pp. 3–12.

[16] Partha Mitter, unpublished paper given at the conference Abstract Space-Concrete Media: Avant-Gardes beyond Western Modernism, Museum Moderner Kunst, Vienna, 2010.

unsuited to the task of evoking the pathos and melancholy of his historicist subjects.[15] However, the choice of his next, and most crucial, visual language was dictated by both personal and political reasons. The Bengal School is identified today with fluid, atmospheric watercolor paintings that one may notice from the works shown at the exhibition in Dessau. Behind this was an avant-garde experiment, which had the ambitions of creating a syncretic Asian art that would resist the Western hegemonic art of academic naturalism.

The global conversations generated among intellectuals in the East and the West—but with a strong Asian accent—were responsible for proposing an anticolonial modernity in the face of Western dominance. An alternative modernist discourse was built around the doctrine of Pan-Asianism aimed at drawing out the common heritage of the East in contradistinction to the West. Pan-Asian ideas were the reaction of the East to the challenges of Western science and material success, as Asian nations began to hit back intellectually following their initial shock. Yet surprisingly, Pan-Asianism was a global tendency that fired the imagination of Western intellectuals as much as it did Eastern ones. Coming to fruition in Japan and India circa 1900, the main architects of this short-lived vision of Asian regional modernity were Rabindranath Tagore and the Japanese scholar Okakura Kakuzō (1863–1913). Tagore's alternative cosmopolitan values, which were based on ancient Indian thought, and Kakuzō's slogan "Asia is one" formed the core of the Pan-Asian movement.[16] A major avant-garde discourse built around Pan-Asian ideas set out to create an alternative mode of art that would pose a challenge to Western colonial aesthetics, which had dominated Asia from the end of the nineteenth century. Just to clarify what I mean by avant-garde here, Pan-Asian art was not concerned with the formalist inventions of the West, such as Cubism, Expressionism, or Surrealism—because European and Asian contexts of art were very different. So, in what way was this Asian movement avant-garde? I have gone back to another, equally resonant definition that is considered to be a key aspect of modernism: "avant-garde" signifies innovation, rebellion, and pushing the boundaries of art against the dominant tradition. These Asian artists created a new radical language of art, though this did not derive from the Western modernism.

The revolutionary aspect of the art lay in its anticolonial strategies. Some of the most resonant cross-fertilization of Pan-Asian ideas took place in art, as networks were established, ideas exchanged, and alliances formed between Indian and Japanese artists in particular. Okakura Kakuzō, Director of the Imperial Art Academy in Tokyo, attempted to replace academic art with the traditional Buddhist art of Japan. Forced to resign around 1900, Kakuzō galvanized international support for his project, arriving in Calcutta in 1902. He stayed with the Tagore family, whose mansion was a meeting place for a host of European and Asian intellectuals. Kakuzō completed his book *Ideals of the East* at the Tagore residence in 1903, which widely disseminated his credo of critical modernity in art. The work described Japanese art as a synthesis of Indian religion and Chinese learning, becoming a classic Pan-Asian text.

Kakuzō's brief stay in Calcutta led to an interesting symbiosis between Indian and Japanese artists that impacted the art of both countries in equal measure. The Tagores were impressed with the simplicity of Japanese taste and design in household objects, replacing heavy and ornate Victorian furniture with simple, functional products. In 1903, after his return to Japan, Kakuzō sent his favorite pupils, Yokoyama Taikan and Hishida Shunsho, to Calcutta to live and work with Abanindranath Tagore, with the aim of forging a common oriental style of art. Shunsho died young but Taikan became a leading exponent of Nihonga, the nationalist style, as opposed to Yōga, the Western mode. Taikan and Shunsho also spent time learning the rudiments of Hindu iconography. In addition, Taikan took lessons in Mughal painting from Abanindranath. The Bengali artist in turn learned to use the Japanese *morotai* wash technique with its fine lines, sparing colors, and understatement. Abanindranath named this fusion of Indian and Japanese styles "oriental art" as an antithesis of Victorian naturalism.

Between 1900 and 1920 the Bengal School of Painters, led by Abanindranath Tagore, produced a body of works that laid the foundations of the first nationalist art movement in India. The movement combined the Indian miniature format and flat treatment, while the variation on *morotai* lent itself to an atmospheric perspective that suited the nationalist narrative.

One of the most powerful slogans of the Indian nationalist art was the "spirituality" of the Bengal School works, unlike the materialism of academic art. What did spirituality in art really mean here? To the British rulers, academic history painting represented the pinnacle of world art. By this token, Indian miniatures were merely the highest form of decorative art. While they had an undoubted appeal, this was of a lower order than the intellectual content of Victorian painting. Since to the British the inferiority of Indian art consisted in its "decorative" quality, for the nationalists this very decorative quality of Indian art came to signify its spirituality. But we should bear in mind here that decorative art did not simply mean the ornamentation of objects. The essential contrast here was between the flat

[17] David Craven, *Art and Revolution in Latin America* (New Haven and London, 2006), pp. 25–73.

[18] Mitter 1994 (see note 5), pp. 332–39.

[19] Stella Kramrisch, quoted in "The Fourteenth Annual Exhibition of the Indian Society of Oriental Art," *RUPAM: An Illustrated Quarterly Journal of Oriental Art* 13–14 (1923), p. 18.

treatment of shapes and colors in decorative art, as seen in Indian miniature painting, as opposed to Western illusionist art. Interestingly, modernism in the West centered on a similar rejection of Renaissance naturalism.

In closing, I now return to the definition of avant-garde art that I had proposed in my introduction. Oriental art sought to create a new visual language that challenged hegemonic naturalism. The revolutionary implications of this new visual language become obvious once we compare these Asian artists with the very different kind of revolutionary art produced in Mexico for instance. Mexico was colonized by the Spaniards at an earlier date than India, and both witnessed a period of nationalist resistance to European powers. In the nineteen-twenties, artists such as Diego Rivera contributed to the Mexican Revolution with ambitious murals glorifying the Aztecs, who had ruled Mexico before the Spanish occupation, his works imbued with Marxist ideology. At the same time, formally these murals belong wholly within the Renaissance tradition even though Rivera incorporated pre-Columbian motifs in his work.[17] The nationalist paintings of the Bengal School were profoundly historicist, their gloomy nostalgia bound up with the nation's bondage, which engendered noble sentiments and deep pathos, quite in contrast to the optimistic history paintings of Varma. The orientalists evoked history and collective memory in a re-creation of a past that had been superseded by colonial rule, creating an ambivalent image of a past that was both desirable and yet full of regrets.[18] The Bengal School shared this aspect with Mexican murals. However, to the Bengal School, no less than to the Japanese artists, resistance to the West took the form of an indigenous "style" that challenged the three-dimensional illusionist art of colonialism.

I would like to conclude my paper with some reflections on the global links between the Western avant-garde and the radical Bengal School. The Indian Society of Oriental Art brought together artists from two different cultural milieux. Wassily Kandinsky, Paul Klee, and other European artists—having spearheaded modernism—were presented side by side with the Indian nationalist artists who had created an avant-garde art of resistance to the colonial academic naturalism. In the catalogue of the 1922 exhibition, Stella Kramrisch urged the Calcutta public to study the Bauhaus artists, so that "they may learn that European art does not mean naturalism and that the transformation of the forms of nature in the work of an artist is common to ancient and modern India."[19] It is not that these European and Asian artists had anything in common in their formal concerns or their choice of themes. What they shared was a common front against figurative painting as hegemonic expression. And that may well be the lasting legacy of the Pan-Asian artistic ideology, which itself became part of the larger romantic challenge to global capitalism and the Western concept of material progress.

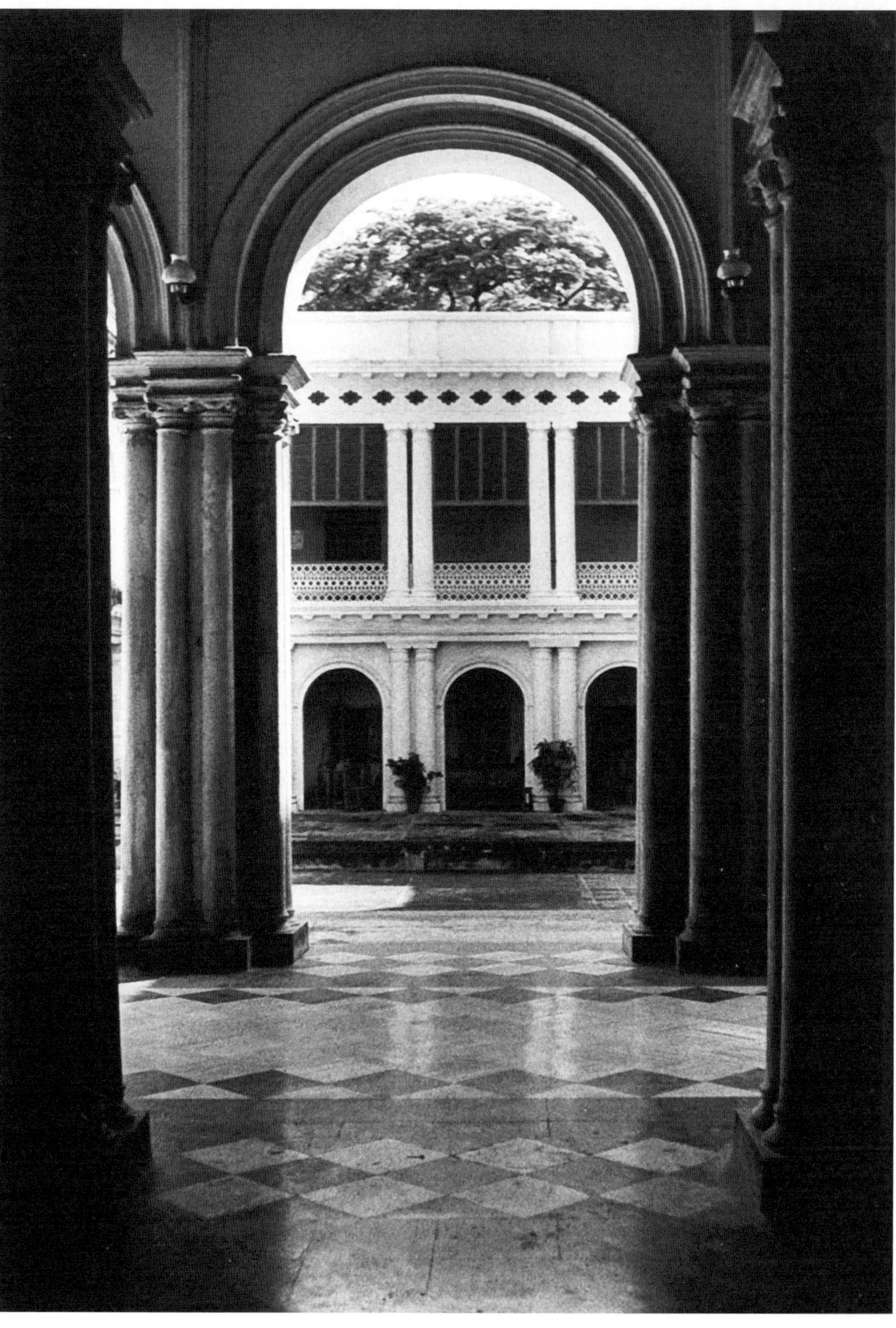

1

Tapati Guha-Thakurta and Sanjukta Sunderason
in Conversation with Regina Bittner and Kathrin Rhomberg

In Search of a New Visual Culture

REGINA BITTNER:
Which institutions, milieus, schools were the most important in fostering this kind of development in the transformation of the arts?

TAPATI GUHA-THAKURTA:
At the time, there had been a modern and a nationalist art movement in place for almost two decades (that in retrospect would be called the Bengal School). It was largely a movement centered around Abanindranath Tagore and his circle: a widening circle of artists, writers, critics, connoisseurs, and patrons, which grew out of the period's thriving network of Orientalist champions of Indian art in the city of Calcutta. I think the institutional sites in which this Bauhaus exhibition featured are defined by the movement of "Indian-style painting" and the spaces it occupied. The Government School of Art, Calcutta, was an important space, but it was one from which many of these other movements had moved away. So some of the artists represented in the show had art school backgrounds and training. Yet by 1915, Abanindranath had left the art school, and his own home at Jorasanko had emerged as a very important alternative center for his art movement—a non-official salon in contrast to the European art salons. This was very much a nationalist art salon. It had a lot of European champions and patrons of Indian art; and out of that grew the Indian Society of Oriental Art, which was of course already functioning from 1907. The Bichitra Art Club and the Jorasanko home became parallel institutions to the Indian Society of Oriental Art, and by 1920 the new art school of Kala Bhavan at Shantiniketan had also been founded. Many of the same artists who had been trained and nurtured at the Bichitra Club and the Indian Society of Oriental Art now gravitated to Shantiniketan. So I think this alternative art space was defined by a set of institutions that were flowing into each other, and their histories dovetailed. Rabindranath Tagore was of course the key figure here, with his travels to Weimar and his deep interest in the Bauhaus, both in its art and design movement and in the educational movement. He was surely a kind of catalyst in bringing on the show. But the context is this larger emergent institutional space, which created a specific division from other worlds of art that were flourishing in Bengal at the same time.

SANJUKTA SUNDERASON:
The catalogue produced for this particular Bauhaus exhibition in Calcutta shows us a broad cross-section of artists represented in the show. An important point to note here is that these were artists limited to particular spaces of institutional and noninstitutional training. For instance, here we have Abanindranath Tagore's students from the Government School of Art, like Nandalal Bose, Debiprasad Roy Chowdhury, and a host of others, and then Bose's students from the Indian Society of Oriental Art and, thereafter, from the newly established art school of Kala Bhavan at Shantiniketan. The location of these artists within the broader art scene in Calcutta during that period reveals that they were positioned directly against and vis-à-vis the academic realist artists of Calcutta. The latter were not organized at this time and felt marginalized from the exhibition spaces and print patronage offered by journals like *The Modern Review* or *RUPAM*, which carried regular reviews and articles on artists from the Bengal School, including detailed coverage of the Bauhaus exhibition. It must be noted that the Bauhaus exhibition provided artists of the "Indian style" with a *front*—a broader spectrum and space to showcase what the Indian art movement stood for at that particular point in time. It was also a way of institutionalizing a kind of artistic modernity, of fostering national and international visibility, and, indeed, of lending legitimacy to "Indian-style" art. From this point onward, the academic artists would have to respond to this organization and this

particular configuration of the Indian modern, upheld at the Bauhaus exhibition of 1922. I think the Bauhaus exhibition was very critical in animating the art worlds of Calcutta and sharpening the aesthetic conflict between artists of the "Indian style" and the academic realists who represented what was seen as the "Western style." I have noted, in my work on the academic artists of Calcutta in the nineteen-twenties and thirties, this lingering anxiety of accessing spaces of exhibition or, for that matter, the need felt by these artists to represent themselves in discourse. The Bauhaus exhibition not only stirred that kind of anxiety, but the liaison between the "national art" of the Bengal School and the modernism of the Bauhaus animated the academic artists to aspire toward a certain kind of national art, a reoriented "national-modern," so to say, which would accommodate realism and naturalistic figuration. This stir within the artistic camps of Calcutta can definitely be seen as a way of contextualizing the Bauhaus exhibition.

TAPATI GUHA-THAKURTA:
There is another point I want to make. If we were to retrospectively look back on the history of modern Indian art during this period, there is a particular canon of modernism of the thirties that comes into profile, that comes to be celebrated nationally and internationally and finds its place in the writing of Indian art history. It is a story of modernism that is centered around the art of Rabindranath Tagore, stretched occasionally to include the paintings of Gaganendranath Tagore. The elder brother of Abanindranath Tagore, Gaganendranath got somewhat lost within the folds of the Bengal School movement, although he clearly was an individualist and did not entirely belong to the dispensations of "Indian-style" painting. He was a very important institutional figure in the Indian Society of Oriental Art and played an instrumental role in bringing the Bauhaus exhibition to Calcutta. He was an exceptionally innovative painter, cartoonist, and printmaker whose career was prematurely stalled in the late twenties, when he suffered from paralysis after a stroke. Gaganendranath produced a series of "cubist" paintings in the twenties that became exemplary of his modernist style. It is interesting to revisit the history of the Bauhaus exhibition of 1922 by looking at the way art history in Bengal evolved at this juncture. In this respect, we may take Partha Mitter's *Triumph of Modernism* book as a very important source, because he begins his story of the "triumph of modernism" with this foundational moment of the arrival of the Bauhaus exhibition in Calcutta.[1] Another scholar, Ratan Parimoo, pioneered a new art-historical attention to Gaganendranath in his nineteen-seventies book on the three Tagores (recently revised and reprinted).[2] Parimoo really believes that, in 1922, the encounter with the Bauhaus produced a new Gaganendranath—a counterpart to the Gaganendranath of the earlier decade—who was deeply inspired by Japanese brush and ink paintings and was engrossed in his parallel experiments with caricature, three albums of which he printed out of the lithograph press he set up at the Jorasanko house. Following the Bauhaus exhibition, there is the Gaganendranath who becomes a kind of "Indian cubist," as the scholar and art critic Stella Kramrisch put it—a Gaganendranath who would not have been conceivable without this exposure to the Bauhaus. In the seventies, Parimoo interestingly compared Gaganendranath's paintings not with Parisian Cubism but much more with the works of the Russian Constructivists and Futurists, with artists like Rodchenko and Delaunay, laying out a ground where Gaganendranath's work could be seen in the context of an international modernist art. When I looked at the Indian artists who were grouped with the Bauhaus artists in this show, I came to realize that the history which we are now discovering is not at all something that rests easily with the way the Bauhaus exhibition has been positioned in relation to the rise of Indian modernism. This was the moment when Indian artists came face-to-face with contemporary European modern art. It was the closest, the first encounter. And its stylistic impact was of course felt most directly in the works of the two Tagores—one of whom then became slightly obscured in art history, while the other emerged as the figure who was misunderstood in his lifetime by his own countrymen, but loved by Europe. The latter was Rabindranath, who openly announced that his writing was for Bengal but his art was for Europe.

Caption

1 Samiran Nandy, untitled (Jorasanko), detail, n.d., photograph

The coming together of the Bauhaus with what—for lack of an official name—we might call the Bengal School, with its many proliferating strands, shows the vast discrepancies in the styles and genres of "modern" art that Calcutta presented to match that of the West. There was clearly no commonality or comparability in art styles. Instead, there was a common ground of ideas, of ways in which art must break out of the academy, the way in which artists must work together with design, with craft, with the environment, with built space. There was a common understanding of how art must be taught, which was clearly bringing together these groups of artists and ideologues in Bengal and Germany. This is where the exhibition's importance lies—not in any stylistic commensurability between the language of Bauhaus modernism and what is then the language of the national modern in Bengal. I think this complex story of the exhibition's context has really not been given its place in Indian art history. It is for this reason that I feel the exhibition in Dessau will have an important impact. Looking at the 1922 exhibition catalogue, which was never very easily available here, was an eye-opener for me. We knew nothing about which Indian art of that time was shown when the Bauhaus show came. A lot was written about what Calcuttans got to see of Bauhaus art. But what was put on view as Calcutta's own versions of the "modern" was less important, yet that should have been just as important. After all, the exhibition was called transnational.

Also, how do we think of the "avant-garde" at that point in time? To me, this is an important question to ask: If the Bauhaus had a more decided place in its own time as avant-garde, do we have an equivalent tag and category in place in India at this time? Critics like Geeta Kapur have been very critical about pushing back categories like modernism and avant-garde to include this period of Indian art.[3] Kapur has a distinct sense of periodization in her arguments about "when was modernism" in Indian art, and she has been very important in defining these terms and these categories. While some of the artistic innovations of these years may qualify as avant-garde (and Rabindranath could certainly be classified in this category), many of the artists who featured in the Indian Society of Oriental Art show can hardly be seen as avant-garde, even by the rubrics of their own time. Yet they were part of a new circle and, as Sanjukta has elaborated, the members of those circles consciously set themselves apart from the worlds of academic art. I think that this is important to note, because, before looking at the catalogue of the exhibition hosted by the Indian Society, I had a rather skewed picture of what was really at stake in the show.

KATHRIN RHOMBERG:

You have not yet mentioned Stella Kramrisch, who surely played an important role in the context of these specific artistic moments in Calcutta and then also in Shantiniketan?

TAPATI GUHA-THAKURTA:

Indeed, the Austrian curator Stella Kramrisch arrived in Shantiniketan in 1921. Rabindranath had met her in London during one of his visits in 1919 to Europe. At the time, she was in London as a wartime émigré. She played a very important and influential role in building up a kind of forum for thinking about European art in Shantiniketan and for developing a language of criticism in writing about both the Indian modern and the international modern. She brought in a certain vocabulary of art criticism that would become very important in the Indian art discourses of the nineteen-twenties and thirties. She was the first local person to write about the art of both Gaganendranath and Rabindranath Tagore.

SANJUKTA SUNDERASON:

In 1922, Stella Kramrisch gave a series of lectures at Kala Bhavan in Shantiniketan, covering a range of artistic and aesthetic issues, providing the newly established art school with a definite exposure to the art of Europe, from Gothic art to the Impressionists and the Post-Impressionists. Kramrisch became a very influential figure in the nineteen-twenties, both through her connection with the Tagore household and her close academic association with the historian Akshay Kumar Maitreya. It can be argued that, with Kramrisch in the twenties, a new vocabulary of formalist consciousness entered art discourse around the Bengal School, marking a departure, as it were, from the orientalizing, spiritualistic rhetoric of the first two decades of the twentieth century. But it must be noted that her formalistic and art-critical lexicon did not sit well with the art teachers within Kala Bhavan in the early twenties. We have instances of Nandalal Bose and Asit Halder, both key formulators of the art curriculum at Kala Bhavan, complaining about the art-critical polemic and modernist aesthetic introduced by Kramrisch in her lectures and student interactions. This reflected, it can be argued, post-Bauhaus-exhibition visibility of European modernism within a pedagogical context at Kala Bhavan, with its parallel dialogues and dissonance with the aesthetic of the "Indian style" still upheld by artists like Bose, Halder, et cetera. In a way, this is a clue into the essentially fluid and dynamic aesthetic formulations of modernism within Kala Bhavan during its first decade, when a reoriented "Indian style" was being developed in various free-floating configurations of romantic pastoralism, nationalist populism, and the specifically interwar aesthetic of ruralism and internationalism. Partha Mitter's influential study on the period, *Triumph of Modernism,* referred to by Tapati earlier, catalogues this wider and complicated aesthetic within the parameters of early twentieth-century artistic primitivism.

TAPATI GUHA-THAKURTA:
At the Kala Bhavan, through the twenties, they were looking more to the Far East for the language of modernism, not to the West at all.

SANJUKTA SUNDERASON:
Yes, Stella Kramrisch's lectures prompted, for the first time, the entry of a language of formalist art criticism—a point she developed in her review of the Bauhaus exhibition, where she can be seen to use this as a bridge connecting the modernist potential of the Bengal School with contemporary European modernism. Her review—celebrating a kind of transcendental aesthetics, uniting these two artistic interventions—appeared in *RUPAM,* the patron art journal of the Bengal School. This modernist sensibility was reflected particularly in her review of the new "cubist" works of Gaganendranath Tagore, who was the brother of Abanindranath and one of the key patrons of the Indian Society of Oriental Art and the Bauhaus exhibition.

TAPATI GUHA-THAKURTA:
That's what the author R. Siva Kumar emphasizes when writing about the "contextual modernism" of Shantiniketan's art.[4] He says Shantiniketan, of course, was a space where a certain language of non-Western modernism was prevalent, a language that was informed primarily by Far Eastern art. Therefore, the visits and travels of Chinese and Japanese artists to Shantiniketan were so crucial. But there was also a modernism based on the indigenous folk and craft aesthetic of Bengal. That is what Shantiniketan's modernism consisted of, into which Stella Kramrisch brought in, during the twenties, an element of European modern art and art criticism. And that is a side of Stella Kramrisch which would not feature so centrally in her later career, when she became the period's most important scholar of Indian temple architecture and sculpture and of Indian aesthetics. Her own prime interest came to center around the collecting of traditional Indian sculpture from a period we call the "early medieval." In the twenties, one of the first publications by Kramrisch was a treatise on ancient Indian aesthetics, on the "Chitra Sutra" of the "Vishnnudharmottara Purana." She actually very quickly made her foray into Indian aesthetics and Indian art of a very different era. While she continued to write occasionally on Indian modern art, her own interest really moved her into the domain of the premodern, into ancient Indian aesthetics and the study of Hindu temple architecture and temple sculpture, resulting in her two-volume magnum opus on *The Hindu Temple* in 1946. And this, in turn, now became a guiding interest for the discipline of Indian art history.
I think the time of the Bauhaus exhibition in Calcutta marks an early moment in Stella Kramrisch's own art-historical transition. She was then very young and had just arrived in India from the University of Vienna. Pramod Chandra, in his art-historiographical survey *On the Study of Indian Art,* locates Kramrisch's writings on Indian architecture and sculpture within a Viennese formalist tradition.[5] Siva Kumar talks about the impact that the lectures on art history given by Kramrisch could have had on the students at Kala Bhavan in Shantiniketan—but it is an impact that has not been documented and studied. That is another layer of Shantiniketan's own pedagogic and artistic development, a part of the story of the emergent modernisms at Kala Bhavan that was of importance in many ways for the nineteen-twenties and thirties and needs to be freshly considered. Stella Kramrisch was a central figure in bringing this strand of influence and exposure to European modernist art into the art milieu of Shantiniketan. Although by the mid-twenties she had relocated to the Department of Ancient Indian History and Culture of Calcutta University, she remained very important to the art pedagogy and practices at Shantiniketan.
In the same years, she also played a crucial role within the Indian Society of Oriental Art, which carried the growing prestige of her name through this period. Its prestigious new journal, *RUPAM,* had just begun

publication from 1920—something needs to be finally written about this one-of-a-kind art publication. I think it made a very important intervention by carrying writing not only on traditional Indian art and aesthetics, but also on folk art and occasionally modern Indian art. Some of Kramrisch's writings on Gaganendranath's "Indian cubist" works and on Rabindranath's art began in this journal.

SANJUKTA SUNDERASON:
RUPAM can also be seen as a site for the gradual unfolding of the changing aesthetic criterions of the "Indian style" and the "Western style" of academic realism in Calcutta. In the early twenties, the precise time of the Bauhaus exhibition, this transformation in the city's art worlds was visible in the reviews and articles published in *RUPAM,* among other contemporary periodicals.

REGINA BITTNER:
This is also something I would like to follow up on. It concerns the very sensitive moment in which the exhibition took place. On the one hand, there was a new orientation toward the Far East—yet, on the other hand, also toward Europe. But, at the same time, this was the moment of the awakening of a new national identity. What is "Indian"? What defined Indian culture and its visual languages under these circumstances?

TAPATI GUHA-THAKURTA:
One could say that the nineteen-twenties was the time when everybody was struggling with a certain baggage (and, one may even say, burden) of being "Indian." The aspirations about being both "national" and "modern" were a concern for artists across all rubrics of styles, whether you were working in an academic style or doing what was then called "Indian" or "Oriental-style" painting, or whether you were attempting to break away from both genres and articulate new styles. And the person who comments on it very interestingly in the nineteen-fifties—and therefore people always fall back to that book—is the art historian William George Archer. In his pioneering book *India and Modern Art,* Archer provides a powerful statement on who qualifies for the first genuine "moderns" of Indian art.[6] For him, this evaluation of the "modern" is entirely defined by the international criteria and the vocabularies of European modern art. So his four "moderns" are Amrita Sher-Gil, Jamini Roy, Rabindranath Tagore, and George Keyt—for him, they represent the brave new moderns of the nineteen-thirties and forties. Archer has an interesting way of looking back on all the possibilities of modernity that the Bengal School generated but never quite fulfilled. In Archer's narrative, Gaganendrath features briefly as one of these unfulfilled promises of the "modern," but the later Abanindranath hardly features, because he was not known. The Abanindranath who, during the late nineteen-twenties and thirties, was painting his *Arabian Nights* series or launching a new series of paintings (the *Kabikankan Chandi* series illustrating the *Mangalkavyas*) based on Bengali folk arts was not known. So I assume that Archer was not even aware of this oeuvre.
The story of the Bengal School is always told as a movement that exhausted itself by the twenties, by which time its work had become stereotyped, formulaic, sentimentalized, and caught up in the repeating trope of mythological classical themes. The art of Shantiniketan broke away from all of that. But the Bengal School during this decade, I would argue, also defined the all-Indian story of the spread and teaching of modern art. By now, the Bengal School artists are in art schools all over the country—the twenties were the time when they radiated outward from Bengal to teaching positions in these different art schools. And that is what a lot of new art historians, who are working on schools of regional modernisms, are having to address, as they track the parallel operations at each of the art schools of the twin worlds of academic art and the local variants of the Bengal School. These multiple strands together constitute and fill out the space of the national modern—it would be important to factor in those stories of regional modernism today as we rewrite the history of India's artistic modernisms.
From a latter-day, cross-country perspective, it is instructive to look back to the first decades of the twentieth century when Bengal's national modern could stand in for the nation. There is a way in which the art of the Bengal School and the art of Shantiniketan, through the nineteen-twenties and thirties, were at the forefront of what was new in the nation's modern art. Rabindranath Tagore as artist alone came to epitomize much of this singularity and novelty of Bengal's modern art. But, if you open up this story beyond Bengal to other locations and regions, in the same period, there were many other variant teleologies that emerged between strands of academic, nationalist, and modern art. The true "modern" identity of Indian

art, in Archer's words, could only evolve, when it could free itself from the stranglehold of the academic and the false burden of "Indianness."

For several years, then, the Bengal School example of "Indian" painting was being bitterly critiqued by several writers, within and outside Bengal, as not being genuinely Indian but a concoction. While the traditionalists criticized Abanindranath's school of "Indian" painting as a distortion of tradition, the modernists condemned it as sterile, repetitive, formulaic, and effeminate. So the criticism of the Bengal School was already forcefully in place in the nineteen-twenties, even before the Bauhaus show was happening. Rabindranath Tagore himself appeared as the strongest internal critic of what he saw as the insular hothouse quality of this "Indian" art movement. One of his great desires was to fling open the closed doors of this movement and bring it into contact with international modern art.

However, little of Rabindranath Tagore's criticisms of the Bengal School and his alternative visions for Indian modern art was reflected in the choice of artists and paintings that went into the exhibition in Calcutta. Alongside the Bauhaus artists, the exhibition featured a body of local artists drawn largely from the networks of the Bichitra Club and the Indian Society of Oriental Art, along with a few from the Government School of Art, Calcutta, and Kala Bhavan. I believe that Rabindranath's major concern was to show Bauhaus artists in Calcutta. But he also needed to mount an Indian show with it—while that must have been important, I doubt that he would have made a claim that the Indian works of art were "modern" on the same terms as the Bauhaus was modern. And I wonder whether any critics were making that claim.

SANJUKTA SUNDERASON:

No, I do not think critics were making such claims. Neither can we find any lengthy discussions on the artistic and aesthetic parameters of the Bauhaus, or any effort at contextualizing the works that were sent, beyond citing them as examples of contemporary European modern art. But Stella Kramrisch's writings around this exhibition can be read as a conscious exercise in making connections between two different articulations of artistic modernity, since she was foregrounding the non-naturalistic aesthetic that lay at the core of modernism, both for the "Indian-style" paintings and the Bauhaus artworks exhibited together. That is where a kind of art-discursive significance of this exhibition can be identified. The exhibition and the Indian artists represented here reveal a conscious attempt at making visible and giving authority to a certain visual aesthetic of the "Indian style" artistic modern.

TAPATI GUHA-THAKURTA:

Looking at it from Rabindranath's perspective, and the perspective of the Tagore household, the Bauhaus exhibition was obviously a very important event. It attracted a small, exclusive circle of scholars, artists, and critics, even as it exhibited the works of a larger pool of lesser-known artists. The show was held on the premises of the Indian Society of Oriental Art, which was situated in the Samavaya Mansions in the area of Park Street. Apart from that venue, the only other place in the city where modern art was then regularly exhibited was the Government School of Art where Tagore's own exhibition would be held in 1932. I would like to say that while this coming together of the Bauhaus with the modern art of Bengal was very important, I doubt that the event had a larger public dimension—especially if you compare it with imperial events like the Calcutta International Exhibition of 1882, which was a spectacular mass event, something like Calcutta's own version of London's Great Exhibition of 1851. A modern art exhibition, by its very nature then, was far more exclusive and small. The Indian Society then regularly hosted these exclusive Indian art exhibitions, and this 1922 exhibition would have been seen as an extension of one of those shows and would have drawn on the same public.

KATHRIN RHOMBERG:

Did the exhibition have an afterlife in Indian modern art history? Did it leave any traces?

TAPATI GUHA-THAKURTA:

The afterlife lies in the importance that is given to it by those art historians who are looking back at the exhibition as the coming of Bauhaus art to India, as the moment of the beginning of a rare dialogue between the two worlds of the Indian and the Western modern. Who were the local artists being shown? Which Indian artists went into the show? These questions have curiously not been of any great concern for these scholars. The main afterlife of the event is centered on the way the show has been positioned as an inaugural event in the history of modernism in Indian art. So it is almost disappointing to now go back to the catalogue and come to terms with the lack of renown and the art-historical "unimportance" of the Indian artists who were shown with the Bauhaus group.

SANJUKTA SUNDERASON:

What we arrive at—and, as Tapati mentioned, disappointingly so—is a fractured spectrum, containing not only the established master artists like Abanindranath Tagore, Nandalal Bose, or Asit Kumar Halder, and the "new" works of Gaganendranath Tagore, but also a wider and more voluminous body of insignificant works from junior artists. Some of them, like Benodebehari Mukherjee from Kala Bhavan, would of course go on to become one of the iconic modernist painters starting in the late-twenties. The catalogue, then, is a document of immense historical importance—an aid to both contextualize the Bauhaus exhibition and historicize the Indian modern beyond sites of triumph and master artists.

TAPATI GUHA-THAKURTA:

The other dimension of the afterlife is the myth about what happened to the works of the Bauhaus artists after the exhibition, and the stories that have circulated about how these works disappeared and never returned—how they became part of Calcutta's invisible art collections where nobody ever saw them again. Yet, as you all now tell us, only one work shown in the Bauhaus exhibition sold, and the rest went back. So what is the status of these works within the history of the Bauhaus? May we ask a counter-question: How important was this incidence of the Bauhaus exhibition traveling to Calcutta to the larger history of the movement? Was it an occasion of any far-reaching impact or significance in the Bauhaus's own international history?

REGINA BITTNER:

I think it changed the grand narrative of the Bauhaus as a movement of European modern art history only. This exhibition also irritated the narration in terms of its impact, of something sent from Europe having an impact in a non-European situation. The 1922 exhibition fostered a different way of thinking; it showed how deeply intertwined the making of the avant-garde was. Especially if you look at the search for the "spiritual" in the arts, the search for alternative ways of teaching and practicing art as a more general worldwide trend of the time, against the backdrop of World War I. A quest for new ways of teaching art and a new notion of art—that is what the alternative art movements of Bauhaus and Bengal had in common. It is reflected in the way they encountered each other; it was probably a fascinating coincidence.

TAPATI GUHA-THAKURTA:

The catalogue is itself such a rare and obscure document. It was not circulated in the way that *RUPAM* and *The Modern Review* were circulated. It almost disappeared off the face of history, and its rediscovery now becomes our only way of reconstructing the show. This fact itself tells us a lot—because while the myths of what happened when the Bauhaus came to Calcutta remained important, the actual context of the exhibition has largely been lost. Was there a more programmatic reason for why the Bauhaus exhibition was brought to Calcutta—a larger international agenda that linked the two histories of alternative modern art practice in these far-flung locations? Perhaps not. It is interesting to see that the catalogue has its two discrete sections—the Indian and the international, two floors, two sections—and then you let the other histories flow. It is also interesting to see how art historians are left struggling to make the connection between the two parts of the show. Yet, for those who brought it together, there appears to have been a self-evident understanding—at least for Tagore and the group from the Bauhaus—that they were on common ground, on a common platform of ideas and values, which, if we knew about, we would struggle less in understanding and recovering the larger context of the exhibition. It is interesting that there is no manifesto of such a show. It has not been put out there for us.

[1] Partha Mitter, *The Triumph of Modernism: India's Artists and the Avant-Garde, 1922–1947* (London, 2007).

[2] Ratan Parimoo, *The Paintings of the Three Tagores: Abanindranath, Gaganendranath and Rabindranath; Comparative and Chronological Study* (Baroda, 1973). New edition: *Art of Three Tagores from Revival to Modernity* (New Delhi, 2011).

[3] Geeta Kapur, *When Was Modernism* (New Delhi, 2000).

[4] Raman Siva Kumar, *Santiniketan: The Making of a Contextual Modernism* (New Delhi, 1997).

[5] Pramod Chandra, *On the Study of Indian Art* (Cambridge, MA, 1983).

[6] William George Archer, *India and Modern Art* (London, 1959).

They rise up like obstructions, and obscure their own backgrounds. But art gives our personality the disinterested freedom of the eternal, there to find it in its true perspective. To see our own home in flames is not to see fire in its verity. But the fire in the stars is the fire in the heart of the infinite; there it is the script of creation.

Matthew Arnold, in his poem addressed to a nightingale, sings:—

'Hark! ah, the nightingale!
The tawn-throated.
Hark! from that moon-lit cedar what a burst!
What triump! hark,—what pain!'

But pain when met within the boundaries of limited reality repels and hurts; it is discordant with the narrow scope of life. But the pain of some great martyrdom has the detachment of eternity. It appears in all its majesty, harmonious in the context of everlasting life; like the thunder-flash in the stormy sky, not on the laboratory wire. Pain on that scale has its harmony in great love; for by hurting love it reveals the infinity of love in all its truth and beauty. On the other hand, the pain involved in business insolvency is discordant: it kills and consumes till nothing remains but ashes.

The poet sings:—

'How thick the bursts come crowding through the leaves!
Eternal Passion!
Eternal Pain!'

And the truth of pain in eternity has been sung by those very Vedic poets who had said, 'From joy has come forth all creation.' They say:—

'Sa tapas tapatvâ sarvam asrajata Yadidam kincha.'

'God from the heat of his pain created all that there is.'

The sacrifice which is in the heart of creation is both joy and pain at the same moment. Of this sings a village mystic in Bengal:—

'My eyes drown in the darkness of joy,
My heart, like a lotus, closes its petals in the rapture of the dark night.'

That speaks of a joy, which is deep like the blue sea, endless like the blue sky; which has the magnificence of the night and its limitless darkness enfolds the radiant worlds in the awfulness of peace; it is the unfathomed joy in which all sufferings are made one with it.

A poet of mediæval India tells us about his source of inspiration in a poem containing a question and an answer:—

'Where were your songs, my bird, when you spent your nights in the nest?
Was not all your pleasure stored therein?
What makes you lose your heart to the sky, the sky that is limitless?'

The bird answers :—

'I had my pleasure while I rested within bounds.
When I soared into the limitless, I found my songs!'

To detach the individual idea from its confinement of every-day facts and give to its soaring wings the freedom of the universal is the function of poetry. The ambition of Macbeth, the jealousy of Othello, would be at best sensational in police court proceedings, but in Shakespeare's dramas they are carried among the flaming constellations, where creation throbs with Eternal Passion, Eternal Pain.

III.—THE AESTHETICS OF YOUNG INDIA.

By BENOY KUMAR SARKAR.

1.—TWO SPECIMENS OF ART APPRECIATION.

A GIFTED Indian painter writes to me, from Calcutta (March 9th, 1921): 'If I had spent years among the museums and exhibitions of Paris, I could never have reproduced a replica of that art in an Indian city.'

The artist's argument is thus worded: 'People, including our greatest men, come back from Europe, with a changed point of view, which they cannot adjust to Indian conditions. Our ideas must live and grow on Indian conditions, however much our education and outlook may be finished and enlarged by foreign travels and intimate

Sria Chatterjee

Writing a Transcultural Modern: Calcutta, 1922

In a format not so far removed from the 2013 exhibition *Bauhaus in Calcutta* in Dessau, the Indian Society of Oriental Art in Calcutta produced a catalogue in 1922 to accompany their exhibition of Indian and Bauhaus works. In the catalogue, Stella Kramrisch, the Austrian art historian in Shantiniketan, wrote: "Whichever nation and whatever artistic mentality these artists may represent, one feature is common to them and this is their training. All of them were brought up in art academies, so well known all the world over. But every one of them was driven by sheer inner necessity to abandon their lifeless scheme. And they struggled each in his own way through decoration and symbolism, through impressionism and post-impressionism and all the various artistic currents which have agitated the surface of European art during the last twenty years."[1]

In this essay, I focus on the 1922 Bauhaus show in Calcutta to illustrate a moment of what, in my view, is not the beginning or middle of a linear history of Indian modernism but rather a "modernism-in-process." I view the artistic exchange between the Bauhaus and Shantiniketan schools neither as artistic transmission, an influence and imitation of the West, nor as a straightforward cultural dialogue with the other. I look instead for a subtext of this modernism-in-process, siting the real event of exchange in an instance of colliding perceptions of the other, in an attempt to define individual notions of modernisms in Germany and India. I further argue that both Germany and India in themselves were loci of multiple encounter and debate. To this end, I propose to lay out a network of object, interaction, and event to explore this moment of a modernism-in-process. Through the processes of the 1922 show, the artists and artworks exhibited, correspondence and debate around the show, it is useful to explore Stella Kramrisch's writings toward a new Indian modern at the cross-section of these collisions, whereby Kramrisch and her contemporaries are flagged up as art-historiographic markers in the understanding of this modernism-in-process.

Destabilizing the notion of Europe as a single, unified entity, I argue that modernism did not come to India from Europe with a time lag as a complete and well-established aesthetic movement. Instead, modernism in 1922 was being negotiated differently in different spaces (such as India and Germany); it took definition in both real and perceived encounters of multiple sources across the world. The 2013 show by the Bauhaus Dessau Foundation also illustrates a critical moment in contemporary curating and cultural theory in that it presents a reconstructed history, not simply of a historic moment but of a moment in the process of being defined as an aesthetic movement.

A leading local newspaper, *The Statesman,* wrote on December 15, 1922 about the forthcoming exhibition: "The third section represents the most novel features of this year's show, namely, the original works of a number of Russian, Swiss and other continental artists who are contributing to the very latest phase to the movements in modern European painting."[2]

For the Indians, a turn to the European avant-garde both stylistically and politically was very much embedded in the anticolonial stance of the intellectual and artistic circles of the Tagore family and the groups that evolved around them. Seen as a break from academic British art, the nonrepresentational avant-garde coincided with a pursuit for shaping an Indian modern. What complicates the issue at hand is that there was no unifying consensus regarding any of these issues, even amongst the Indian intellectuals. Rabindranath Tagore's essay "Nationalism in India" claims: "India has never had a real sense of nationalism. Even though from childhood I had been taught that the idolatry of Nation is almost better than reverence for God and humanity, I believe I have outgrown that teaching, and it is my conviction that my countrymen will gain truly their India by fighting against that education which teaches them that a country is greater than the ideals of humanity."[3] Breaking away from the British academic tradition, Rabindranath turned not specifically toward a nationalist but rather a more universal, unfettered alternative, which spoke for the liberation of the people just as much as Abanindranath Tagore's nationalist art, yet it transcended notions of nationalist boundaries to embrace the human.

[1] Stella Kramrisch, "The Fourteenth Annual Exhibition of the Indian Society of Oriental Art," in *RUPAM: An Illustrated Quarterly Journal of Oriental Art* 13–14 (January–June 1923), p. 18.

[2] *The Statesman,* Dezember 1922.

[3] Rabindranath Tagore, "Nationalism in India," in *Nationalism* (London, 1917), p. 127.

Captions

1 Benoy Kumar Sarkar, "The Aesthetics of Young India," *RUPAM: An Illustrated Quarterly Journal of Oriental Art* 9, ed. Ordhendra C. Gangoly (January 1922), p. 8

2 Stella Kramrisch, "The Aesthetics of Young India: A Rejoinder," *RUPAM: An Illustrated Quarterly Journal of Oriental Art* 10, ed. Ordhendra C. Gangoly (April 1922), p. 66

ago the Faculty of Arts accepted a scheme proposed by myself for giving art an equal position to Science in its "arts" curriculum. The daring scheme was promptly suppressed by the higher powers.......

Tempora Mutantur and the new Professor of Fine Art, I am glad to think, is not likely to meet with the same difficulty.

I am yours obediently,
E. B. HAVELL.

16th January 1922.

VII.—THE AESTHETICS OF YOUNG INDIA: A REJOINDER.

By STELLA KRAMRISCH.

TO all the definitions of art one may add another one, equally true and relevant, namely, that art is a substance subject to discussions *ad infinitum* with impunity. Works of art are taciturn and do not take revenge for they are merged into the eloquent silence of perfection.

The statement, that "what the fishing canoe is to the submarine, that is all classic and Christian art to the art of the last two hundred years, and that is, all the Hindu art to European art since the Renaissance" is the underlying idea of Mr. Sarkar's essay on the Æsthetics of Young India. "Rupam," No. 9).

The assertion that any period of art surpasses all others by its artistic merit is not only obviously against all insight into the nature of art, but it also proves a rhetoric presumption gained by an acquaintance with the current art-terminology of Western critics. Surveying from this high pedestal the art of the world, Byzantine art for instance, appears to have influenced Asia Minor, although the "historical" relation is exactly the opposite, etc.

Mr. Sarkar on the other hand is right in repeating the dogma of modern æsthetics that only the "how" of artistic realisation is essential and Agastya who pleads for the Indianness of Indian art is right too.

However justified these claims may be, they do not help to secure an objective standard of æsthetics which ought to lie at the root of the Indian point of view. Undoubtedly the art and the outlook of the European middle ages have many features in common with the Indian thought and creation in so far as both are spiritualistic. But why did Europe never invent a work of art corresponding to the sitting Buddha, or quite apart from its subject-matter—why did a scheme of composition like that of the sitting Buddha, never find an interpreter in the West? Why although subject-matter and composition are very intimately connected in the representation of any Japanese and any Indian Buddha, why is it impossible to mistake even the back view of either the one or the other? Why, for example the Buddha from Sarnath needs must be Indian. What is so unmistakably Indian about this sculpture? May be that if we become aware of it we will find out the degree of its inner relation with the temple of Kandarya, for instance, or the perforated stone-window of Sidi-Sayyid's mosque. How does the creative instinct of India work, and through what combination of visual elements does it manifest itself?

The æsthetics of us, the young generation, whether in India or anywhere else, have to be scientific and are therefore of international validity. Their structure might be pointed out in a few words.

Every art is possible only through some kind of material. What belongs to the material of art? Stone, bronze, paper, colour, brushes and so on; (for instance, to what natural conditions and æsthetic necessity does the use of earth colours in Indian painting correspond; what is the significance of the rock-cut caves and temples of India; why are Egyptian monumental statues made of the hardest, the most permanent stones; why were stained glass windows introduced together with Romanesque and Gothic architecture and how is it possible that wood-cut did not develop into an independent branch of Western art before the fourteenth century although wood-cut blocks were used for printing cloth long ago).

In this way the selection of material and technique is not merely of a technical interest. But besides the few materials mentioned many others have to be put under consideration, which belong to different categories. Subject matter with regard to creation is such a material. As subject matter, however, have to be classified not only the episodes of the Ramayana or "Ganesa with elephant-head, three eyes, pot-belly and dwarfish form, holding in his four hands a lotus, his own tusk, a battle-axe and a ball of rice-cake"; landscape or portrait-painting, but also the general ideas and conceptions of the age and nation to which the artist belongs, nature, men and things which surround him and the experiences and knowledge he possesses whether grown in his own country or imported from somewhere else. All these are given facts in a chaotic mixture. They constitute the raw material which awaits creation. Ultimately all art results from the union of intuition and personality. The first universal, unlimited and unchangeable consists in intensity and tends towards expression, the latter confined in temporal, national and individual limits enables

The Indian Society of Oriental Art was founded in Calcutta by Abanindranath and his brother Gaganendranath Tagore in 1907. The Society as an institution emerged within an organic discourse around a specific "nationalist" ideology that grew out of the prevailing trends of aesthetic discourse in Bengal, linking itself closely with Orientalist knowledge.[4] Setting in some ways the scene for Kramrisch's arrival in India, the period between 1905 to the early twenties saw an oscillation between and negotiation with notions of the national, the Indianness of the Indian, and, in an anticolonial stance, a complicated approach to the West. The constructive Swadeshi movement, in which the Tagores were keenly involved in 1905–06, propelled the notions of "self-development" and "self-expression." When the impetus for nationalist claims waned into a more active preoccupation with universalist notions, the same concepts of the "lyricism" and "sentiment" of Indian art and the Indianness of its subject matter looked to slightly different motivations. From 1906–07 onward, a number of other artists who came to form the "New School" or the Bengal School around Abanindranath Tagore enrolled as students of the Government School of Art. Among them were Asit Kumar Haldar, Kshitindra Nath Mazumdar, Sailendranath Dey, Samarendranath Gupta, Surendranath Kar—all of these names recognizable from the Calcutta Bauhaus show. Through this first inner circle of students, the semblance of new art emerged, with works that broadly conformed to the master's formula of an "Indian style."[5] By the nineteen-twenties, Abanindranath, however, claimed to move away from art as direct propaganda, retreating into his private sphere of images. His students in the later years, each following their individual artistic trajectories, moved back and forth in terms of style and subject matter from the early tenets of the Bengal School to an interest in the Pan-Asian and the European avant-garde, as we see so variously and richly illustrated in the Indian works on display in 1922. Still concerned with the dream of an independent India, the languages of the national and the universal overlapped and underwrote each other—competing claims, in a polyphonic arena of debate in Bengal, toward much the same end: a notion of the modern.

[4] Tapati Guha-Thakurta, *The Making of a New "Indian" Art: Artists, Aesthetics and Nationalism in Bengal, c. 1850–1920*, vol. 52: *South Asian Studies* (Cambridge, 1992), p. 185.

[5] Ibid.

[6] Stella Kramrisch, "The Aesthetics of a Young India: A Rejoinder," in *RUPAM: An Quarterly Journal of Oriental Art* 10 (April 1922), pp. 66–67.

[7] Kramrisch 1923 (see note 1).

[8] Ibid.

[9] Kramrisch 1922 (see note 6).

This variance of artistic production within the same networks of aesthetic debate and discourse opened up another realm—that of criticism. The sociologist Benoy Kumar Sarkar in his attack on orientalist parochialism (in revivalist, stylistic groupings such as of the Bengal School) came out with an unabashed celebration of modern art in his essay "Futurism of Young Asia." He also published his essay "The Aesthetics of Young India" in the art journal *RUPAM* in January 1922. Writing from Paris after the Swadeshi movement, and with a clear understanding of contemporary European culture, Sarkar aims for a methodology of art appreciation that was concerned purely with the internal form and structure of a "work of art." Criticizing the search for the Indian in Indian art, he claims that "Young India" in rejecting the West had shut itself out from the aesthetic revolution in modern Europe. The "internationalism" that Sarkar proposed was not quite the same as what Stella Kramrisch had in mind. In her article "The Aesthetics of a Young India: A Rejoinder," published in April 1922, she took up Sarkar's formalistic approach to argue that all art grew out of the dual forces of intuition and personality—while the first is universal, unlimited, and unchangeable, the latter is confined in temporal, national, and individual limits,[6] enabling the variety of visualizations and the breeding peculiarities of design and composition. Regardless of an opening up to the West, the Indianness of Indian art, for Kramrisch, could not be compromised.

Intellectual thought and artistic activity in Bengal were therefore clearly caught up, on the one hand, in this constant negotiation of ideals, hashings, and rehashings of India's relationship to its past, its present, and to colonial Britain and, on the other, in the new, rebellious Western avant-garde. The modernism-in-process of 1922 is well illustrated not only in the artworks shown in the Bauhaus exhibition but also in the forces and motivations for the exhibition, as well as in the literature of negotiation that grew around it. For instance, the anonymous review of the 1922 show in the art journal *RUPAM* claims: "That the ideas of the West are destined to bring about a new renaissance in India, and in fact are sowing seeds for such a consummation under our very eyes, will be readily admitted. But that should not discount the value of the contribution of Indian thought itself to the synthesis of the coming era."[7] Stella Kramrisch's note in the catalogue is less convinced about any dubious rebirth. She writes: "Kandinsky is the first to paint pictures without any subject matter . . . The Indian public should study this exhibition, for then they may learn that European art does not mean naturalism and that the transformation of the forms of nature in the work of an artist is common to ancient and modern India."[8]

Further, Kramrisch claims in her rejoinder to Sarkar that "to know her own necessity of significant form should be the first endeavour of artistic young India."[9] She identifies the "significant form" of the European avant-garde in their move toward abstract expression, while at the same time suggesting that it is the spirit or personality of the artist on which this significant form is contingent.

Placing the moment of the 1922 exhibition in what I have identified as modernism-in-process, I suggest that the literature of negotiation traps this modernism-in-process in both a constructed past and a constructed future, existing in empty time. For people like Benoy Kumar Sarkar, the West had arrived at a future that India should follow. Dissidents to Sarkar's view, such as authors like Agastya, claimed that young India should return to its roots, much like the revivalist notion of the artist Abanindranath Tagore and the art historian Ernest Binfield Havell in the early Bengal School phase. Stella Kramrisch, on the other hand, believed that it was the personality of the individual that held the key to a historical and cultural consciousness, and it was this personality of the artists that made an artwork local or national. In seeking the creative spirit of the individual embedded in the past and looking to the future, her interaction with the Bauhaus artists becomes most significant. Whilst she finds common ground and seeks a future for Indian art in the European avant-garde, her basis of dialogue with the Bauhaus School is very different from Sarkar's push toward adopting the forms of the modern West.

Various members of the Bauhaus group had turned to theosophy as a Western adaptation of Eastern tenets and to an engagement with the Vedas and ancient Indian texts. Whilst artists such as Johannes Itten and Wassily Kandinsky strove toward a "spiritualism in art," India for them became a locus that was perceived as the pinnacle of the spiritual ideal. The decision to exhibit in India had just as much to do with the show taking place in real time in India as it did with the perception of the ancient East. Kandinsky, Piet Mondrian, Kasimir Malevich, and others invested in what has been termed the "primitive"—a spiritual dimension of human culture absent in urban modernity.[10] They attributed, I suggest, an otherworldliness to what they viewed as natural human impulse, drawing a rather stark and sometimes undiscerning distinction between the primitive and the modern, similar to the distinction between the spiritual and the material dimensions of human existence. In an odd clash of perceptions, both the Bauhaus avant-garde artists and the Bengal School artists strove toward an integration of abstract thought and abstract form, looking to the other for

[10] Rolf Bothe, ed., *Das frühe Bauhaus und Johannes Itten* (Ostfildern, 1994).

inspiration but in very different ways and to very different ends. The European avant-garde, who saw primitivism as a universal phenomenon, sought it as a critique of rationality, whilst Rabindranath Tagore juggled his universalism and search for the spiritual with the German Romantic discovery of India as an ideal land. It is only against the background of this conflictual situation that the euphoric responses may be understood which Rabindranath's visits elicited from the German public. Gaganendranath, Rabindranath's nephew—though one of the driving forces of the nationalist Bengal School—in the early twentieth-century took up caricature to satirize the Westernized middle class of urban Bengal. He used a curious mix in style of the popular Kalighat and Japanese prints. The 1922 exhibition was positioned in this context of negotiation of the modern, where a perception of India as the eternal land of the spirit further served to collapse the temporal spaces within the moment of a modernism-in-process in Bengal.

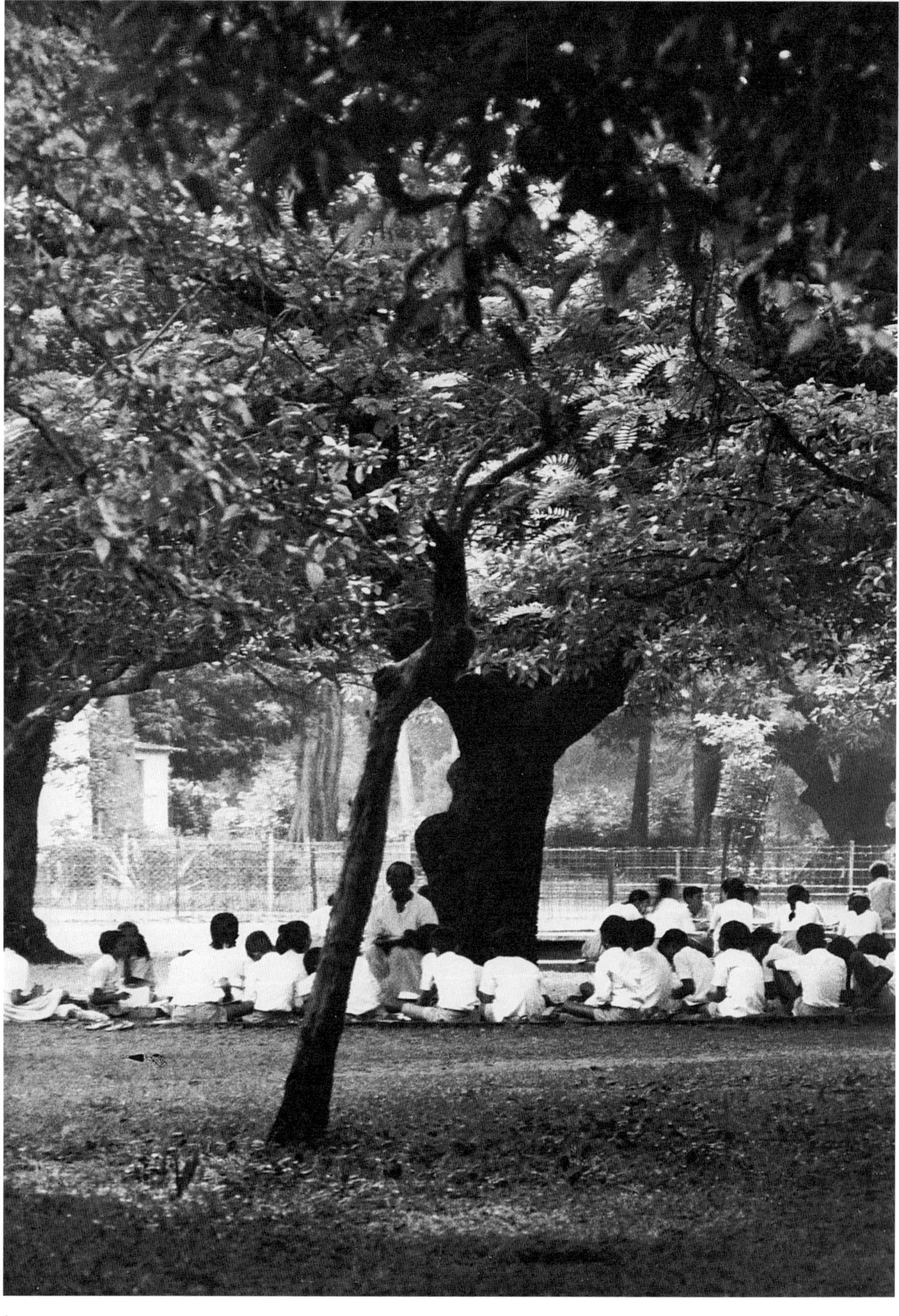

1

R. Siva Kumar in Conversation with
Regina Bittner and Kathrin Rhomberg

Shantiniketan: A World University

REGINA BITTNER:
It would be very interesting for us if you could explain a little bit about the Shantiniketan art school—its establishment, the pedagogic concepts, the teaching. We assume that there are a lot of similarities to the Bauhaus.

R. SIVA KUMAR:
Yes, there are certain similarities. In fact it begins with the year of their founding. Kala Bhavan, the art school at Shantiniketan—like the Bauhaus in Weimar—was founded in 1919. They were also guided by similar ideas, at least similar in certain respects. These ideas were broadly developed by Rabindranath Tagore and expanded into a pedagogic practice by Nandalal Bose, whose role in Shantiniketan was like that of Walter Gropius at the Bauhaus. They both developed similar approaches to art education.

KATHRIN RHOMBERG:
Without knowing about each other?

R. SIVA KUMAR:
Yes, without knowing about each other. What was happening in Indian art before this institution came into existence was largely initiated by Rabindranath's nephews Gaganendranath and Abanindranath Tagore. They were involved in what was largely seen as a nationalist revival of Indian art. Rabindranath Tagore also played a part in that cultural resurgence of which the new art movement was a part. But he found their goals somewhat limited, and not in agreement with certain things he felt strongly about. One of the things he believed in was that contact with other cultures was necessary for sustaining creative vitality. The other thing that he felt strongly about was that art should have a robust contact with life around.

KATHRIN RHOMBERG:
Do you mean daily life?

R. SIVA KUMAR:
Yes, contact with daily life, but also with the environment at large. The nationalist school was largely historicist. Their paintings were based on myths and stories gathered from ancient literature; the kind of things on which our image of the past is based. Tagore thought that contact with life around was as important as, or even more important than, awareness of history. This was what he had learned as a writer.
He was a city man and was sent to the villages, against his wish, by his father who wanted him to look after the family estates. But when he came into contact with village life, he came to know another India. And this did him good as a writer. He thought that the artists should also try to come in contact with nature and the larger life around them. He also thought that artists should not remain confined to their studios and that art should play a larger cultural role. He came to it partly by his own thoughts, and partly by what he saw in Japan in 1916. In Japan he found that some of the ideas he was trying to develop were in practice. Japanese artists were keen observers of nature and designed functional objects that were not merely beautiful but added refinement to everyday life.
That was the kind of thing he wished to see in India. He wanted art to move out of the studios into the public space, and into the lives of people. But the artists in Kolkata, who were trying to revive a national identity through contact with historical antecedents, were not very responsive to this idea. This led him to think about starting a new art school which was not to simply teach art but to achieve all of this. So he invited Nandalal Bose, who was one of the students of Abanindranath Tagore—perhaps his most talented student, but also the one who was most responsive to Rabindranath Tagore's ideas—to take charge of the school

and to put these ideas into practice. So that is how the school began in 1919.

It did not begin either with a manifesto or a structured program leading toward an all-encompassing master art as envisaged at the Bauhaus, but it developed, if only gradually, the same kind of amplitude of purpose and practice. Kala Bhavan was primarily an art school, but its teachers and students were encouraged to erase the borders between art and craft, and to be as versatile as possible. Nandalal and Rabindranath worked on this side by side. They realized that colonization had alienated Indians from their traditional visual culture, and what replaced it was not suited to Indian conditions and to the life pattern and needs of the emerging India. Shaping a new visual culture needed artists who were not simply professional artists or individuals committed to self-expression but also designers of various kinds, interested in functional designing and communication.

So Nandalal and his colleagues illustrated books, designed the stage and costumes for plays written by Rabindranath and enacted in Shantiniketan, planned and designed the new secular festivals that Rabindranath introduced in Shantiniketan, and designed textiles, furnishings, and functional objects suitable for interiors, and so on. They also did murals and outdoor sculptures that embellished and transformed public spaces. Taken together, this represented a wide panorama of activities that brought art out from the studio into social spaces and even into domestic life. They got the students involved in all this, each according to his or her skill and inclination.

But it took place in a less organized and programmed way than at the Bauhaus in Germany. For instance, all this did not happen under one roof. While at Kala Bhavan, Nandalal tried to give a broad orientation to his art teaching and get his students involved in the different things I have mentioned. Much of the professional training and production of craft was carried on at Sriniketan, a kilometer away from Kala Bhavan. This center was set up as part of Tagore's rural reconstruction program. Its initial aim was to revivify the rural crafts, but it also tried to introduce new skills and practices. And some of it came from outside India. Besides artists like Nandalal, professional potters from Germany and Scandinavian weavers were also closely associated with it.

So there were two programs: the art school Kala Bhavan and the craft center at Sriniketan. But there were informal interactions between the two, and they benefited from each other's close presence.

REGINA BITTNER:

Could you please describe how the relationship of Western art and Eastern art was negotiated in this school? That would explain the Austrian art historian Stella Kramrisch's commitment to teaching Western art history.

R. SIVA KUMAR:

It was largely Rabindranath's idea to use Stella Kramrisch's firsthand knowledge of Western art for the benefit of the artists and students at Shantiniketan. Even during the nationalist years he was someone who thought that you ought to have contact with as many cultures as possible—including cultures that are different from yours. He had this very modernist idea that cultures which are very different from yours are important for bringing about innovative transformations within one's own culture. So, in fact, he made it compulsory for everyone to attend her lectures and he himself was present. And sometimes he acted as her translator.

Because of her association with Max Dvořák, Kramrisch on her part was also interested in modern art and played a role, as we now know for sure, in bringing the Bauhaus exhibition to India. Less noticed but equally important is the fact that she brought the formalist approach of the Viennese school to bear on her analysis of traditional Indian art. This was a departure from earlier scholars of Indian art like Ernest Binfield Havell and Ananda Kentish Coomaraswamy, who had stressed the differences between Oriental and Western art. And Kramrisch's views made an impact on young artists, especially on someone like Benodebehari Mukherjee and a little later Ramkinkar Baij, who were to become two of the most important teachers at Kala Bhavan after Nandalal Bose. This was remarkable because in 1922 very few artists in India were aware of developments in modern Western art.

Caption

1 Samiran Nandy, untitled (lessons under mango trees), detail, n.d., photograph

So Kramrisch's lectures were very important from that point of view.

However, it would be wrong to say that Indian artists were unaware of modern developments in Western art before Kramrisch's arrival. We know from William Rothenstein's memoires, *Men and Memoires* published in 1931, that he found books on modern Western art in the personal library of Abanindranath and Gaganendranath Tagore when he visited them in 1910. But their interest in Western modernism was more aesthetic than stylistic. Stylistically, they were interested in those areas of Oriental art to which the early Western modernists were also drawn, such as Japanese and Mughal and Persian painting. And they appreciated the same qualities, like pictorial flatness and freedom of spatial articulation, which appealed to Western artists. So their affinities with Western modernism were oblique. To a great extent this was also true of Nandalal Bose.

While Nandalal developed a pedagogy that erased the division between art and craft, seeing art not merely as self-expression but as visual communication, Kramrisch provided Benodebehari with the theoretical apparatus that helped him to relate different styles with different expressive or communicational purposes.

Cross-cultural interest also contributed to Tagore's development as a painter. But this, as I have pointed out, antedated his contact with Kramrisch. He was drawn to "primitive" and Western art just as he was drawn to Japanese art. He looked at this art in books and in museums during his travels. He saw the Armory Show in Chicago in 1913, and this should have given him a good introduction to modern art. He was also familiar with Wassily Kandinsky's writings. Inviting Stella Kramrisch to Shantiniketan was part of this larger interest. And she definitely helped in furthering it and bringing about broader contact with Western art.

If in the beginning Shantiniketan was looking toward Oriental antecedents for inspiration, it gradually became more open to the West. It became a space where the East and the West were looked at with equal interest, though the stress might have differed from artist to artist.

REGINA BITTNER:

That is very interesting: the concept of internationalism made artists get in touch with other cultures to become innovative and creative. There was a similar attitude at the Bauhaus. Many international artists joined the Board of Masters. It is quite fascinating that they shared the spirit of this cosmopolitanism.

R. SIVA KUMAR:

Yes, that's right. Tagore believed that cross-cultural contacts can spur innovation and revitalize cultures. However, it needs to be clarified that for him knowing other cultures did not mean abandoning the local. For him it was important to know other cultures, but getting to know other cultures did not mean erasing one's own culture or erasing cultural differences and replacing them with internationalism.

He was against cultural insularity. He wanted culture to become an instrument for a people to reach out to the world. And he believed that by knowing other cultures, by knowing each other, we can bring a larger human perspective to our political, economic, and social projects. This was something that the modern world made possible, and we ought to use it. Modernism for him was not about looking alike; it was about freedom of mind, freedom from insular histories that dehumanize others and limit our possibilities. He was working toward a "cosmopolitan local."

REGINA BITTNER:

Let me ask you a question regarding everyday life on the campus of Shantiniketan in the nineteen-twenties. Could you tell us a little bit about what it was like in those days?

R. SIVA KUMAR:

It was very simple. During the twenties Shantiniketan was very rural, with very few modern amenities. Its cosmopolitanism was in its intellectual pursuits, but not in the lifestyle. One of the things Shantiniketan definitely lacked was money. It did not have the financial resources it needed. Tagore refused to accept assistance from the colonial government because, although he kept his institution away from active nationalist agitation, at heart it was both a nationalist and an anticolonial project. It was run with sporadic assistance from native and international well-wishers and earnings from the sale of his books and personal assets. After he received the Nobel Prize, his books were also widely translated. In fact, in the early nineteen-twenties more than a million copies of his books were sold in Germany. The royalty from his translations also went into the financing of the school. But it was seldom sufficient. Old photographs of the place will show you how simple it was. Most of the buildings you see today were not there in the twenties. There were a few small buildings and large open spaces around them. Most of the classes, especially of the school, were held under trees. Early Shantiniketan had very little by way of material resources, but there were great teachers and scholars, so it was rich in human resources.

REGINA BITTNER:
Where did the students come from?

R. SIVA KUMAR:
Most students came from different parts of India, but a few also came from other parts of the world. As I have said, Tagore kept his institution away from nationalist politics, but many of the students who came to Shantiniketan were nationalist-spirited. As it was not government-funded and thus outside the purview of colonial administration, nationalists who were thrown out of government schools and those who did not want go to colonial educational institutions found refuge in Shantiniketan. For a long time it was not a degree-giving institution. Later, those who were interested were allowed to sit privately for the Calcutta University examinations. And, even later, it became a regular degree-giving institution.

KATHRIN RHOMBERG:
What was the main teaching language?

R. SIVA KUMAR:
Initially Tagore wanted the school education to be in Bengali, but later English was introduced as a second language. And it remains so even today. Under Tagore, besides the school and the study of cultures, there were three other areas of thrust: the visual arts, the performing arts, and rural reconstruction. And their linguistic needs were different.

REGINA BITTNER:
So rural development was an integral part of the teaching?

R. SIVA KUMAR:
Yes, rural reconstruction was an integral part of Tagore's educational experiments. When Tagore was sent to the villages to administer the family estates, he was charmed by the natural beauty of rural Bengal but also equally pained by the poverty and suffering he saw. These were also the years of nascent nationalism, and he realized that without addressing the issues of the rural peasants who formed the vast majority of its population, the fight for the political freedom of India would be meaningless. So he began to take interest in improving their life.
So when Tagore started the school at Shantiniketan—by setting it up in rural Bengal and by using nature as an open textbook—he hoped to create an educated class sensitive to nature and to rural life and its needs. Simultaneously, he also wanted to bring the benefit of modern science to agriculture in the villages around his school. For this reason, he sent his son to Urbana, Illinois, in 1912 to learn agriculture. He also found other people who were interested in similar things, especially Leonard Knight Elmhirst. Tagore met him in America where Elmhirst was an agriculture student. He joined Shantiniketan in 1922 and took charge of the rural reconstruction work at Sriniketan. The craft program that we spoke of earlier was part of the rural reconstruction program. The emphasis was on activities, not on teaching; the training in crafts was only a small part of it. The main thing was the regeneration of the rural economy and the improvement of village life. Rabindranath's efforts in this direction, which began in his estates and included rural banking, found an institutional framework at Sriniketan.

KATHRIN RHOMBERG:
Rabindranath Tagore was obviously a pioneer in considering art, craftsmanship, agriculture, and rural life as a united whole.

R. SIVA KUMAR:
Yes, he was a pioneer. In fact his efforts at rural reconstruction and the creation of a peasant cooperative movement actually predated similar efforts by Mahatma Gandhi. He definitely was one of the first Indians to think about such things.

REGINA BITTNER:
Can you tell us something about Shantiniketan today? How does this institution rely on its heritage?

R. SIVA KUMAR:
Well that is a different story altogether. After Tagore's death it gradually moved away from what he had envisaged. In 1940, when Mahatma Gandhi visited Shantiniketan, Tagore placed a letter in his hands which said that Visva-Bharati was his most important

creation and that hopefully his countrymen would consider it worthy of preservation and that Gandhi would take it under his protection after Tagore's death. And Gandhi readily accepted this responsibility. After Gandhi was assassinated in 1948, Jawaharlal Nehru thought a permanent way of helping the university would be to bring it under government protection. And it was made a central university in 1951. Nehru and his colleagues were aware of the special aspects of Tagore's institution, but gradually it became assimilated into the national educational system and was governed by the educational policies of the day. Though this brought in economic stability, Shantiniketan lost its independence, which Tagore had wanted to preserve even at the cost of economic hardship.

KATHRIN RHOMBERG:
Does Shantiniketan follow government directives?

R. SIVA KUMAR:
Yes, absolutely. It is not an autonomous institution anymore. The government—through the University Grants Commission, which funds all universities—has set the rules and we have to follow them. These obviously are prompted by political and social expediencies and are not in keeping with the ideals of Rabindranath Tagore. So the uniqueness it once had is gradually disappearing. Some of the old practices, rituals, and festivals remain, but its administrative structure and educational goals have changed.

KATHRIN RHOMBERG:
And the involvement in the rural area, does that still exist?

R. SIVA KUMAR:
Yes, it's still there. Sriniketan continues to exist and has grown a little bigger even. It has an agricultural department, a social work department, a department for extension work in the villages around, and a craft and design center that is in the process of transforming itself into a design school. But it is now more academically oriented and gives degrees; and it trains students who can be employed by the government in its programs for rural and social uplift. It is more teaching-driven than activity-driven. Tagore's emphasis was on work that brought about changes in the life of the people around.

KATHRIN RHOMBERG:
And is the international exchange still going on?

R. SIVA KUMAR:
Yes, it is happening to an extent. But there is a difference in quality and purpose. Shantiniketan does not have ample resources to invite foreign scholars, but scholars and students who get funded do come. In the past, though there was even less money, Tagore's personality and ideas attracted like-minded scholars from different parts of the world to Shantiniketan. There was also the specific goal of promoting cross-cultural understanding, which is different from the exchange of professional knowledge that guides most global exchanges today.
There is also one other thing about this institution that has changed, something that was important for achieving the goals it had set. Tagore saw Shantiniketan as an experiment in education and community-building. And interpersonal contact was important in his plan of things. I personally believe that to achieve what he set out to do, the institution has to remain small. But as a government-funded university, this is not possible. The government is interested in providing education to the masses, which is necessary. But in the process it fails to see the importance of supporting small experimental institutions that have other goals. Under government funding, Visva-Bharati—like every other university—is forced to take more and more students. For instance in its early days, the art college had twenty or thirty students at a time. Now it has five hundred students. So it has grown more than fifteen times. And when you are so big, you can't have that same interpersonal relationship between teachers and students and that sense of community.
The idea of community was very important for Tagore. When he started the school at Shantiniketan in 1901 the model he had was that of the "tapovana," the forest hermitage schools of ancient India, which he saw as a small community of teachers and students living together. When it became Visva-Bharati, a world university, in 1921 he still saw it as a place where the world gathered in a single nest. He still saw it as a small community. Now it has grown so much, it is no longer a close-knit community.

REGINA BITTNER:

This is again a very interesting similarity to the Bauhaus, where 150 students lived close together, outside the city. So the idea was also to form a community.

R. SIVA KUMAR:

And also a kind of culture of its own. When Rabindranath Tagore established his school here, the place was draught-prone barren land. It was transformed into a lush green place by Tagore and some of his associates. It was, in a way, an environment built from scratch. Alongside this transformation of the environment, he also set himself to building a culture. He wrote songs and plays that made one take note of the landscape; he also created new secular festivals that welcomed the spring, the rains, and the autumn. If you take all this activity together, it amounted to building a culture from scratch within the framework of a community.

Captions

2 Photographer unknown, painting class in Silpa Sadan (Sriniketan), n.d., photograph
3 Photographer unknown, painting class, n.d., photograph
4 Photographer unknown, weaving workshop, n.d., photograph
5 Shambhu Shaha, Udayana, 1939, photograph
6 Samiran Nandy, untitled (public festival near Shantiniketan), n.d., photograph

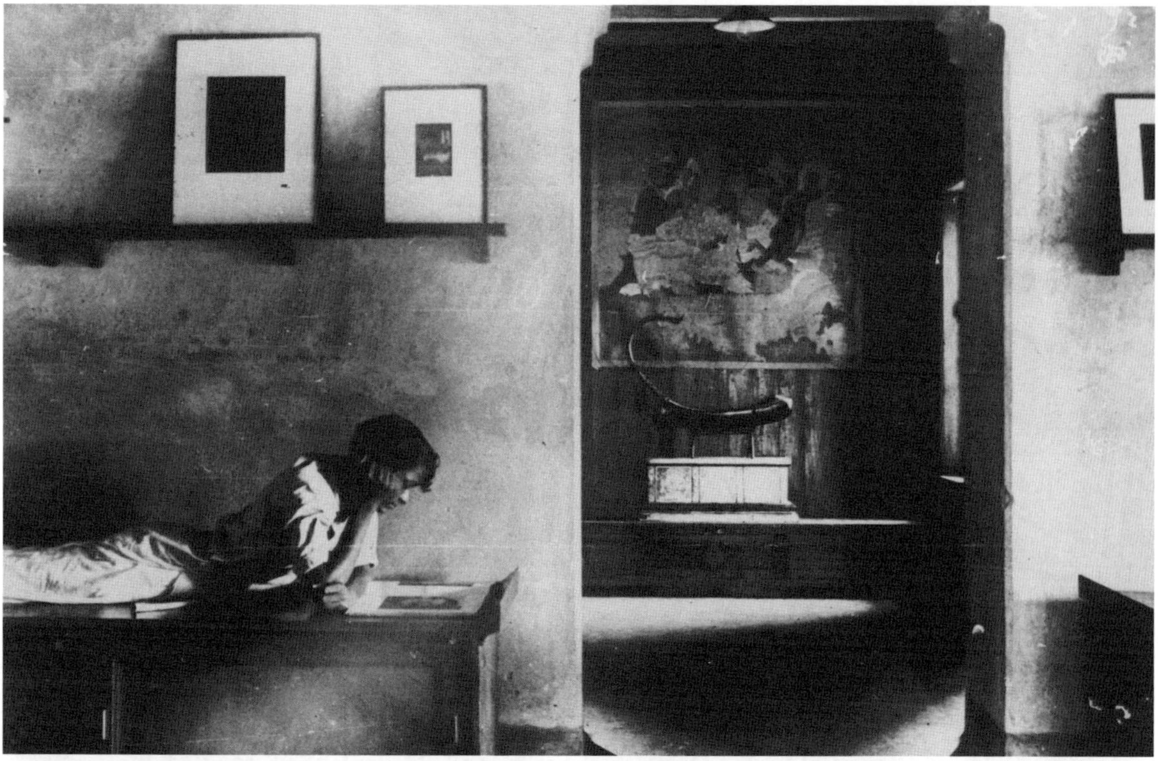

2

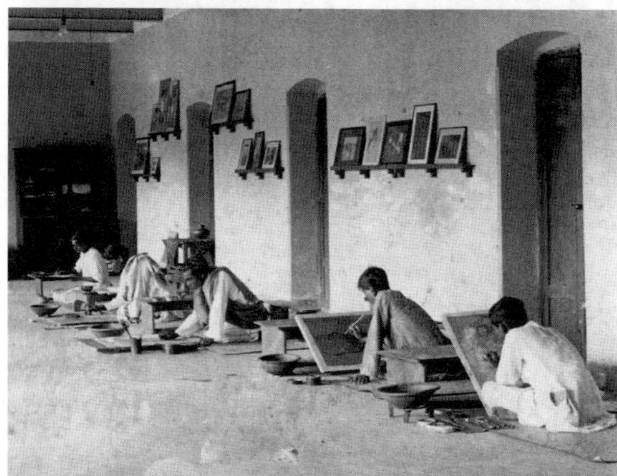

3

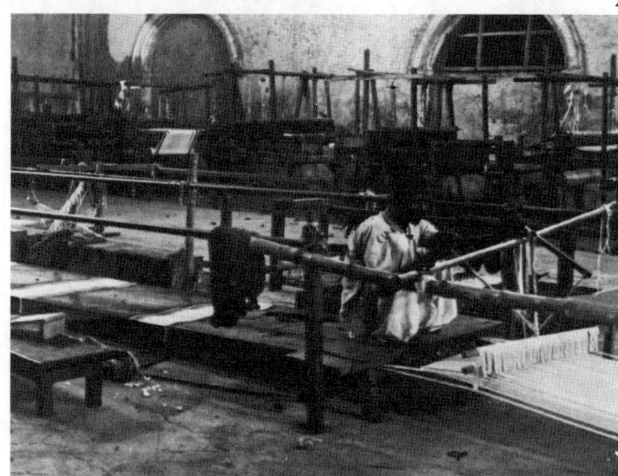

4

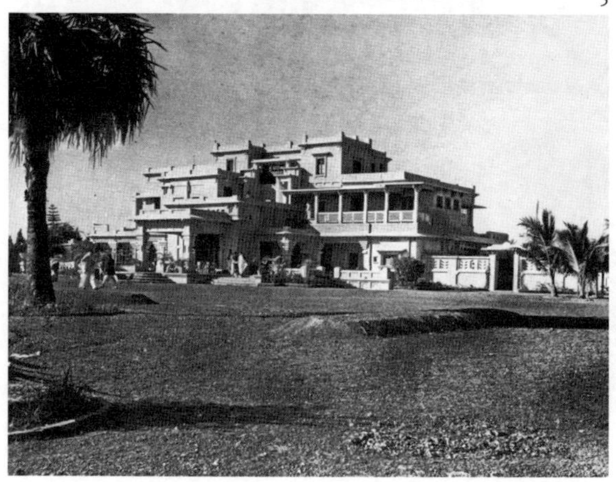

5

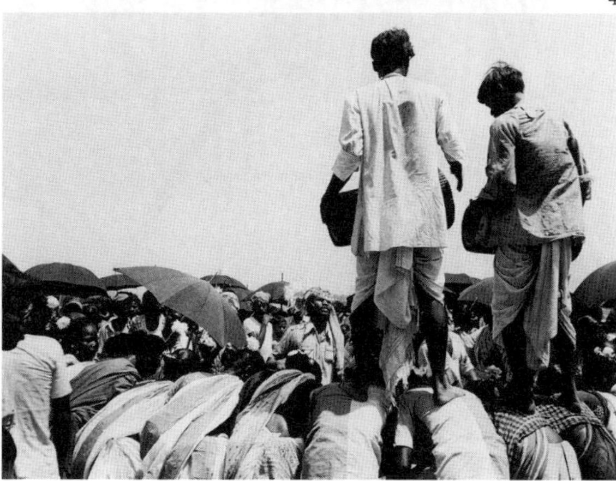

6

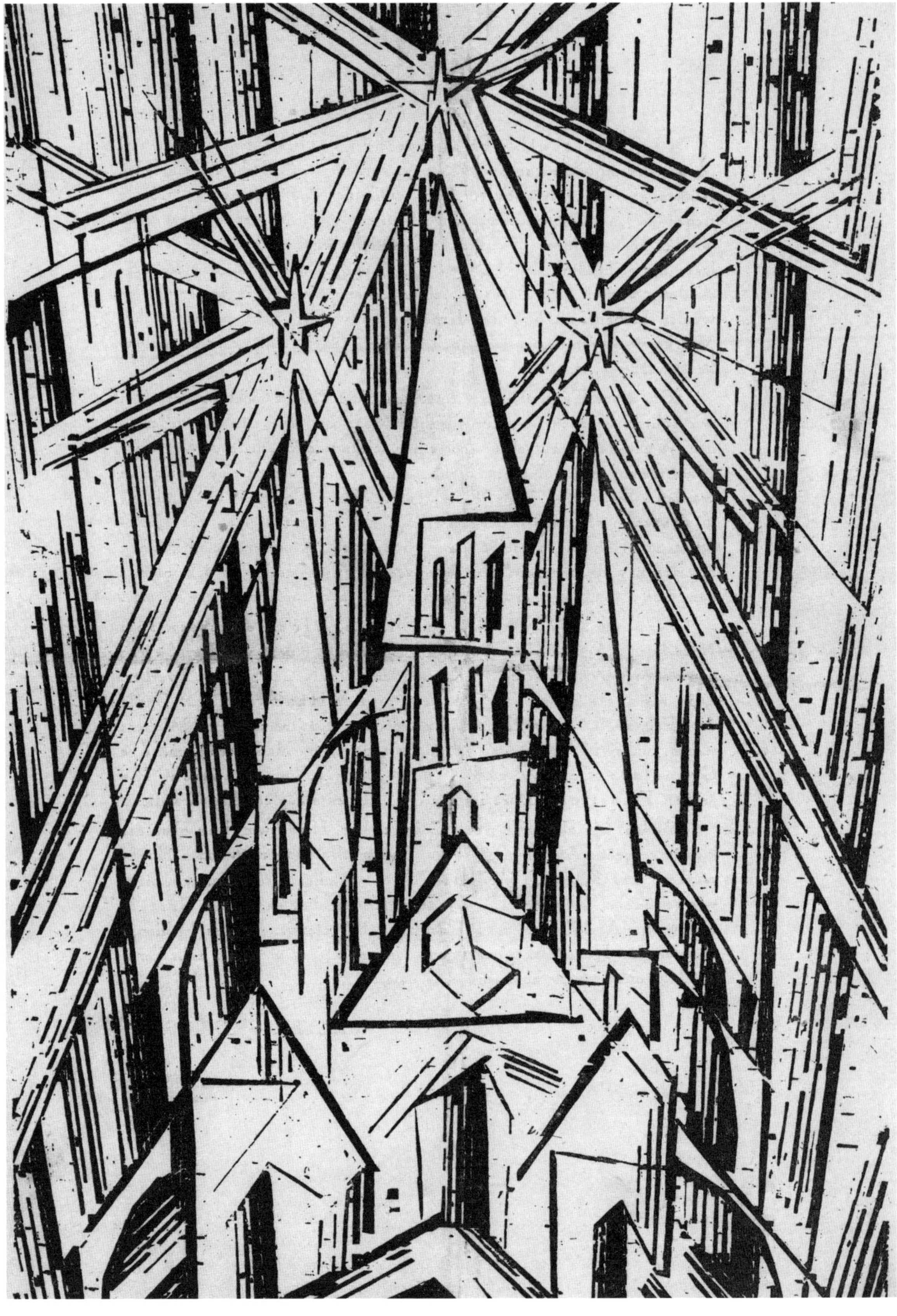

1

Boris Friedewald

The Bauhaus and India: A Look Back to the Future

"Building! Design! Gothic—India!"

In the beginning was longing—the longing to overcome the materialism and horrors of the "Great War" and at the same time to create something new and modern—even a new human being. What guise this newness should take was, however, something that most of the young people drawn to the Bauhaus in Weimar, founded in 1919, were less sure about. Inquiry and experimentation were therefore very much in the air. That some things nevertheless soon took shape goes down to the founder of the Bauhaus, Walter Gropius, who had something that was invaluable at the time: a sense of optimism. While he did not have a blueprint at hand, he did have ideas and other, even more valuable, things: utopias! Thus, the title page of the Bauhaus manifesto shows a cathedral, which reaches to the stars, and the first sentence of the program announces: "The ultimate aim of all artistic activity is the building!"

Gropius dreamed of a small, lodge-like community in which artists and skilled craftsmen of various disciplines would, hand in hand and on equal footing, create a new architecture: architecture as a *Gesamtkunstwerk* and communal project that would serve a new, future society. Like many other Expressionist architects, he thereby looked to the Gothic cathedral, which he believed was informed by the mysterious Masonic knowledge of the artists and artisans of the cathedral workshop.[1] For Gropius, this made architecture the "mother of all arts." Nonetheless, a number of years passed before an architecture class was introduced at the Bauhaus in Dessau.

In May 1919 Gropius delivered his inaugural speech in front of one hundred and fifty Bauhauslers. As the concept for this speech reveals, he once again adopted collective design work on the building and Gothic architecture as a guiding principle but added to this a further dimension: "Building! Design! Gothic—India!"[2] Gothic and India—these were everything but opposites for Gropius, who must have thereby been thinking of the temples of India, which had also been built by collectives of craftsmen and artists. And when he opened the first exhibition of students' work at the Bauhaus, he again testified to the fact that "all great artworks of the past, the Indian, the Gothic wonders, were born of the mastery of craftsmanship."[3] It comes as no surprise that at the time, Gropius gave his close colleague, architect Adolf Meyer, the gift of a book about Indian architecture. For critic and author Paul Westheim, the huge enthusiasm for Indian architecture that Gropius shared with some of the avant-garde architects of the day was clearly rooted in the cultural pessimism of the age. In the introduction to this book, he stated: "It is natural that the embattled people of Europe, who have every reason to doubt the superiority of their civilization and, on a higher plane, are worried by something like the 'decline of the Western world,' turn toward the East. That, which is first revealed in the art of East Asia and most palpably in the art of India is the creative power of spiritual driving forces, without which, as can be seen, art is condemned to decline."[4] The young architect Fred Forbát, who in 1920 became an assistant in Gropius's architecture office, surmised that the enthusiasm for India certainly also had an impact on the designs of Gropius and Meyer at that time: "The design vocabulary confounded me, for until then I knew of Gropius and Meyer only buildings of clear-cut cubes and glass . . . That it was not exclusively informed by the special timber structure, but also had to accommodate Gropius' attitude of mind at the time, was something I first noticed later when he gave me a book about Indian sculpture for Christmas, inscribed with the dedication: 'an aspiration!' "[5]

[1] See Annemarie Jaeggi, "Ein geheimnisvolles Mysterium: Bauhütten-Romantik und Freimaurerei am frühen Bauhaus," in *Das Bauhaus und die Esoterik,* ed. Christoph Wagner (Bielefeld and Leipzig, 2005), pp. 37–45.

[2] Concept by Walter Gropius for the inaugural speech at the Bauhaus on May 6, 1919, Bauhaus Archive Berlin, Archive Walter Gropius, GS 3, File 12.

[3] Speech by Walter Gropius for the first exhibition of students' work at the Staatliche Bauhaus on June 25, 1919, in *Das Staatliche Bauhaus in Weimar: Dokumente zur Geschichte des Instituts 1919–1929,* vol. 15: *Veröffentlichungen der Historischen Kommission für Thüringen, Große Reihe,* ed. Volker Wahl (Cologne et al., 2009), p. 243.

[4] Paul Westheim, ed., *Indische Baukunst* (Berlin, ca. 1919), p. 14. Originally published by Orbis Pictus / Weltkunst-Bücherei.

[5] Fred Forbát, "Erinnerungen eines Architekten aus vier Ländern," pp. 46–47, typescript, Bauhaus Archive Berlin.

[6] Letter from Hermann Graf Keyserling to Franz Singer, March 13, 1920, Bauhaus Archive Berlin, File Gropius / Letters to personages GS 19/346.

[7] Hermann Graf Keyserling, *Das Reisetagebuch eines Philosophen,* vol. 1 (Darmstadt, 1922), p. 402.

[8] Letter from Paul Klee to Lily Klee, October 27, 1917, in *Paul Klee: Briefe an die Familie 1893–1940,* vol. 2: *1907–1940,* ed. Felix Klee (Cologne, 1979), p. 885.

Caption

1 Lyonel Feininger, *Cathedral,* 1919, woodcut, 32 × 19.7 cm, title page, manifesto, and program of the Staatliche Bauhaus Weimar, Stiftung Bauhaus Dessau

The Guest from a Higher Spiritual Dimension

The communal life of the Bauhauslers was not over at the end of the school day—Gropius had even set this out in the Bauhaus program. Masters and students therefore went on walks together, celebrated vibrant parties, and engaged in discussions—for example, in the Indian tea room in Weimar's Marienstraße, where they were served by ladies clothed in batik robes. The Bauhauslers attended "Bauhaus evenings" to hear lectures or performances by poets or musicians. The Bauhausler Franz Singer had evidently invited the Baltic aristocrat Hermann Graf Keyserling to deliver a lecture, for in a letter to Singer, Keyserling expressed a wish to speak about "spiritual reincarnation."[6] His *Reisetagebuch eines Philosophen* (Travel Journal of a Philosopher), in which he described at length his world tour before the First World War, had been published the year before, promptly making him famous. On this adventurous journey to Asia and elsewhere he had seen "tropical kings" and "intellectual giants"; in Calcutta he had also encountered a man who, to him, seemed otherworldly—the musician, poet, philosopher, and founder of a progressive school, Rabindranath Tagore: "Rabindranath, the poet, seemed like a visitor from a higher spiritual dimension. Perhaps never before have I seen such robust spiritual substance in one man."[7] At the time that Keyserling described this encounter, Tagore knew almost no one in Europe, but when he was awarded the Nobel Prize in Literature in 1913 for his collection of poems *Gitanjali,* he became famous overnight. But Tagore was not yet loved by the German masses. And in a letter to his wife Lily in 1917, Paul Klee, whose father had previously composed a German version of Tagore's *The Gardener,* described a work by Tagore as follows: "The Indian book is not all that powerful, weakly erotic, a bit stiff. For that, we don't need an Indian."[8]

It is not known whether Keyserling actually held his lecture at the Bauhaus. After all, he had great plans: in autumn 1920 in Darmstadt he founded the "Schule der Weisheit" (School of Wisdom), with which he created a meeting place for spiritual figures where practical counter models were to be found for a world increasingly characterized by rationalism and technology. For Keyserling this was inextricably linked with the endeavor to build a bridge between the Eastern and Western spiritual worlds. Keyserling shared this unorthodox philosophy with Rabindranath Tagore, who, after being awarded the Nobel Prize, increasingly also saw himself as an ambassador between the East and the West and was convinced that India and the East could bring peace to the world. On May 12, 1921, Tagore took a three-day trip to Germany—and also visited Keyserling in Darmstadt. A few days later, Keyserling announced in the press: "The Indian and I have reached such agreement on our mutual objectives that Shantiniketan, Tagore's Bengali university, and the School of Wisdom will henceforth work together in order to create a brotherhood between East and West."[9] Tagore was now the talk of the town, first and foremost among the bourgeoisie who felt dispossessed and sought spiritual orientation. This enthusiasm will have been the reason why the German National Theater in Weimar dedicated one of their Sunday matinees on May 29 to Tagore, although the program announced that this was "To celebrate his 60th birthday," when he had in fact celebrated it on May 3. Weeks before the matinee, the Bauhaus master Johannes Itten had already noted in his diary: "Rabindranath Tagore to appear on his 60th birthday with a program . . . in the German National Theater."[10] Evidently, Itten had misread the announcement, for the matinee began with a welcome speech by Carl Stanz, the theater's dramaturge. This was followed by a recitation of some of Tagore's works at the public premiere of composer Carl Schadwitz's *Zyklus nach Gedichten Rabindranath Tagores* (Cycle after the Poems of Rabindranath Tagore). One thing is, however, clear: Tagore was not present at the celebration in Weimar—he had traveled via Hamburg to Sweden, where he belatedly accepted the Nobel Prize in person. Finally, also in May of that year, Itten had completed a small drawing, which he called *Tagore*. This, however, does not show a man with flowing hair and a long beard, but a music-making tabla player entirely free of such sumptuous locks. While Germany's fascination with Tagore at the time also focused heavily on his outer appearance, which was often associated with the figure of prophet and savior, for Itten it was obviously more about the emotion associated with Tagore's nature—which he perceived as equally ascetic and artistic. From Northern Europe, Tagore returned to Germany and visited Berlin, Munich, and finally Darmstadt once more, where, from June 9 to 14, Keyserling had organized a so-called "Tagore Week" with great pomp and ceremony.

[9] Hermann Graf Keyserling, "Rabindranath Tagore und Deutschland," *Der Tag* 21, no. 117 (May 22, 1921).

[10] Quoted from Patha Mitter, "Bauhaus in Kalkutta," in *bauhaus global*, vol. 3: *neue Bauhausbücher, neue Zählung*, ed. Bauhaus Archive Berlin (Berlin, 2009), p. 157, footnote 9.

Captions

2 Louis Held, Indian tea room in Weimar, Marienstr. 4, postcard, ca. 1919–23, photogravure on off-white card

3 Auguste Léon, Rabindranath Tagore, winner of the Nobel Prize in Literature 1913, 1920, photograph

4 Deutsche Nationaltheater, invitation to the tenth morning ceremony in celebration of Rabindranath Tagore's sixtieth birthday, Deutsche Nationaltheater, Weimar, May 29, 1921

2

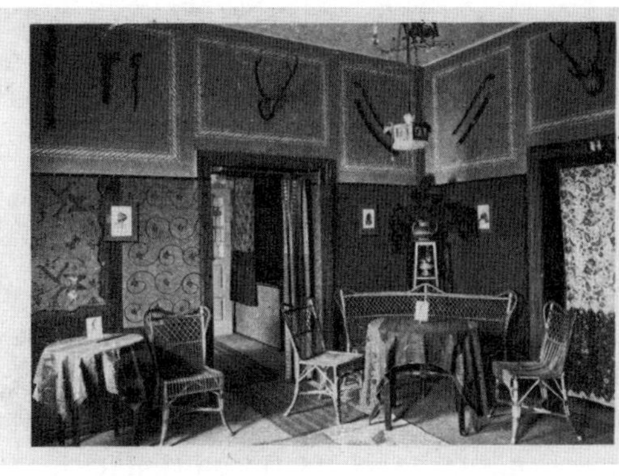

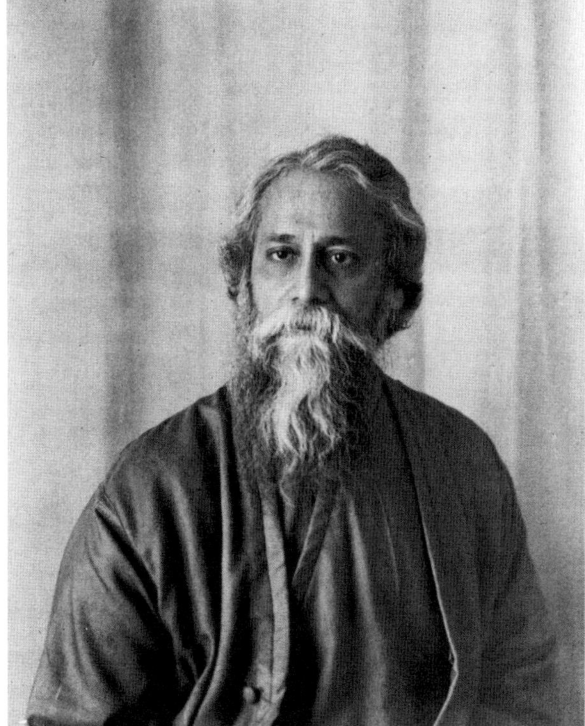

3

Deutsches Nationaltheater

Sonntag, den 29. Mai 1921
Vormittags 11½ Uhr

Zehnte Morgenfeier
Rabindranath Tagore

(zur Feier seines 60. Geburtstages)

Vortragsfolge:

I. Einleitender Vortrag: Rabindranath Tagore
Carl Stang

II. Rabindranath Tagore:
a) Ich lieb dich (aus „Der Gärtner")
b) Der Anfang
c) Der böse Postbote (aus „Der zunehmende Mond")
Kaete Nadel
d) Es war einmal ein König (aus „Erzählungen")
Claus Clausen

III. Carl Schadewitz: „Der Gärtner." Ein Cyclus nach Gedichten Rabindranath Tagores für Sopran und Bariton, Violine, Flöte, Klavier (op. 17)
Mali Trummer, Hans Bergmann, Arthur Rösel, Otto Braun, Julius Maurer — **Zum ersten Male**

Konzertflügel: Bechstein, aus dem Thüringer Musikhaus Hermann Mensing (Inh.: Karl Heßler), Weimar, Marktstraße 24

Die Werke von Rabindranath Tagore sind im Verlag Kurt Wolff, München, erschienen.

Preise der Plätze 5.—, 3.—, 2.—, 1.— M.

Kassenöffnung 10¾ Uhr Ende gegen 1 Uhr

Wochen-Spielplan

Montag, den 30. Zu ermäßigten Preisen: **Die Bohème,** Szenen in vier Bildern von G. Giacosa und L. Illica Deutsch von L. Hartmann Musik von G. Puccini Anfang 7, Ende 9¾ Uhr

Freitag, den 3. Juni **Das Rheingold,** Vorabend zu dem Bühnenfestspiel „Der Ring des Nibelungen" von R. Wagner Anfang 5, Ende gegen 8 Uhr

Sonntag, den 5. **Die Walküre,** erster Tag des Bühnenfestspiels „Der Ring des Nibelungen" von R. Wagner Anfang 3½, Ende gegen 8 Uhr

Montag, den 6. Im Foyersaal: **Siebenter Kammermusikabend** (Schumann: Streichquartett; Pfitzner: Klavierquintett [zum ersten Male]) 10, 8, 6 und 3 M Anfang 8, Ende 10 Uhr

Dienstag, den 7. **Siegfried,** zweiter Tag des Bühnenfestspiels „Der Ring des Nibelungen" von R. Wagner Anfang 3½, Ende gegen 8 Uhr

Freitag, den 10. **Götterdämmerung,** dritter Tag des Bühnenfestspiels „Der Ring des Nibelungen" von R. Wagner Anfang 3, Ende 8 Uhr

Nibelungen-Ring (3., 5., 7. und 10. Juni): Der Vorverkauf für den **geschlossenen** Ring beginnt Montag, den 30. Mai. Einzelkarten sind erst von Donnerstag, den 2. Juni ab käuflich

Kartenvorverkauf: Wochentags von 11–1½ Uhr, Sonntags von 3–4 Uhr
Telephonische Bestellungen (Nr. 49) täglich von 9–11 Uhr, **außer Montags**

Während der Vorträge bleiben die Türen geschlossen

An- und Abfahrt nur an den Seitentüren

235 Weimar — G. Uschmann

4

The Preliminary Course and Johannes Itten

For all its enthusiasm for experimentation, the Bauhaus had meanwhile rejected many a controversial path and also parted with some teachers—moves that were frequently accompanied by intense discussions among the Bauhaus masters and Weimar's conservative citizens and artists. At the same time, in the public and ongoing search for the contemporary, some things had taken firm shape at the school. In addition to the original departments—the metal, graphic printing, bookbinding, and weaving workshops—further workshops were added in 1920, which the students could choose between: workshops for ceramics, glass painting, wood carving, stone carving, and wall painting. A carpentry workshop and a stage workshop were then set up in 1921. That same spring, the introductory course became the preliminary course, which from then on was obligatory for every new Bauhaus student. This six-month course was designed to liberate the students from any traditional ways of thinking and stimulate their inherent artistic potential. The preliminary course was developed and led by the Swiss artist Johannes Itten, a man with an abiding interest in the mysticism, esotericism, and spiritual teachings of diverse cultures. Before he arrived at the Bauhaus, he had been the director of his own private art school in Vienna. Here, in this city on the Danube, Itten had also met Alma Mahler, whose interest in theosophy he soon came to share. Shortly before the First World War, Mahler had become so fascinated by the theosophy that permeated the spiritual doctrines of India that she enrolled on a Sanskrit course in Benares, India, with Annie Besant, President of the Theosophical Society.[11] However, the outbreak of the First World War put a stop to these plans. At the time, Mahler's circle of friends included art historian Josef Strzygowski, who in 1912 had

[11] See Alma Mahler, *Mein Leben* (Frankfurt am Main, 1989), p. 67.

[12] Manuscript of the lecture in Eva Badura-Triska, *Johannes Itten: Tagebücher. Stuttgart 1913–1916; Wien 1916–1919* (Vienna, 1990), vol. 1, pp. 225ff.

[13] See "Zwischen Lebensreform und Esoterik: Johannes Ittens Weg ans Bauhaus," in Wagner 2005 (see note 1), pp. 67–68.

[14] See Manfred Metzner, ed., *Ré Soupault: Bauhaus; Die heroischen Jahre von Weimar* (Heidelberg, 2009), pp. 38–39 and 46.

[15] During his trip to Germany in 1921, he was usually introduced as Murshid Inayat Khan. However, his worshippers called him Pir-o-Murshid, a title of respect for Sufi leaders. After his death, he was given an honorary title to precede his name, according to the Sufi tradition for high-ranking Sufis. Today he is therefore generally known as Hazrat Inayat Khan.

[16] *Jenaische Zeitung* 248, no. 236 (October 8, 1921).

[17] See minutes of the masters' council meeting on October 12, 1921. Document in the Thüringisches Hauptstaatsarchiv Weimar, ThHStA Weimar, Staatliches Bauhaus Weimar 12, sheet 105–106.

[18] The transcript of the unpublished lecture is now in the archive of the Nekbakht Foundation, Suresnes, France. While the Bauhaus had announced Khan's lecture for October 22, 1922 (see ThHStA, Staatliches Bauhaus Weimar, no. 14, sheet 144 r), the transcript mistakenly gives October 24 as the lecture date.

established an East Asia department at Vienna's Kunsthistorisches Institut. In May 1917, Itten presented a lecture here on composition theory,[12] in which he made reference to many aspects that he was to take up shortly afterward in his preliminary course at the Bauhaus. It is likely that Itten had met Strzygowski through Alma Mahler, who had married Walter Gropius in 1915 and recommended Itten to him as a suitable man for the Bauhaus.[13]

Once in Weimar, Itten became increasingly involved with the Mazdaznan movement, a "life school" founded in nineteenth-century America that aimed to draw on the secret doctrines of the Persians, Greeks, and Egyptians. As a result of his involvement with this movement, Itten began to do breathing exercises with his students and introduced a purely vegetarian diet to the Bauhaus canteen. But his interest in everything Indian did not end there, as illustrated by his journal on temple mansions, among other things. Here he notes the canons of the Tattva that symbolize the "basic principles" of the cosmos, expressed in different base colors and forms. The journal also includes notes on the fate of Brahma, the god of creation, who on committing his first sin wept tears so hot that they formed the first sapphires. He also cultivated an interest in Pali, the literary language of the original Buddhist texts. Itten's devotion to India also stimulated some of his students: the Bauhaus student Erna Niemeyer, for instance, began to simultaneously study Sanskrit in Jena and subsequently wove many of the Sanskrit symbols that she learned there into a carpet she was making in the Bauhaus workshop.[14]

The Bauhaus Visit of the Indian Poet-Philosopher

Just a few months after Rabindranath Tagore's first visit to Germany, another Indian gentleman traveled through Germany in autumn 1921. This was Murshid Inayat Khan, musician, poet, philosopher, and founder of the International Sufi Movement.[15] He visited Munich, Hagen, Berlin, Frankfurt, and Darmstadt, where he also met Keyserling. On October 21, Khan arrived in Jena, where he held a lecture at the home of a publisher and admirer of Eastern philosophy, Eugen Diederichs. The local press had already announced his arrival some weeks earlier and connected his visit with Tagore's: "Khan's visit to Germany . . . is, like Tagore's, a sign of the convergence of Indian spiritual life and German thought."[16]

After his visit to Jena, Khan went on to Weimar. There, he was invited by Elisabeth Förster-Nietzsche to give a lecture at the Nietzsche Archive on October 23. He was also invited to visit the Bauhaus: Eugen Diederichs had recommended the Sufi master to Gropius for the Bauhaus—a suggestion that was unanimously welcomed by all the Bauhaus masters.[17] Khan finally arrived at the Bauhaus on October 22, where, in the Oberlichtsaal, he sang, played the vina, and spoke freely on "The Nature of Art."[18] Khan spoke on the beauty of god and life and described the two best-known Eastern paths of enlightenment: the path of the Yogi and the path of the Sufi, which, unlike the former, found great pleasure in art. The Sufi recognized the divine in art, which therefore could become something religious for him. Finally, Khan declared: "The call of the Sufi to the Western world and to the whole world today is to harmonize and combine in the beauty of God . . . For during this age materialism and commercialism increased to the greatest disaster the world ever has seen."[19] This evening made an impact at the Bauhaus. Many years later, Bauhausler Heinrich Konrad was to recall: "One day an Indian poet-philosopher appeared to give a lecture; everything about this man emanated the metaphysical, which we were hungry for." Konrad wrote further about his fellow student Kurt Schwerdtfeger: "Schwerdtfeger modeled this manifestation in one day, also by the dark of night, and later realized this imposing study in granite."[20]

The very next week, Itten penned an ardent letter to Diedrichs: "You were so kind to send us the Indian musician last Saturday. Because of illness I was unfortunately unable to attend the lecture, but a friend told me about it. Since the way of thinking that this man expressed is in essence precisely in line with what I have intuitively known and taught for 5 years, you can imagine how happy I am to know of a second man, or indeed a whole order, that has for a long time thought and felt the same way . . . would you be so kind as to let me know where the Sufi . . . will be in the next 3–5 days, so that I can seek him out."[21] But Itten's interest in spiritual matters of all kinds, which was also transferred to the students, was soon to lead to conflicts at

[19] Murshi Inayat Khan, "The Nature of Art," transcript of the English-language lecture of October 22, 1922, Nekbakht Foundation Archive, Suresnes, p. 6.

[20] Letter from Heinrich Konrad to the Bauhaus Archive, February 11, 1956, p. 3. The letter regarding the Heinrich Konrad questionnaire is located at the Bauhaus Archive Berlin.

[21] Letter from Johannes Itten to Eugen Diederichs, n.p., n.d. Available as a copy in the Deutsches Literaturarchiv Marbach, Handschriften, Medien-Nr. HS000626289.

Captions

5 Johannes Itten, *Rabindranath Tagore* (?), May 1921, pencil on paper, 17.5 × 22.0 cm, Itten-Archiv Zurich

6 Alfred Bischoff, Hazrat Inayat Khan (Pir-o-Murshid) in Jena, 1921, photograph

7 Announcement of the event *Umlauf* (Circulation): "Tonight at 8 p.m. in the Oberlichtsaal, lecture, songs and lute music by the North Indian musician Murschid Inayat Khan, Weimar, October 22, 1921"

5

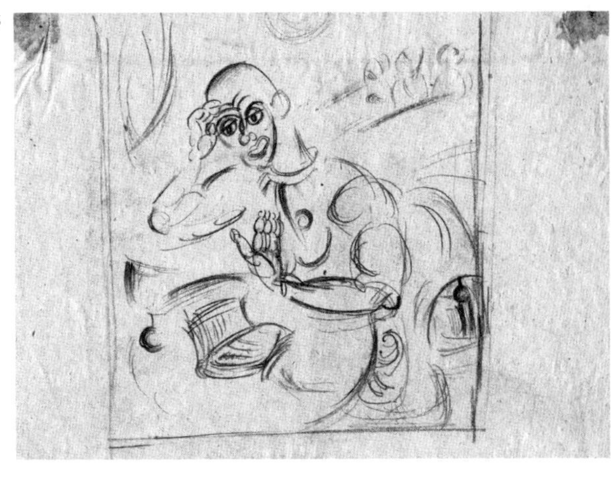

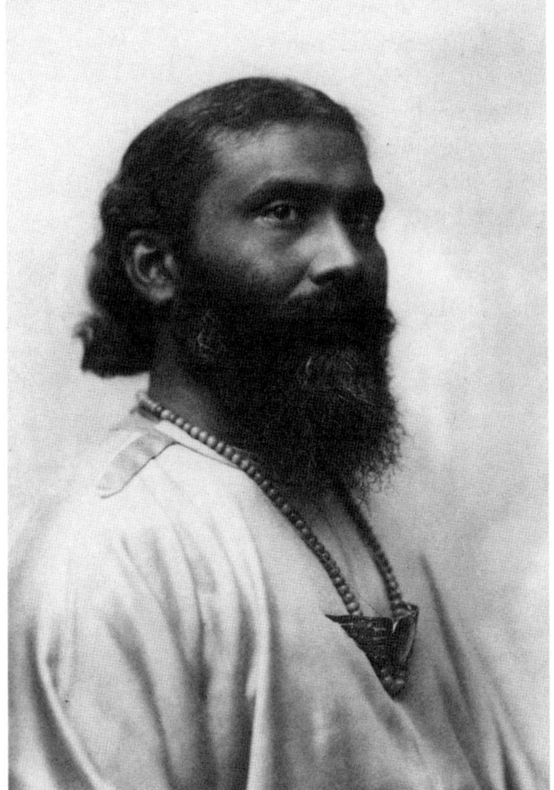

6

Umlauf. 000144

Heute Abend 8 Uhr im Oberlichtsaal Vortrag, Gesang und Lautenspiel des nordischen Musikers Marschid Inayad Khan.

Weimar, den 22. Oktober 1921.

Vorzulegen:

Meister Lyonel Feininger,
" Johannes Itten,
" Paul Klee,
" Gerhard Marcks telephonisch erledigt
" Georg Muche,
" Oskar Schlemmer
" Lothar Schreyer
" Adolph Meyer verreist
" Josef Hartwig
" Josef Zachmann
" Max Krehan telephonisch erledigt
" Carl Schlemmer z.Zt. Berlin
" Helene Börner
" Carl Zaubitzer
" Otto Dorfner

7

the Bauhaus, the reasons for which are implied as early as December 1921 in a letter written by the Bauhaus master Oskar Schlemmer to his artist friend Otto Meyer-Amden: "But Gropius says that that we may not place ourselves outside life and reality, whereby the risk (if it is one) of Itten's method is that, for example, the workshop students find meditation and rites more important than work." Schlemmer continues: "This duality appears to be fundamental to present-day Germany. On the one hand, the advent of Eastern culture, the India-cult, also the return to nature of the wayfarer and others, settlement, vegetarianism, Tolstoyism, reaction to the War—and on the other, Americanism, progress, the marvels of technology and invention, the metropolis. Gropius and Itten are the quasi-typical advocates and I must say, I find myself once more happily-unhappily in the middle. I approve of both, or indeed wish that one were informed by the other."[22]

[22] Oskar Schlemmer in a letter to Otto Meyer-Amden, Weimar, December 7, 1921, in *Oskar Schlemmer: Idealist der Form; Briefe, Tagebücher, Schriften, 1912–1943*, ed. Andreas Hüneke (Leipzig, 1990), pp. 81–82.

Captions

8 First page of handwritten notes for the lecture "The Nature of Art" by Hazrat Inayat Khan (Pir-o-Murshid) at the Staatliche Bauhaus Weimar, 1921, manuscript

9 Joost Schmidt, *Die sieben Chakras* (The Seven Chakras), 1931, pencil and colored pencil drawings and typewritten notes on transparent paper, from *Natur- und Menschenwerk: Die Sinne als Steuerungswerkzeuge; Studien zum Thema "Mensch und Raum," Elemente einer Gestaltungslehre, Aufzeichnungen für den eigenen Unterricht*

8

Pir-o-Murshid Hazrat Inayat Khan 1882 – 1927

corrected by Murshida Goodenough

The nature of art

The Sufi thinks that art is divine for the very reason that the source of art is divine. As the source of art is divine, art depends more on intuition than on study. ~~In the language of the Mystic there is one great attribute of the Creator and that attribute is art.~~

There are two things, nature and art. Nature is the art of the creator and in the nature one sees the perfection of the creator's art. The variety of colours and forms that one can notice in the nature can show one that God is the perfect artist. If there is anything that has given the proof of God it is Nature and the beauty of nature.

No, doubt there are two kinds of individuals, the major and the minor and this does not depend on age. There is an individual who lives in the beauty, ~~…~~ he is not conscious of it. He does not feel, he only lives in his grave. But there is another who is open to feel the beauty of colour and form in nature and to him nature is a paradise. And when that person goes a step forward, he asks what appeals to him, is it the colour, the form? And he wishes to recreate, so to speak, the nature which is already there. And it is this tendency to create again in which is the origin of art.

This tendency comes in two forms:

20.361

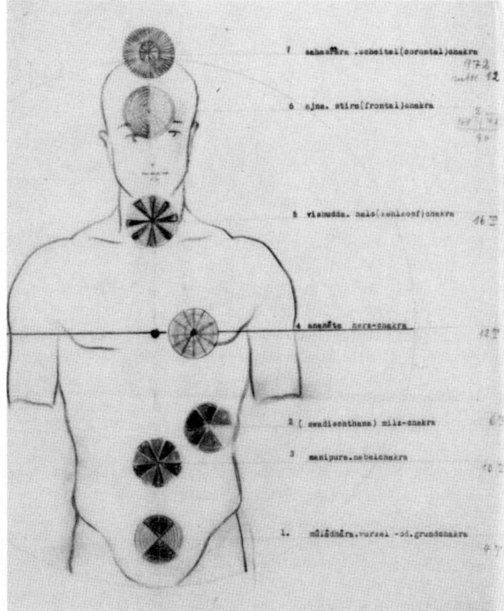

9

A Letter from Calcutta

In May 1922 a letter from Calcutta arrived at the Bauhaus. This was from Stella Kramrisch, who had been working at the International University in Shantiniketan, founded by Rabindranath Tagore, since 1921. She had studied under Josef Strzygowski in Vienna, where, in 1919, she drafted her dissertation on the early Buddhist art of India. Kramrisch was fascinated by theosophy and anthroposophy. In 1920, she wrote an article about the painter Sophie Korner, who had studied under Itten in Vienna and who, as a student, had moved with him to the Bauhaus.[23] Kramrisch's letter included an invitation to the Bauhaus masters and students to participate in a commercial exhibition with works by contemporary Indian artists, organized by the Indian Society of Oriental Art—it was addressed not to Gropius but to Itten. This suggests that Kramrisch already knew Itten from Vienna.

Among the works by the Bauhauslers that were eventually sent to Calcutta in August were several copies of the art book *Utopia: Dokumente der Wirklichkeit* (Utopia: Documents of Reality). Compiled by Itten in 1921, this contained philosophical and religious texts from different cultures, as well as his own painting studies. Itten followed the introduction with the beginning of the creation myth from the Rigveda, the oldest part of the Hindu Vedas. This was followed by a text that refers, among other things, to the book *Chitralakshana,* one of the earliest books on the history of Indian art. This text was accompanied by an illustration that shows the interior of an Indian temple in Ahmedabad.

The packages sent to India also included three works by Wassily Kandinsky, who in 1922 had just joined the group of Bauhaus masters. As early as 1911 in his book *Concerning the Spiritual in Art,* with which the

[23] Stella Kramrisch, "Sophie Korner," in *Die Bildenden Künste: 1920,* vol. 3 (Vienna, 1920), pp. 104–07.

[24] Wassily Kandinsky, *Concerning the Spiritual in Art,* trans. M.T.H. Sadler (New York, 1977), p. 13.

[25] Letter from Lyonel Feininger to his wife Julia, September 6, 1922. A copy of the letter is located in the Bauhaus Archive Berlin, inv. no. 11830/1-4. The original is at the Houghton Library of Harvard University, Cambridge, MA.

[26] Thüringisches Hauptstaatsarchiv Weimar, Staatliches Bauhaus Weimar, no. 57, page 79a.

[27] Oskar Schlemmer in a letter to Otto Meyer-Amden, Weimar, June 1922, in Hüneke 1990 (see note 22), p. 93.

[28] Ibid.

Bauhauslers were most familiar, he had written critically about "materialistic science" and praised those contemporaries who looked to other peoples with different, nonscientific methods of exploring the phenomena of existence and the world: "However, these very methods are still alive and in use among nations whom we, from the height of our knowledge, have been accustomed to regard with pity and scorn. To such nations belong the Indians, who from time to time confront those learned in our civilization with problems which we have either passed by unnoticed or brushed aside with superficial words and explanations."[24]

What might the Bauhauslers have felt when their pictures for the first joint exhibition abroad went to the much-revered India, of all places? Perhaps a healthy mix of trepidation about the distance their works were to travel, and great delight. In a letter from Lyonel Feininger to his wife Julia in September 1922, there are echoes of both: "I have been advised by Fraulein Heckmann that the 35 watercolours, woodcuts, etc. are happily on the way to Calcutta . . . Oh, girlie—."[25]And Paul Klee, who even prior to his Bauhaus days had often engaged with matters Indian, and whose bookshelves contained titles on Indian sagas, Indian sculpture, and Indian miniatures of the Islamic era, at that time painted a picture that he christened Indian Flower Garden. In spring 1923 there was a long wait for the works to arrive back from India. Then, in April, the secretary of the Bauhaus, Lotte Hirschfeld, noted in a small handwritten memo: "Works arrived on 23.4."[26] There was just one work that failed to make its way back to Weimar: a watercolor by the student Sophie Korner, which was the only one to find a buyer—Rabindranath Tagore.

"Art and Technology—A New Unity"

In summer 1922, there were already indications that Itten might soon leave the Bauhaus. He now imagined that the Mazdaznan doctrine might inspire the Bauhaus more strongly than ever. Itten's Mazdaznan dream "met with resistance, especially from Gropius, who feared sectarianism at the Bauhaus," as Oskar Schlemmer noted in a letter.[27] Shortly afterward, Schlemmer outlined what the Bauhaus was now moving toward: "Rejection of the utopia. We can and may aspire only to the most real, to the realization of ideas. The *Wohnmaschine,* as opposed to the cathedral. Rejection, therefore, of the medieval and the medieval concept of craftsmanship."[28] Itten, who advocated craftsmanship and the handmade object, finally handed in his resignation and left the Bauhaus in spring 1923. With this, the Bauhaus's initially very open search for the new had departed from many of its early utopian ideals, and the fascination for "Americanism, progress, the marvels of technology and invention, the metropolis," once referred to by Schlemmer, led to a change of direction that was articulated in the slogan "Art and technology—a new unity."

Spirituality and Technology—A New Unity?

With the Bauhaus's new orientation, the collective reconnaissance of the East, of India, was quickly consigned to the past, with mysticism and esotericism becoming the private preserve of individual Bauhauslers. Some of it nevertheless continued to reach the Bauhaus crowd through the spiritual world view of the masters Klee, Schlemmer, and Kandisky. But in 1931—Ludwig Mies van der Rohe was by now director of the Bauhaus, and Schlemmer and Klee had left—something unexpected happened: Joost Schmidt, who had initially studied under Itten and other masters at the Bauhaus in Weimar, and who was now junior master of the advertising department and head of the sculpture workshop, introduced a special course for students, in which he aimed to convey the "quintessence of his learning."[29]

While Schmidt in his workshops was involved with practical typography, advertising photomontages, the exploration of elementary spatial figures, and exhibition design, this course was to be about the comprehensive analysis of the human being—his relation not only to nature, but also to the cosmos. From this course, or from its preparation, stems a work by Schmidt that shows the seven chakras of the body—materially intangible energy centers through which human energy flows. The chakra teachings were first referred to in the Upanishads, where each of these energy centers had its own name. Schmidt, too, gave the Sankrit name to each of these. For all the zeal that Schmidt applied to the technique, he also saw the risks associated with it. As early as 1928 in the journal *Bauhaus,* he had warned: "A look at the social discrepancies of the technological machine age should suffice to make all its splendor seem highly questionable!"[30] And he was convinced that the end of the nineteen-twenties would herald a new age that would have the physical-psychological wholeness of the human being at its core. For Schmidt, the knowledge of the chakras evidently belonged to this amplified, new image of humanity—an image that the early Bauhaus had already longed for.

[29] See Lutz Schöbe, "Joost Schmidt: Die Sieben Chakras," in Wagner 2005 (see note 1), p. 109.

[30] Quoted from ibid., p. 110.

[31] Walter Gropius, opening of the new building at the Ulm School of Design (HfG), September 1955, typescript, Bauhaus Archive Berlin, GS 20/File 161, p. 4.

Four years later, with the Bauhaus long since closed, the Ulm School of Design (HfG), which initially saw itself as an extension of the Bauhaus, was founded. Walter Gropius held the inaugural speech for the opening of the new school building in 1955, in which former Bauhauslers such as Josef Albers, Walter Peterhans, and Johannes Itten taught. Now, Gropius—as if he could hear the words of Joost Schmidt in his ear—spoke about how the technological advances of past decades had convulsed humanity, had dissolved the people's sense of community, and emphasized the importance of a new cultural orientation. Gropius's vision looked back to the early days of the Bauhaus and, at the same time, presented a utopia for the present: "On a world tour last year I became familiar with the oriental mode of thinking in Japan, Siam and in India, which reveals itself so differently, more internalized and magical than that of the logical-practical Western man. Will the future with its greater generosity on earth bring the gradual merging of these two modes of thinking and henceforth lead to a more mature democracy of balance between the spiritually divine and intellectually logical? The artistic being with his predisposition for human completeness is predestined to nurture this interpenetration and to achieve for himself an aim that is truly worthy of enthusiasm."[31]

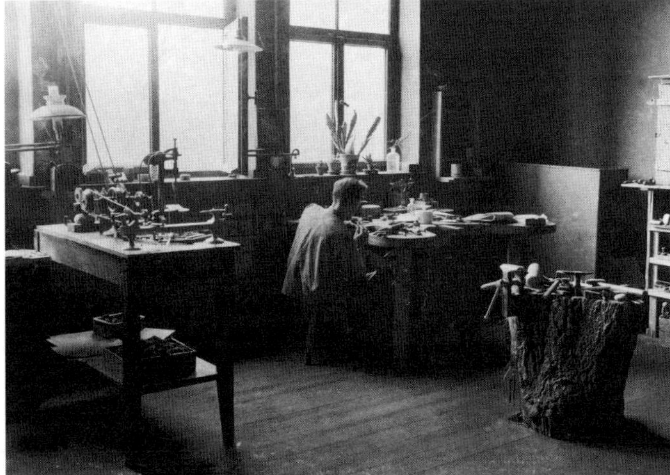

2

1

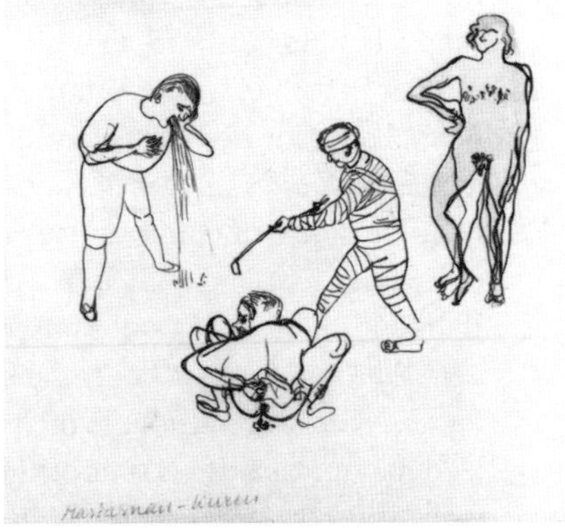

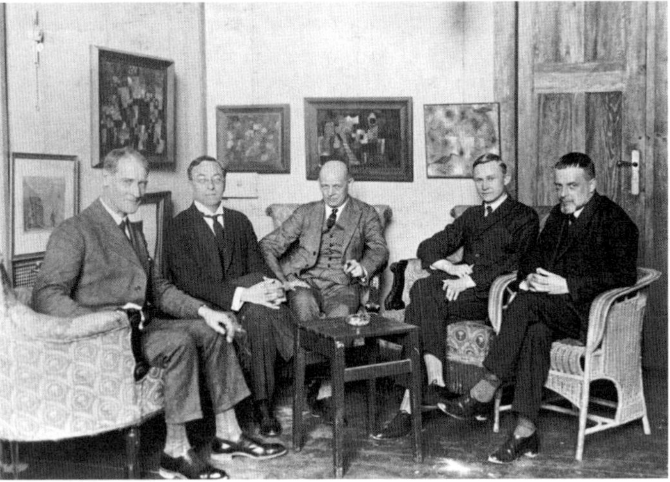

3

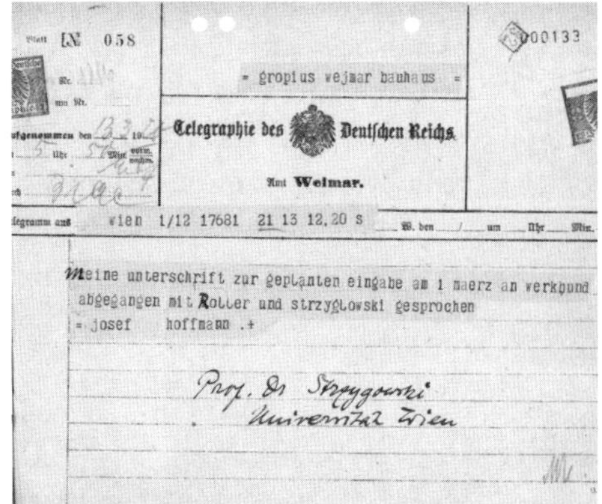

058

00133

= gropius wejmar bauhaus =

Telegraphie des Deutschen Reichs

Amt Weimar.

Telegramm aus wien 1/12 17681 21 13 12.20 s

Meine unterschrift zur geplanten eingabe am 1 maerz an werkbund abgegangen mit Roller und strzyglowski gesprochen = josef hoffmann .+

Prof. Dr Strzygowski
Universität Wien

4

Captions

1 Paul Citroen, *Masdasnan-Kuren* (Mazdaznan Cures), pen-and-ink drawing and watercolor on transparent paper, ca. 1922
2 Photographer unknown, Bauhaus master Naum Slutzky in his workshop, ca. 1922, photograph
3 Photographer unknown, Bauhaus masters in Paul Klee's Weimar studio, 1925, photograph
4 The telegram shows the message of protest against the closure of the Bauhaus in the context of the declaration of directors and professors of the Austrian art schools for the Staatliche Bauhaus Weimar, 1920
5 Photographer unknown, kite festival in Weimar, 1921–22, photograph
6 Photographer unknown, Indian festival in front of the Prellerhaus in Weimar, February 4, 1913, photograph
7 Photographer unknown, life at the Bauhaus Weimar with Bauhauslers in front of the Bauhaus Weimar, 1921, photograph. From left to right: unknown, Alexa Röhl, Peter Röhl, Felix Kube (or Fritz Kuhr), Lou Berkenkamp (later Lou Scheper), unknown, Hinnerk Scheper, Käthe Reichelt, unknown
8 Photographer unknown / Carl Schlemmer (?), life at the Bauhaus Weimar with Bauhauslers and guests, ca. 1922, photograph. Bauhauslers: Oskar and Tut Schlemmer, Casca Schlemmer, Gunta Stölzl, Benita Koch-Otte, Marcel Breuer, Josef Albers, Josef Hartwig, Kurt Schmidt; guests: Willi Baumeister, Werner Gilles (?)

5

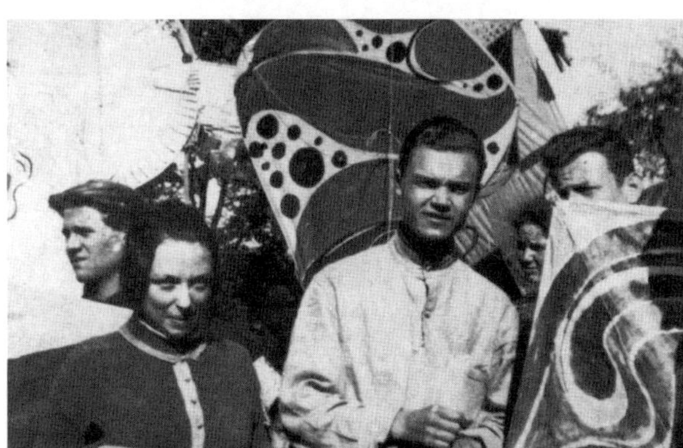

7

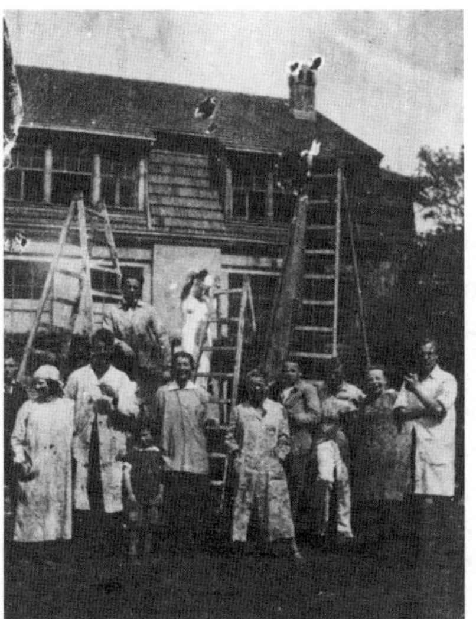

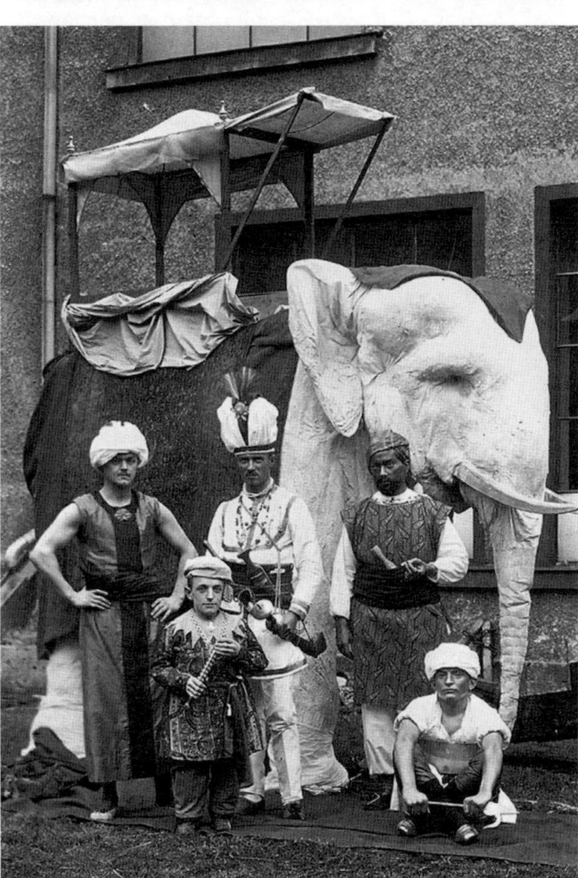

6

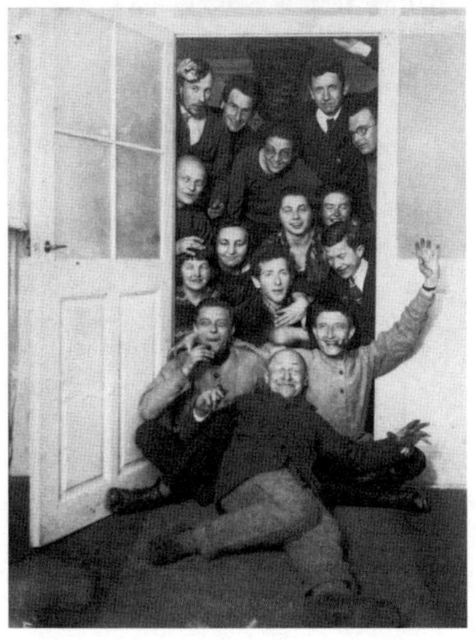

8

Torsten Blume

Mazdaznan and Racial Theory

"The liberal racial theory of Dr. O.Z. Hanisch is as relevant to the research into the history of development as perhaps the spinal cord is to mankind." This emphatic statement opens the article on "Racial Theory and Art Development," which was published by Johannes Itten in 1923 in the *Masdasnan* journal under the subheading: "Guide to the highest level of development of body and mind, to the elevation of the white race, to the achievement of youth, health, self-confidence, neurological strength, serenity and happiness." Itten's article ends with the sentences: "Only the white race is offered the opportunity to create complete, that is, harmonious artworks as symbols and models of the advancement to human completeness, to sanctity. Visual art (painting, sculpture, architecture), the art of tones and of the word, comes to full fruition only in the white race."[1] The foregoing argumentation, which portrays art history as the reflection of higher development from the "black," "brown," "olive-skinned," and "grey-red" up to the "white" race, is already found in almost identical form four years earlier in a manuscript, undated but written in 1919, titled "1st Lecture Weimar: The Art of the Present and the Threefold Nature of the Human Being (Phrenology—Racial Theory)." And on February 4, 1919—fourteen days before Walter Gropius appointed him at the Bauhaus—the designated Bauhaus master presented a lecture in Munich on "Human Development, Art Development, Power of

[1] Johannes Itten, "Rassenlehre und Kunstentwicklung," *Masdasnan* 16, no. 5 (1923), pp. 89–92.

[2] Johannes Itten, "1. Vortrag Weimar: Die Kunst der Gegenwart und die dreifache Veranlagung des Menschen (Phrenologie—Rassenlehre)," in *Das frühe Bauhaus und Johannes Itten,* ed. Rolf Bothe, Peter Hahn, and Hans Christoph von Tavel, exh. cat. Klassik Stiftung Weimar, Bauhaus Archiv Berlin, and Kunsthaus Zürich (Ostfildern, 1994), pp. 446–47.

[3] See Bernd Wedemeyer-Kolwe, *"Der neue Mensch": Körperkultur im Kaiserreich und in der Weimarer Republik* (Würzburg, 2004), pp. 154ff.

Concentration" with similar content.[2] Both when he started at the Bauhaus in 1919 and when he finished there in 1923, Johannes Itten therefore repeatedly and publicly theorized about the Mazdaznan idea and maintained thereby that "all possibilities and levels of development [are, or could be] concentrated and harmonized in the white race."

The founder of the Mazdaznan theory and movement was Otto Hanisch, an American of German and Russian descent. Hanisch came from a modest background but reinvented himself in his new homeland as the son of a Russian ambassador to Persia and an Iraqi princess. He had also, in a Tibetan monastery, rediscovered and thenceforth studied for twenty-five years the ancient Mazdaznan religion of the Persian proto-Aryans, founded by Zarathustra. This, Hanisch maintained, justified his claim to be the rightful successor of Zarathustra, authorized to disseminate the Mazdaznan doctrine once again. In 1890 in Los Angeles, he founded the "Reorganized Mazdaznan Temple Association of God" and called himself Dr. Otoman Zar-Adusht Ha'nish. He explained that the term "Mazdaznan" originated from Middle Persian and meant "master thought" or "masterfully concentrated thought"—but that it above all signified the oldest "universal religion of the white race" which, although it had been spread throughout the world by "young" Zoroastrian prophets such as Moses, Jesus, Buddha, and Mohammed, sadly had been corrupted by "racial intermixture," the wrong diet, the wrong breathing, and religious crises, thereby becoming obsolete. If only the "white man" were now to decide, through "sexual hygiene and racial breeding" and the new breathing and nutrition theory, to eliminate "the bad juices from the body and thereby also the bad thoughts and impulses," then he would not only further his own personal development but also help the Aryan race recapture its leading role as the chosen "master race"—and thereby ultimately promote human progress.[3]

The Mazdaznan racial theorists—according to their theosophical model based on Helena Blavatsky's "root race theory"—consistently emphasized the movement's pacifist, nonaggressive character. In fact, their new religious, esoteric figures of thought—unlike the contemporaneous racial theories influenced by social Darwinism and colonial-political ideas—hardly constituted direct, politically orientated concepts but instead addressed the individual who sought "meaning" and a misplaced "wholeness." Mazdaznan was especially appealing for many members of the bourgeois middle class, for this religious culture dedicated to health, lifestyle, and body movement offered numerous practical formulas with a view to achieving, through work on one's own body, a new feeling for life in the "unity of body, mind, and spirit." When in 1907 the movement—with its eclectic mix of Far Eastern, theosophical, and racial theory elements—began to recruit followers in Germany, too, it thereby interacted in a contentual and personal context with other new religious and body-orientated reform movements that took a critical stance toward civilization, which were organized along communal and sectarian but also commercial lines. Quite often these were led by charismatic figures who, like Otto Hanisch, possessed "prophet status." At the end of the Weimar Republic, this heterogeneous so-called "body culture movement" had more than one hundred thousand devotees. They were all united by the hope of finding, through training and shaping the body, the one, universal path from which they might completely redress all the conditions of modern life that they perceived as unsatisfactory.[4]

One of the foundations of Mazdaznan theory is the classification into three types of temperament: material, spiritual, and intellectual. This was derived from phrenology, according to which different facial and cranial forms are assigned a priori to different types of people. Based on this, in racial theory the "black, brown, and olive-skinned races" were characterized as natural and materially orientated ancient races, and the "grey-red and yellow races" as already spiritually sensitized, balanced races—but only the members of the "white race" were in a position to harmoniously combine material and spiritual orientation with intellectualism, to recognize in themselves the interplay of these temperaments, and to sustain themselves with the appropriate basic diet. There were dietary recommendations for each type: carbohydrates for the material type, phosphates for the spiritual type, and proteins for the intellectual type. Detailed instructions regulated the daily dietary program, and colonic irrigation was recommended as a cleansing ritual for the body, to combat "spiritual imperfection." As an important means to the improvement of the whole sensitive faculty and for increased vitality, the movement embraced a series of rhythmic breathing exercises adopted from Indian yoga, which were combined with auto-suggestion exercises. In Germany in 1910 there were already fifteen Mazdaznan centers that organized lectures, "reincarnation," breathing and cooking classes, and "harmony evenings"; Mazdaznan was also practiced in more than ten natural healing centers and sanatoriums. During the First World War, the European branch relocated to Switzerland, and Leipzig once again became the movement's headquarters. From the German publishing center in the twenties,

[4] Ibid., p. 158.

[5] Ibid., p. 164. See also Paul Scheurlen, *Die Sekten der Gegenwart*, 4th ed. (1921; repr., Stuttgart, 1930).

[6] Itten, "1. Vortrag Weimar," in Bothe et al. 1994 (see note 2), p. 446.

[7] Johannes Itten, *Mein Vorkurs am Bauhaus: Gestaltungs- und Formenlehre* (Ravensburg, 1963).

the movement then issued countless flyers, books, and magazines, with circulations sometimes reaching sixty thousand. Even a mail-order business with Mazdaznan products was established, offering almost everything that a Mazdaznan-orientated body culture specialist might need, ranging from underwear, spices, oils, and other health products to colonic irrigation kits and special cooking pots. In his comprehensive study of the German body culture movement in the German Empire and the Weimar Republic, Bernd Wedemeyer-Kolwe graphically described how the Mazdaznan culture was thoroughly embedded in the life reform movement of the day. And although the National Socialists banned the Mazdaznan movement, at first provisionally in 1935 and then once and for all in 1941, many of the Mazdaznan devotees—like numerous other life reformers—had initially welcomed the Third Reich and its "Führer principle," offering Mazdaznan up as a potential "common property of all members of the German nation" and to some extent also attempting to promote the "eugenic principles of the Zoroastrian theory of reincarnation" as a possible means of "improving" the German race.[5]

Johannes Itten's Weimar Mazdaznan manuscript, which was probably drawn up as a kind of inaugural lecture, also formulates the idea of a series of lectures: "The lectures should serve the objective of self-awareness."[6] This call for "self-awareness" as human being and artist, which is known to be central to the preliminary course that Itten introduced at the Bauhaus, has, in the reception of Itten to date, been based on the progressive educational background of his earlier activities as a primary school teacher and, above all else, on his artistic apprenticeship in Adolf Hölzl's circle. The fact that Itten's artistic concept—also in his classes at the Bauhaus—is at its core an earnestly meant, esoteric one, and that he advocated and consistently taught the Mazdaznan theory not only as one of many other sources of inspiration, but as a universally valid world view, has been rarely and, if so, only peripherally discussed to date. Moreover, Itten himself—above all in later presentations of his Bauhaus pedagogy[7]—contributed significantly to the fact that his virtually obsessive preoccupation with theosophy and especially the new religious Mazdaznan movement around 1920 has been thematized only as a minor, rather curious by-note.

Nonetheless: in his time as a Bauhaus master, Johannes Itten's involvement with esoteric theories was anything but peripheral. On the one hand, he integrated the practical applications of the Mazdaznan sect in his lessons; and he also advocated the Mazdaznan ideology and its fundamental beliefs regarding racial theory, which he consistently promoted at the Bauhaus, although he was ultimately only really able to reach a manageable—albeit highly visible and active—circle of dedicated devotees. Itten regularly used the semester breaks for long stays at the Mazdaznan center in Herrliberg or visited the Mazdaznan center in Leipzig, where he also held lectures. And in November 1921 Johannes Itten endeavored to invite the German "ambassador" of the Mazdaznan movement, David Ammann, to lecture at the Bauhaus, who would have then perhaps proclaimed his message: "It is not the triumph of the races, but the triumph of the spirit alone, which will bring you health: world power begets only struggle and strife, while spiritual power begets unity!"[8] Ultimately, the Itten-supported appointment in 1920 of the acknowledged Mazdaznan devotee Georg Muche, who among other things pushed the Bauhaus canteen to switch to a vegetarian Mazdaznan menu in 1921, reflected the efforts to "Mazdaznanize" the Bauhaus to the greatest possible degree. Oskar Schlemmer wrote about this in his letters: "Itten and a few Bauhaus stalwarts have lived according to the Mazdaznan principles for some time . . . He sees it as the only possibility to produce 'the new human being,' believes in a transformation of the way of thinking and feeling as a precondition for everything." . . . "As I have already mentioned, Itten has allowed the Mazdaznan doctrine to become established here."[9]

Walter Gropius first met Itten through his then wife Alma Mahler, who toyed with the idea of becoming a "Sanskrit pupil," studying under the chairman of the Theosophical Society. When he appointed Johannes Itten as Bauhaus master in February 1919, the Bauhaus director was not only familiar with his symbolic-esoteric artistic concept, but was also initially sympathetic to it and at the very least supported it.[10] Something similar will have applied to Wassily Kandinsky's engagement with theosophy or the theosophical work of his erstwhile colleague, the architect Adolph Meyer. However, among the avant-garde artists in search of modern individualization,

[8] D. Bezner-Heilbronn, "Zur Selbsterkenntnis der anglischen Gruppe in der weißen Rasse," *Masdasnan* 16, no. 5 (1923), pp. 92–93.

[9] Oskar Schlemmer, letter to Otto Meyer-Amden on December 7, 1921, in *Oskar Schlemmer: Idealist der Form; Briefe, Tagebücher, Schriften*, ed. Andreas Hünecke (Leipzig, 1990), p. 79.

[10] See Christoph Wagner, "Johannes Itten und die Esoterik: Ein Schlüssel zum frühen Bauhaus?," in *Esoterik am Bauhaus* (Regensburg, 2009), pp. 108–49, esp. pp. 109–11.

[11] Walter Gropius, "Rede bei der ersten Ausstellung von Schülerarbeiten des Bauhauses im Juni 1919," in Karl Heinz Hüter, *Das Bauhaus in Weimar* (Berlin, 1976), p. 211.

[12] Wagner 2009 (see note 10), pp. 113–16.

[13] Ludger Busch, "Das Bauhaus und Mazdaznan," in Bothe et al. 1994 (see note 2).

[14] See Ullrich Linse, "Mazdaznan: Die Rassenreligion vom arischen Friedensreich," in *Völkische Religiösität und Krisen der Moderne: Entwürfe "arteigener" Glaubenssysteme seit der Jahrhundertwende*, ed. Stefanie von Schnurbein and Justus H. Ulbricht (Würzburg, 2001), pp. 268–91.

meaning, and spirituality in the nineteen-twenties, there was scarcely one who had not engaged with esoteric ideas, at least for a while. This also applied to Theo van Doesburg, who then (especially from 1921) became a catalyst for the debate about the rationalization of the Bauhaus, which led to Walter Gropius's coining of the slogan "Art and technology—A new unity" in 1923 and forced Johannes Itten's departure from the Bauhaus. In June 1919, Gropius also said that the solidarity of the sect was his ideal for the Bauhaus: "small, secret, internal associations, lodges and conspiracies that protect a secret and aspire to creative design." For Johannes Itten, this must surely have sounded like a direct confirmation of his vision of influencing the Bauhaus in the sense of an artistic realization of the Mazdaznan movement, or, respectively, of even perhaps transforming the Bauhaus into an artistic Mazdaznan center.[11] Not only his classes, where Itten appeared before his students in self-made Mazdaznan garb with his head shaved like a guru, and his relaxation or breathing exercises and countless other body training methods may be interpreted in the Mazdaznan context, but also his artwork. To whit, *Turm des Feuers* may be interpreted as a manifestation of the Mazdaznan concept of higher development, and his *Farbenkugel in 12 Tönen und 7 Lichtstufen* as a human model of the Mazdaznan teachings on elements and temperaments.[12] But Itten's belief in the Mazdaznan doctrine and its racial theory is presented with most clarity through repeated quoting of Otto Hanisch in his texts and images, as in his contribution to the first Bauhaus portfolio in 1921: "House of the white man: greet and hail the heart that is illuminated by the light of love and is not led astray by the hope of a heaven or the fear of a hell."[13]

Johannes Itten, whose paintings were treated as "degenerate art" by the National Socialists and who had to leave Germany in 1933, had understood, along with many of his contemporaries, the crude racial theory that he advocated as a positivistic concept or hypothesis concerning development—surely without suspecting the terrible consequences that this entailed. For precisely this reason, this racial theory should no longer be suppressed but brought into ever-sharper focus.[14]

Christoph Wagner

Johannes Itten and India

I. Johannes Itten as Many-Armed Shiva

A seemingly good-natured and humorous photomontage by Hans Finsler from the end of the year 1948 shows Johannes Itten as a many-armed Shiva (fig. 1): tongue in cheek, the assiduous artist, who simultaneously worked as a painter, educator, and museum man,[1] is portrayed as a quasi-mythical, "many-armed" entity in the iconographic reference. Perhaps Finsler, with his comparison between Johannes Itten and Shiva as Nataraja, who evolves as the Lord (or King) of Dance in his cosmic dance over the "demon of ignorance," also alluded to Itten's fascination with Expressionist dance dating back to the nineteen-twenties, as well as to his wide-ranging, artistically

[1] From December 1, 1938 onward, Johannes Itten was head of the Kunstgewerbemuseum (museum of applied arts) alongside the Kunstgewerbeschule (arts school) in Zurich. Since the referendum on the restructuring of Villa Wesendonck into the Museum Rietberg of June 3, 1949, he additionally headed the latter. Willy Rotzler, ed., *Johannes Itten: Werke und Schriften,* catalogue raisonné by Anneliese Itten (Zurich, 1978), p. 429; Christoph Wagner, "Johannes Itten: Leitmotive einer Künstlerbiografie," in *Johannes Itten: Alles in Einem—Alles im Sein,* ed. Ernest W. Uthemann (Ostfildern, 2002), pp. 11–81.

[2] Christoph Wagner, *Das Bauhaus und die Esoterik: Johannes Itten, Paul Klee, Wassily Kandinsky,* ed. Christoph Wagner (Bielefeld, 2005). Christoph Wagner, "Johannes Itten und die Esoterik: Ein Schlüssel zum frühen Bauhaus?," in *Esoterik am Bauhaus: Eine Revision der Moderne?,* vol. 1: *Regensburger Studien zur Kunstgeschichte,* ed. Christoph Wagner (Regensburg, 2009), pp. 108–49.

[3] Christoph Wagner et al., eds., *Itten – Klee: Kosmos Farbe,* exh. cat. (Regensburg, 2012). The exhibition ran from November 30, 2012 to March 31, 2013 at the Kunstmuseum Bern and from April 25 to July 29, 2013 at the Martin-Gropius-Bau, Berlin.

[4] See the short review by Ernst-Gerhard Güse, "Der Einfluss ostasiatischer Philosophie und Kunst auf Lehre und Werk von Johannes Itten," in *Johannes Itten: Gemälde, Gouachen, Aquarelle, Tusche, Zeichnungen,* exh. cat. Westfälisches Landesmuseum für Kunst und Kulturgeschichte (Münster, 1980), pp. 13–19.

[5] Copper alloy h. 82.4 cm, Museum Rietberg, Zurich, RVI 501, donated by Eduard von der Heydt. On the iconography of the dancing Shiva and on the history of the Museum Rietberg: Johannes Beltz, "The Dancing Shiva: South Indian Processional: Bronze, Museum Artwork, and Universal Icon," *Journal of Religion in Europe* 4 (2011), pp. 204–22.

[6] Rotzler 1978 (see note 1), p. 260. See the short notice in *Eduard von der Heydt: Kunstsammler, Bankier, Mäzen,* ed. Eberhard Illner (Munich et al., 2013), pp. 106–7.

minded, and sometimes esoterically inclined, reflections,[2] in which the entire existence of humankind and the world[3] were frequently invoked. Certainly, the photomontage also implies Itten's at the time very active commitment to non-European art in general and his efforts toward the establishment of the Museum Rietberg in particular. To which extent, however, do these connections with the Indian culture inform Itten's art?

Despite all appearances to the contrary, the aforementioned photomontage, which originated on the occasion of Johannes Itten's sixtieth birthday on November 11, 1948, is not the mere product of chance. It may instead be understood as an iconographic and biographic key for the theme of Johannes Itten and India, which has hitherto been completely neglected in research.[4]

The photograph manipulated in the photomontage shows a characteristic, almost one-meter-high Indian bronze sculpture of a Shiva "Nataraja," the dancing Shiva, which emerged from the twelfth century Chola dynasty in the Indian state of Tamil Nadu (fig. 2), and which Johannes Itten was more than familiar with: the large sculpture is one of the best known holdings of the former collection of Eduard von der Heydt, whose donation to the city of Zurich Johannes Itten had pursued insistently for many years and by the achievement of which he was able to lay the the foundation of the Museum Rietberg, which had been established after a referendum on June 3, 1949. It is certainly not a coincidence that the referendum was also advertised with a picture of Shiva "Nataraja," which was to become the emblem of the museum thereafter.[5] The photomontage showing Itten as Shiva "Nataraja" may be seen as the starting point of the visual adoption of Indian art in the Museum Rietberg. Another part of the collection of von der Heydt was brought to Zurich by Johannes Itten from the depot of the East Berlin art museums in rather adventurous circumstances in 1951, in exchange for "a tea glass, a tea strainer and two butter knives" belonging to Lenin, which were received as coveted political "relics" in East Berlin in those days.[6] Itten himself described the bizarre facts surrounding this transfer of artworks, which he also, if nothing else, personally chaperoned during the three-hour truck journey to Zurich. These Chinese sculptures transferred to Zurich back then are now also part of the important collection of non-European art at the Museum Rietberg in Zurich, which Johannes Itten built up from 1949 and curated from its opening in 1952 to 1956.

Given this biographical background, the pictorial comparison of Johannes Itten and Shiva, as realized in the photomontage, is to be understood as a programmatic visual reference to the artist, to non-European art in general, and to Indian art in particular in the context of his artistic and political activities as art curator at the Museum Rietberg: Itten's spiritual and artistic affinity with Indian art may be traced back over several decades and important stages in his life.

II. "Concerning Composition"

The extent to which Johannes Itten's interest in Indian art informs his own artistic and theoretical reflections is already documented in his early diary entries: influenced by Adolf Hölzel and his lessons at the Stuttgart Academy from autumn 1913, Johannes Itten had kept so-called diaries, in which he noted his thoughts on art theory.[7] Itten was one of the few artists who endeavored to consider the history of art—following the major teleological historical models of the nineteenth century, such as, for instance, Hegel's *Aesthetics*—as a world-historical development process. He thereby attributed individual quality and meaning to Indian art.

An important key to this deep appreciation of Indian art as a distinct and specific part of a world art history is documented in Itten's lecture "Concerning Composition," which he presented in Vienna on May 7, 1917 to the Verein der bildenden Künstlerinnen Österreichs, or Austrian Association of Women Artists.[8] In October 1916, Itten relocated from Stuttgart to Vienna, where he founded a private art school.[9] It was the well-connected Stuttgart student Agathe Mark-Kornfeld who had encouraged Itten to move to Vienna and who had then continued to support him financially: from autumn 1916 onward, it was Mark-Kornfeld who introduced Itten to Vienna's artistic avant-garde circle. Here, he quickly got to know artists, architects, composers, poets, philosophers, and art historians, such as Carl Moll, Josef Hoffmann, Adolf Loos, Franz Werfel, Arnold Schönberg, Alban Berg, Josef Matthias Hauer, Hans Pfitzner, Rudolf Steiner, Hans Tietze, Josef Strzygowski, and Alma Mahler. That Johannes Itten repeated this lecture on May 21, 1917

[7] Eva Badura-Triska, ed., *Johannes Itten: Tagebücher Stuttgart 1913–1916, Wien 1916–1919* (Vienna, 1990).

[8] The lecture survives in Itten's words in three versions: as a postscript in Diary II, as a revised edition in Diary VI, and as a clean copy with additional illustrations, probably drafted by Emmy Anbelang, on which Rotzler (1978, see note 1, pp. 212–19) based his transcription (Badura-Triska 1990 [vol. 2], see note 1, p. 97).

[9] Dieter Bogner and Eva Badura-Triska, eds., *Johannes Itten: Meine Symbole, meine Mythologien werden die Formen und Farben sein*, exh. cat. Museum moderner Kunst Stiftung Ludwig Wien, Kunsthaus Zürich, and Museum Folkwang Essen (Vienna and Zurich, 1988). Christoph Wagner, "Johannes Ittens 'private Kunstschule' in Wien: Ein Modell für das Bauhaus?," in *Bauhaus global: Gesammelte Beiträge der Konferenz bauhaus global vom 21. bis 26. September 2009*, vol. 2: *New Bauhaus Books*, ed. Bauhaus Archive Berlin [new numbering system] (Berlin, 2010), pp. 59–68.

[10] Heinrich Lützeler, *Kunsterfahrung und Kunstwissenschaft: Systematische und entwicklungsgeschichtliche Darstellung und Dokumentation des Umgangs mit der bildenden Kunst*, vols. 1–3: *Orbis academicus I/15* (Freiburg and Munich, 1975), vol. 2, pp. 1494–95.

[11] Rotzler 1978 (see note 1), p. 409 (note referencing p. 212).

[12] Ibid., p. 212.

[13] Ibid., p. 213.

[14] Ibid.

[15] Ibid., p. 214.

[16] Ibid.

at the Department of History of Art of the University of Vienna at the request of Josef Strzygowski—then a prominent art historian advocating a non-European art historiography in Vienna, who later on admittedly embodied through his "racism the hitherto unsurpassed high point of a constructivist distortion of comparative art history"[10]—shows how much attention the presentations of the then twenty-nine-year-old artist attracted.[11] Moreover, the fact that Johannes Itten had planned his lecture, as the side notes show, as a "slide presentation" with diagrams, proves that he was also well versed in the recent media developments of the day. Unfortunately, we do not know the visual material he used, but the transcriptions give a clear impression of his specific understanding of Indian art, at a time when there was a dearth of comparable material from other avant-garde artists.

Itten already emphasized at the beginning of his presentations that he did "not wish to develop a manifesto on composition theory, but to teach the development of composition."[12] Itten understood artwork to be "living, animated, exciting, for which the human being creates an organism in his work by words, sound or form."[13] In this interplay, Itten saw artist and work profoundly historically conditioned in the context of an alterable situation in the history of perception: "We people of today living here in Vienna in the spring of 1917 are the product of a long development, are complex and abstruse, often completely beyond our own comprehension."[14] At the beginning of this long development process in cultural and art history, Itten viewed Indian art as high culture—perhaps comparable with the Egyptian culture and in some ways superior to contemporary art: "The young Indians were clear-sighted, sharp-eared, extraordinarily sensitive individuals, whose young senses were attuned to the path of the original movement. The intuitive creative power was immense, compared with ours. The Indian knows only rhythm, endlessly ser pentine linear rhythm, this steadily interflowing movement. Perhaps so [fig. 3]: please pay more attention to the movement of the hand than to the emerging line. Try to feel the movement."[15]

In 1917, this prompt to "feel the movement" already formulated the artistic program that Johannes Itten went on to award a more prominent role in his "Analysen Alter Meister" (Analyses of Old Masters) in the *Utopia* almanac of 1921, which was also exhibited in Calcutta. And it is astonishing how directly Itten's empathy for the "endlessly serpentine linear rhythm" of Indian art, the "chaotic rhythm of the Indian,"[16] corresponded with the artistic language of his own drawings at this time (fig. 4).

While one may deride Itten's subsequent ambitious attempt to locate Indian art in a wide-ranging historico-cultural development, it simultaneously shows how hard he tried to historically categorize the topicality of Indian art in relation to contemporary art: after the "Indian cultural epoch followed the Persian" with its sense of dark and light, thereafter the Egyptian, with a new sense for the mathematical proportions of the form, and so forth.[17] By way of Cézanne and the Cubists, Itten finally arrived at the "futuristic outlook," to which he assigned a "longing to return to the strong emotional experience of the Indian."[18]

III. ". . . to express his insight into the rhythm of all visible things . . ."

This background casts a somewhat different light on why it was not Walter Gropius, but Johannes Itten, who received Stella Kramrisch's written invitation to the exhibition project in India in May 1922.[19] As a doctoral student under Josef Strzygowski, Kramrisch—who had completed her doctoral thesis in Vienna in 1919 and was moreover in touch with women painters at Itten's school in Vienna—was probably present at Johannes Itten's lecture in 1917 or had, at the very least, heard about it.

This puts the choice of works in a new context, and especially the text commentary that Itten provided for the *Indian Society of Oriental Art*'s catalogue for the 1922 exhibition in India. Here, the portrait of Itten, which he himself undoubtedly subedited or authorized, proceeds as follows: "Itten, the Swiss Artist is possessed by all the zeal of conviction. He does not stop unless he reaches the very essence of appearance. He visualises, for instance, the scent, freshness and colour of a rose in a few pencil strokes; this utmost economy however is the outcome of numberless experiments as to the structure of a rose, the movement of rose petals, the touch of their cool and smooth surface and the atmosphere in which they breathe. And his sketch confesses that unless you feel your own existence merged into that of the rose and lost in it, you fail to know what a rose means. Itten gains his artistic vocabulary by intuitive abstraction and moulds his compositions by its help and with the logic of a masterbuilder. His method is scientific and serves to express his insight into the rhythm of all visible things, as well as of his own soul. His work has religion."[20]

[17] Ibid., pp. 214–15. See also Christoph Wagner, "Klees 'Reise ins Land der besseren Erkenntnis': Die Ägyptenreise und die Arbeiten zur 'Cardinal-Progression' im kulturhistorischen Kontext," in *Paul Klee: Reisen in den Süden; 'Reisefieber praecisiert,'* ed. Uta Gerlach-Laxner et al. (Ostfildern, 1997), pp. 72–85.

[18] Rotzler 1978 (see note 1), p. 219.

[19] The letters are reproduced in the publication at hand (see page ##) and also in the German version of this catalogue: Regina Bittner and Kathrin Rhomberg, eds., *Das Bauhaus in Kalkutta: Eine Begegnung kosmopolitischer Avantgarden*, vol. 36: *Edition Bauhaus* (Ostfildern, 2013), p. 69.

[20] Cited according to the exemplar in Lahore, Pakistan; ibid., pp. 11–14. With many thanks to Regina Bittner for surrendering a PDF copy of *Das Bauhaus in Kalkutta*.

[21] Rotzler 1978 (see note 1), pp. 214–15. See Christoph Wagner, "Chaos und Naturgenese bei Paul Klee, Wassily Kandinsky und Wols," in *Naturentwürfe: Arbeiten auf Papier von Cézanne bis Beuys*, ed. Jörg Becker (Albstadt, 2000), pp. 99–117.

[22] Christa Lichtenstern and Christoph Wagner, *Johannes Itten und die Moderne*, from the series *Materialien zur Moderne* (Ostfildern, 2003).

The conceptual-artistic aspiration formulated here, that is, "to express his insight into the rhythm of all visible things, as well as of his own soul," is remarkably consistent with the idea of a "chaotic rhythm of the Indian."[21] There is some evidence that, for this exhibition in Calcutta, Itten did not simply select works indiscriminately from the perspective of the current avant-garde positions in Western art,[22] but that he attempted to conform to his own historico-culturally based paradigm of Indian art as a strongly dynamic-rhythmic visual language. The European avant-garde artist, in the selection of works, demonstrated his solidarity with Indian art!

Johannes Itten's body of work from 1922, the year of the Calcutta exhibition, in fact includes a drawing titled *Rosen* (Roses, 1922, fig. 5, Rotzler CR 290) among a series of plant studies, whereby the aforementioned lines from the exhibition catalogue describe what he might have been aiming for. Itten had exemplified this aesthetic aspect of the empathetic concept in exaggerated form a year earlier in the *Utopia* portfolio, in the prominent work *Distel* (Thistle, fig. 6). This portfolio was also on show in Calcutta: "A Copy of the Magazine 'Utopia' 2 £." The lithography that Itten likewise presented for the exhibition, *Flowers on the edge of the Forest (Litho.)* (1919, fig. 7, CR 160), listed in the catalogue as No. 49 at a price of two pounds, may also be categorized in this context.

All of the works in the exhibition catalogue that may with some confidence be ascribed to Johannes Itten adhere to this concept in that they show the dynamism of a chaotic and free rhythm of forms, which Itten associated with Indian art, in the visual language of an abstracting rhythmization of Western avant-gardes:

48. Landscape in Tyrol (Lithography), 2 £	CR 159, 1919
49. Flowers on the edge of the Forest (Litho.), 2 £	CR 160, 1919
50. Old Woman, 2 £	CR 161, 1919
51. Bridge, 2 £	CR 79/80 1916
52. Maiden, 2 £	CR 162/3 (?), 1919 [fig. 8]
53. Man, 2 £	CR 164, 1919
54. Composition I, 2 £	CR 166, 1919 (?)
55. Composition II, 2 £	CR 165, 1918 (?)
56. Composition III, 2 £	CR 167, 1918 (?) [fig. 9]

Interestingly enough, connections can be made between these reflections regarding content and some of the works from the exhibition in Calcutta that cannot be directly attributed to Itten: on the list of exhibited works, a few abstract compositions are catalogued with the description "Action Picture" or "42. Coloured painting depicting action":

43. Action Picture I	7 £
44. Do. II	7 £
45. Do. III	6 £
46. Do. IV	7 £
47. Do. V	6 £

Although we can no longer attribute the general entries in the exhibition catalogue to specific works with complete certainty, it is nevertheless clear from Itten's oeuvre in those years that these are works—like *Farbige Rhythmen*

(Colored Rhythms, 1916, CR 84), *Das Entzweite* (The Sundered, 1916, CR 102), *Rhythmen* (Rhythms, 1916, fig. 10, CR 107), or *Flecken und Bewegungen* (Spots and Movements, 1918, CR 140)—which depict, on an abstract level, the dynamism of an "endlessly serpentine linear rhythm" based on a "primal movement" in the sense of Itten's vision of a modern adaptation of the Indian sense of rhythm.[23]

If, in this context, one carefully rereads the opening remarks of the exhibition catalogue, it becomes clear that introducing the avant-garde positions of the Western world to India was just one aim among many: "It is for the first time that Western Art is represented in India by a number of the most advanced and most sincere works of leading Continental Artists. They do not belong to any school, but come from different parts of Europe, each having his own manner and technique. . . . Neither masters nor students are the followers of any 'isms' although they are bound to make use of them to a greater or smaller extent. For 'Cubism' or 'Post-impressionism' are conventions of form, developed out of the need of the moment, and no artist in whom the present is alive can escape their formulae."[24]

Moreover, Johannes Itten and his colleagues set great store in raising awareness of the artistic correlation between the abstraction of European art and the vital rhythm of the Indian use of form—which Itten reflected on early and intensively in his lecture "Concerning Composition": "The Indian public should study this exhibition for then, they may learn that European Art does not mean 'naturalism' and that the transformation of the forms of nature in the work of an artist is common to ancient and modern India and Europe as an unconscious and therefore inevitable expression of life of soul and of artistic genius."[25]

That Itten above and beyond this also focused sharply on the philosophical-spiritual background of Indian culture is verified by the notes and extracts to this effect in his so-called *Tempelherrenhaus-Tagebuch,* a diary that he kept during his years at the Bauhaus Weimar and in which he relates drawings and diagrams to key words such as *Yoga, Atma, Prana, Tejas, Puthiv,* or *Ahankra.*[26]

The beginnings of Itten's artistic-spiritual involvement with Indian art are thus to be located within the time frame of his early Bauhaus years. From that point on, the lines of development of his involvment with Indian art can be pursued uninterruptedly into the late nineteen-forties and early fifties, where they led to his prominent efforts toward the presentation of non-European art in the Museum Rietberg.

[23] Christoph Wagner, "Bauhaus Before the Bauhaus? Johannes Itten's Painting *The Encounter,*" in *Bauhaus: A Conceptual Model; 1919–2009,* ed. Bauhaus Archive Berlin, Klassik Stiftung Weimar and Bauhaus Dessau Foundation (Ostfildern, 2009), pp. 23–26.

[24] See note 20.

[25] Ibid.

[26] See also Christoph Wagner, *Itten, Gropius, Klee am Bauhaus in Weimar: Utopie und historischer Kontext,* vol. 3: *New Bauhaus Books,* ed. Bauhaus Archive Berlin [new numbering system] (Berlin, 2013).

1

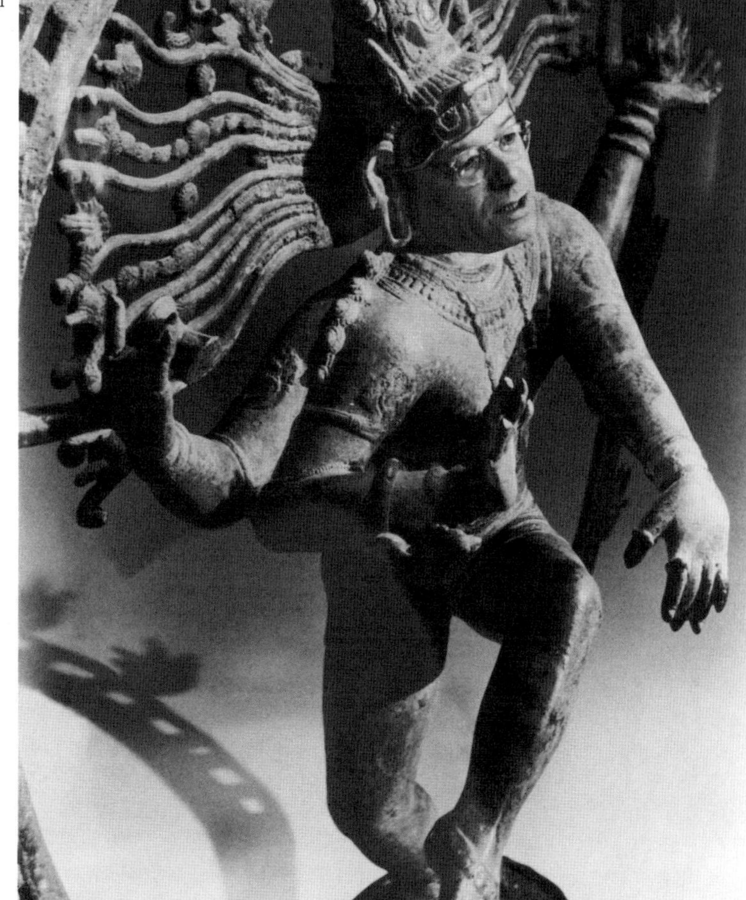

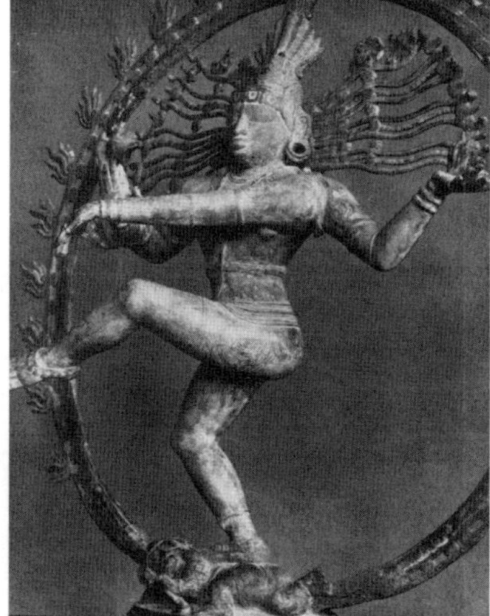

2

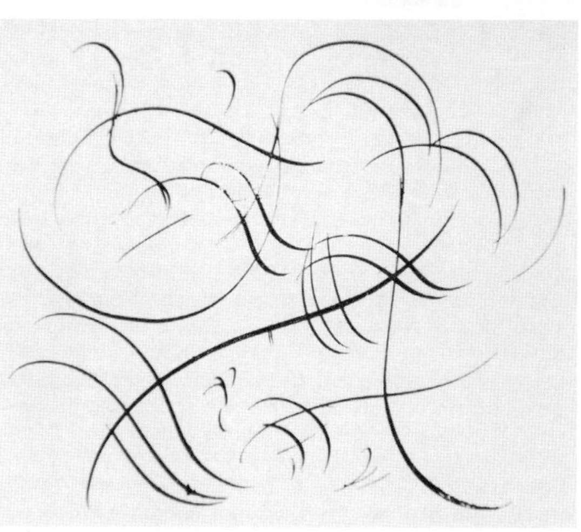

3

Captions

1 Hans Finsler, *Johannes Itten as a Many-Armed Shiva,* 1948, photomontage
2 Shiva Nataraja, 12th century, bronze, Museum Rietberg, Zurich
3 Johannes Itten, illustration for his lecture "Concerning Composition," 1917

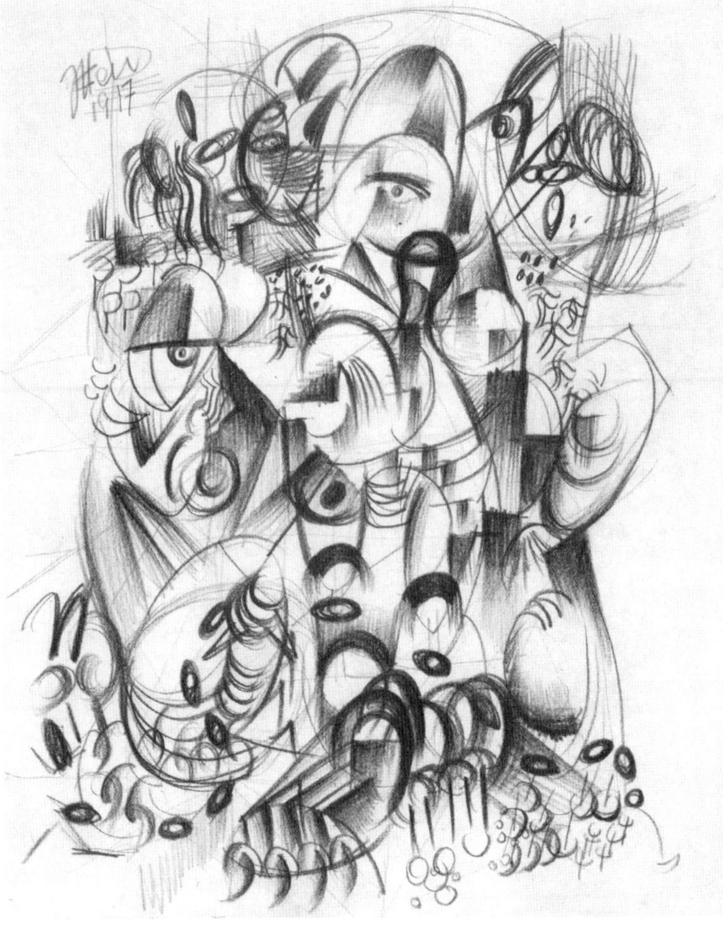

4

5

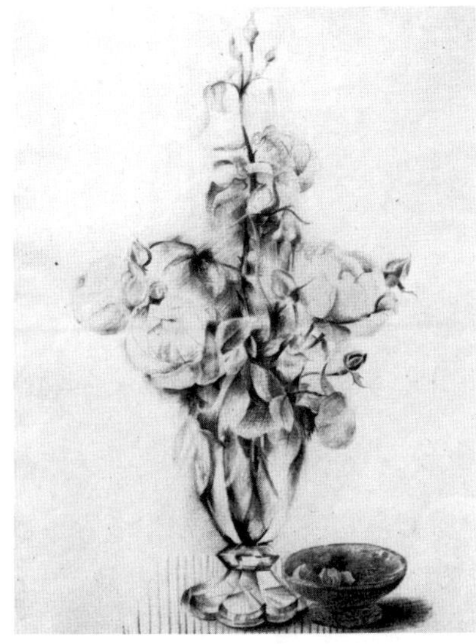

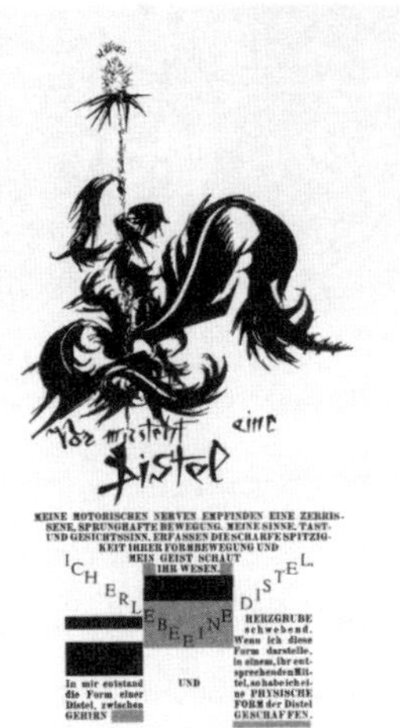

6

Captions

4 Johannes Itten, *Hören und Sehen* (Listening and Seeing), 1917, pencil
5 Johannes Itten, *Rosen* (Roses), 1922, pencil and colored pencil
6 Johannes Itten, *Die Distel* (The Thistle), 1921, lithograph from "Analysen Alter Meister" in the Utopia almanac of 1921
7 Johannes Itten, *Flowers on the edge of the Forest,* 1919, lithograph
8 Johannes Itten, *Mädchen* (Girl), 1919, lithograph
9 Johannes Itten, *Komposition III* (Composition III), 1919, lithograph
10 Johannes Itten, *Rhythmen* (Rhythms), 1916, pencil

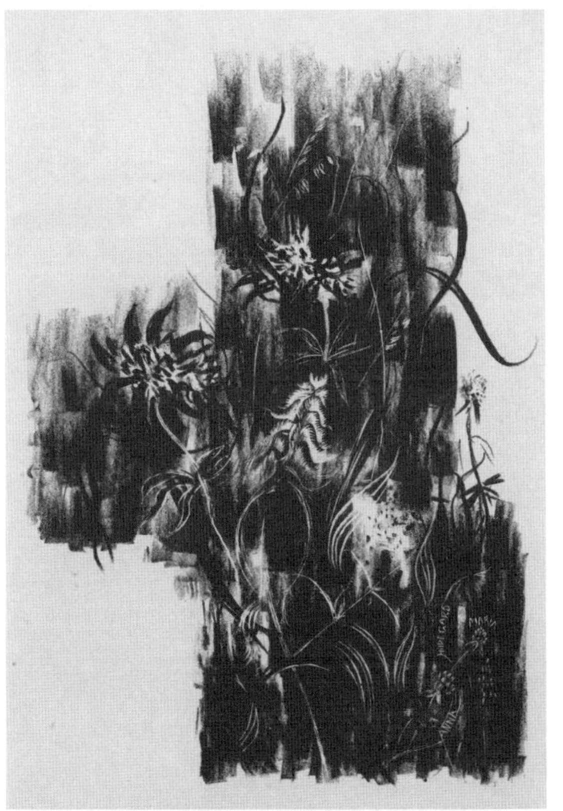

7

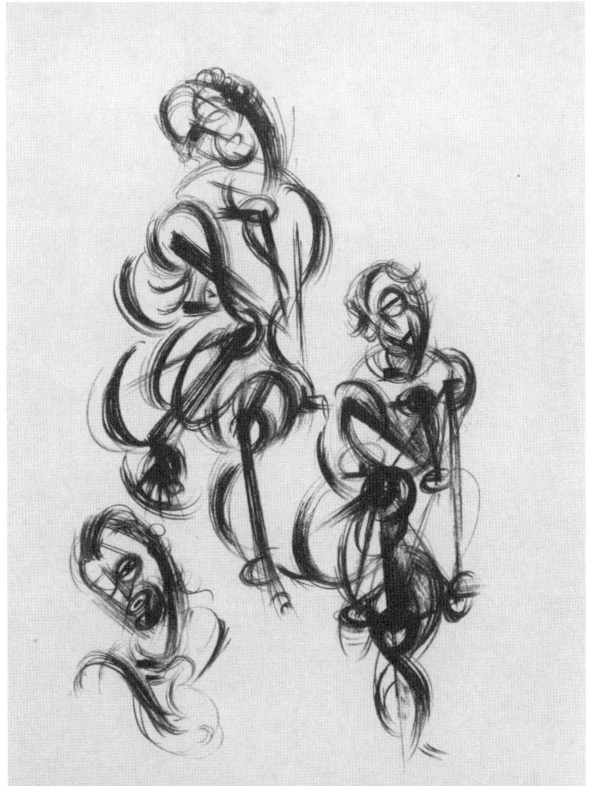

8

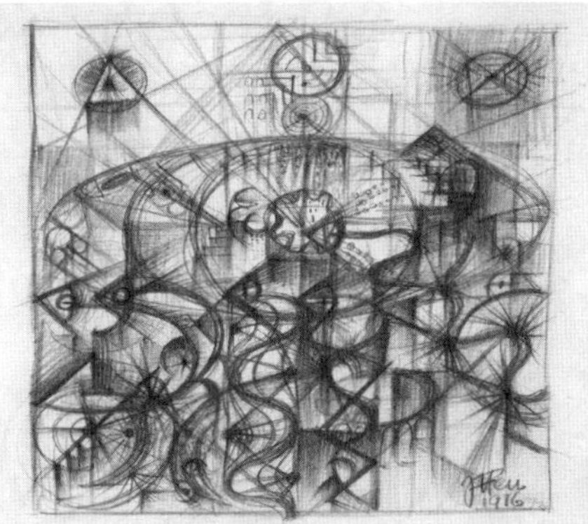

10

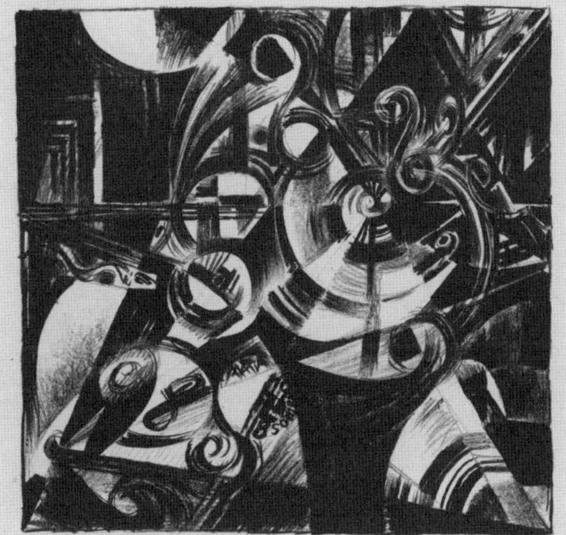

9

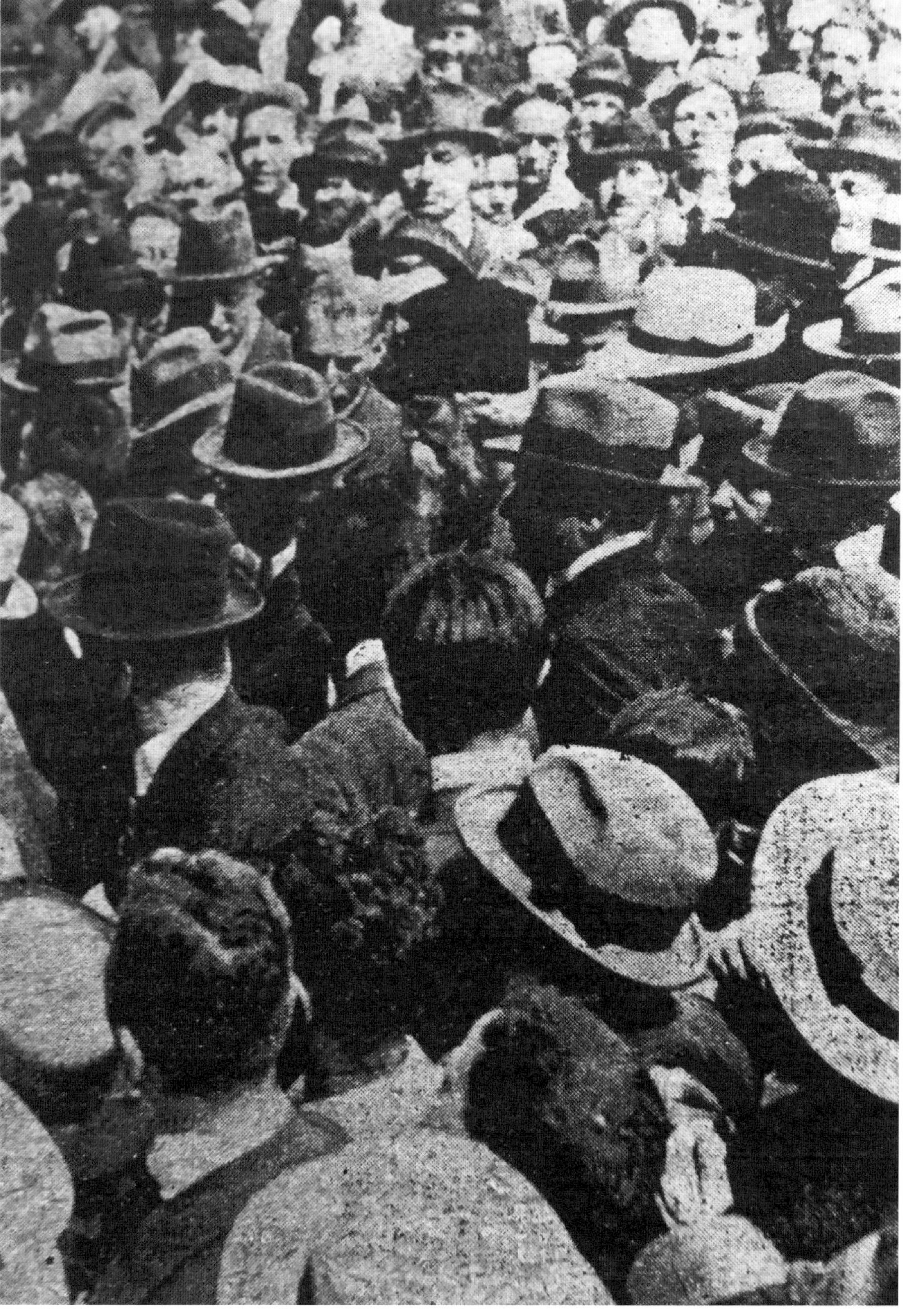

1

Kris Manjapra

The Anticolonial Laboratory

Indian Nationalist Diaspora in German-Speaking Europe

Asian Immigration to Continental Europe

Just as the Chinese and Vietnamese diasporic communities in Paris and Berlin in the nineteen-twenties produced political and intellectual figures of great importance, such as Zhou Enlai, Deng Xiaoping, and Ho Chi Minh, the same is true in the Indian case.[1] Counted among the Indian diaspora to Germany in the twenties were Manabendra Nath Roy (1887–1954), Benoy Kumar Sarkar (1887–1949), Meghnad Saha (1893–1956), Satyendranath Bose (1894–1974), Taraknath Das (1884–1958), Virendranath Chattopadhyay (1880–1937), Zakir Husain (1897–1969), and Subhas Chandra Bose (1897–1943), among many others, all of whom made critical contributions to Indian anticolonial politics in the years leading up to and including the Second World War.

Radical forms of thought and politics characterized the mental worlds of these diasporic figures. But there are many other anticolonial travelers and students who also journeyed outside the imperial axis to interwar Germany, and their story should not be occluded by the looming shadow of "great men." A perspective that emphasizes the sociopolitical relations between individuals, as well as between groups of individuals and their urban geographies and social institutions, helps us to understand the rise of Indian deterritorial nationalism, and its significance for freedom struggle in the interwar years.

As Kavalam Madhusudan Panikkar commented long ago, "technology has helped to make distances and space relative . . . with the advance of technology space has contracted."[2] While large flows of Indian and Chinese migrants began arriving in Britain by the mid-nineteenth century,[3] Asian immigration to France and Germany only began in significant numbers with the advent of the First World War.[4] But the number of Indian "sojourners" in Germany was augmented by the large number of Indian prisoners of war from the British army, held at camps outside Berlin.[5] Prisoners were allowed to exit the camps if they entered the service of the German Foreign Office during the war. And after the war's end, some POWs chose to remain in Berlin rather than return to colonial India. This small contingent of radical activists and ex-POWs formed the kernel for a significant Indian community in Berlin in the twenties.

The First World War made continental Europe a site for Asian diasporas, especially for the pursuits of work and study, but also anticolonial political activity. But not just the war was at work here. Another reason for Indian emigration to Germany in the twenties was the closure of North America, as well as other Anglo-Saxon settler colonies, to Asian migrants during these years. The quota laws instituted in Canada, Australia, and the United States from the turn of the century intensified in the interwar years, bringing about a degree of "deglobalization" that pressed Indians into alternative migration

[1] On Chinese intellectuals in Paris, see below. On Ho Chi Minh and the Vietnamese political diaspora to France and Moscow, see Hue-tam Ho Tai, *Radicalism and the Origins of the Vietnamese Revolution* (Cambridge, MA, 1992) and Sophie Quinn-Judge, *Ho Chi Minh: The Missing Years, 1919–1941* (Berkeley, 2003).

[2] K. M. Panikkar, *Geographical Factors in Indian History* (Bombay, 1955), p. 14.

[3] The first Chinese arrived in Britain in the eighteen-sixties and seventies but greatly rose in numbers at the turn of the nineteenth century. See Gregor Benton and Edmund Terence Gomez, *Chinese in Britain 1800–Present: Economy, Transnationalism, Identity* (Basingstoke, 2007), pp. 24–27. Indian migration to Britain stretches back to the beginning of British economic interests in India starting in the seventeenth century, in the form of both wealthy nabobs and house servants. But the diasporic Indian community in Britain in the mid-nineteenth century developed when "several hundred Indians" were living in Britain. See Rozina Visram, *Asians in Britain: 400 Years of History* (London, 2002), pp. 44–104. Sumita Mukherjee, *Nationalism, Education, and Migrant Identities* (New York, 2010).

[4] Jeffrey G. Williamson and Kevin H. O'Rourke, *Globalization and History: The Evolution of a Nineteenth Century Atlantic Economy* (Cambridge, MA, 2001), p. 135.

[5] On "sojourning," see Sunil Amrith, *Migration and Diaspora in Modern Asia* (Cambridge, 2011).

[6] Norbert Wenning, *Migration in Deutschland: Ein Überblick* (Münster, 1996), p. 102.

[7] Lala Hardayal, *Forty-four Months in Germany and Turkey, February 1915 to October 1918* (London, 1920), p. 20.

[8] The Nachrichtenstelle für den Orient was located first on Savigny-Platz and then at Tauentzienstrasse. See Karl Emil Schabinger, *Reportage über die Nachrichtenstelle für den Orient*, September 21, 1915, R1502: 13643.

[9] Hardayal 1920 (see note 7), p. 17.

[10] For information on the Hindustan House dormitory on Uhlandstraße, the Association of Indians in Central Europe house on Knesebeckstraße, and places of worship, see Ausländer-Kartei Indien, 1928–38, Humboldt University Archive (henceforth HUA); on the cricket field at Baumschulenweg, see I.B., Orientals in Berlin, Oriental and India Office Collections of the British Library (henceforth OIOC), September 3, 1923, L/P&J/12/102; on homes of senior émigrés, see Orientals in Berlin, OIOC, May 22, 1923, L/P&J/12/102.

Caption

1 Photographer unknown, Rabindranath Tagore at the University of Berlin in *The Modern Review* (August 1921), p. 258

patterns. And Berlin was not the only port of call in German-speaking Europe. Chempakaraman Pillai led a political center, called the Pro India Committee, in Zurich starting in 1912. In Hamburg, Munich, Kiel, Heidelberg, and Vienna there were also major subsidiary centers of the diasporic anticolonial laboratory that concentrated in Berlin, around its powerful institutions and embedded within its imperial infrastructures.

In comparison to the over two hundred thousand Poles, Czechs, and Austrians who immigrated to Germany in 1926 alone, the absolute numbers of Asian immigrants to continental Europe seems relatively insignificant.[6] However, the political significance of these Asian populations was immense. Continental European diasporic populations were the source of a new, more radical, deterritorial nationalism in the nineteen-twenties, which served as an important catalyst for politics in the subcontinent. The rise of a new era of radical politics in India in the thirties must be traced to the effects of political radicalization in the continental European diaspora in the decade previous. It was from among these diasporic communities that anticolonial entanglements with Marxism and totalitarian nationalism ensued.

A Center for Diasporic Nationalism

In the aftermath of the destruction of the First World War, émigré communities from various Eastern lands collected in Charlottenburg, one of Berlin's western boroughs. Charlottenburg became Berlin's "little Asia," partly because the Foreign Office had set up its Committee for the Orient in that region during the war.[7] Government officials, such as Max von Oppenheim, had ensured that the colonial subjects invited to Berlin to work with the Indian Committee in 1914 were housed in the vicinity of the Information Service for the East (Nachrichtenstelle für den Orient) to facilitate surveillance.[8] Of his time in Charlottenburg in 1914, Lala Hardayal recalled that "all the peoples of Asia could be seen on the streets."[9] After the war, the most powerful and respected colonial émigrés involved with the Foreign Office—such as Virendranath Chattopadhyaya and Bhupendranath Datta among the Indians, Mansur Rifat of the Egyptian community, and the Persian leader Seyyed Hasan Taqizadeh—remained in Berlin, living in the same homes and establishing salons for nationalist activity. The social imprint of wartime experience kept Indians in this same region of Berlin throughout the nineteen-twenties and thirties. Social spaces that were established in the war years for anticolonial activists—dormitories for Indian students, community meeting houses, parks to play cricket, places of worship, the homes of the older generation of émigrés—now served a burgeoning community of Indian students in the Weimar period.[10] Another reason for the dense social clustering of Indian diasporic communities in Charlottenburg was the proximity of homes in this region to the Technical University and the Friedrich Wilhelms

University (today's Humboldt University), where most students studied.

Berlin was a city of well-differentiated neighborhoods. Many Eastern Jews lived in the Scheunenviertel district around Orianenburger Straße, while the communist quarter centered around Alexanderplatz. Charlottenburg, in contrast, was the area for political émigrés and foreign students. It was home to the foreign, elite, and educated.[11]

The Berlin Indian émigrés became the main engine of anticolonial politics outside territorial India in the nineteen-twenties, numbering at least five hundred individuals by 1923.[12] Just as the intellectual avant-garde of other national communities, such as Vietnam's Ho Chi Minh, China's Zhou Enlai, and Russia's Vladimir Nabokov, lived in Berlin in the early twenties, the same can be said for the Indian group.[13] Highly influential Indian modernist thinkers like Manabendra Nath Roy and Benoy Kumar Sarkar, figures who would chart a radical intellectual agenda for Indian nationalism in the interwar period, were embedded in the social life of Berlin in these immediate postwar years. Berlin was a central node in the nervous system of Indian anticolonialism and modernism.

[11] Karl Schlögel, *Berlin, Ostbahnhof Europas: Russen und Deutsche in ihrem Jahrhundert* (Berlin, 1998), p. 55; also see Karl Schlögel et al., eds., *Chronik russischen Lebens in Deutschland 1918–1941* (Berlin, 1999).

[12] A British surveillance report from 1923 recorded 363 Indians present at a nationalist meeting; see HW, Orientals in Berlin, OIOC, January 13, 1923, L/PJ/12/102, pp. 9–10. Another report records that the Indian Association (Verein der Inder) house had space to accommodate four hundred visitors; see I.B., Orientals in Berlin, OIOC, September 3, 1923, p. 43.

[13] On Ho Chi Minh and the Vietnamese political diaspora to France and Moscow, see Hue-tam Ho Tai 1992 (see note 1) and Quinn-Judge 2003 (see note 1). On Zhou Enlai and the Chinese intelligentsia, see Marilyn Levine, *The Found Generation: Chinese Communists in Europe during the Twenties* (Seattle, 1993). Also see Arif Dirlik, *The Origins of Chinese Communism* (New York, 1989); on Nabakov in Berlin, see Dieter E. Zimmer, *Nabokovs Berlin* (Berlin, 2001).

[14] Stauer to the Foreign Office, October 26, 1921, AA, R63011, unnumbered. Students of medicine, chemistry, and technical fields in particular are reported as having expressed interest.

[15] See the calling card of Chattopadhyaya from 1922 in the folder "Deutsches Generalkonsulat in Kalkutta," AA, R63011, n.d.

[16] See report by Ruth, Deutsches Generalkonsulat in Kalkutta, February 19, 1922, AA: R63011, unnumbered.

[17] Daniel Headrick, *The Invisible Weapon: Telecommunications and International Politics, 1851–1945* (New York, 1991), pp. 39ff.; Laura Otis, *Networking: Communicating with Bodies and Machines in the Nineteenth Century* (Ann Arbor, 2001), p. 56; Dieter Basse, *Wolff's Telegraphisches Bureau 1849–1933* (Munich, 1991).

[18] According to British intelligence reports, the first volume of M. N. Roy's magazine *The Vanguard of India*, dated May 15, 1922, was intercepted in India in early June. Similarly, the August 15, 1922 issue of the *Vanguard* was quoted in the August 31 edition of the Calcutta newspaper *Amrita Bazar Patrika*. See Cecil Kaye, *Communism in India* (Calcutta, 1971), pp. 9–10.

[19] See Ausländer-Kartei Indien, 1928–38, HUA. This source consists of enrollment cards of Indian students to the Humboldt University in these years. I have tallied various statistics from them for the information provided in this section.

The Indian Community

In the context of the political upheavals in Berlin and Munich after the war, the majority of Indians had left Germany. However, beginning in 1921, the numbers began to rise again. In October, the German consulate in London reported that a significant number of Indian students were interested in studying in Germany and that a bureau should be opened in Berlin to welcome them.[14] Soon afterward, Virendranath Chattopadhyaya started the "Indian News and Information Bureau" on Burgstraße, right next to the Hackescher Markt metro station.[15] The swift timing suggests the enduring connection between Chattopadhyaya and German officials, which stemmed from his involvement with the Foreign Office during the war. Surely, the German government was not only acting out of benevolence in inviting Indians to Berlin. In the postwar period it also wanted to combat the anti-German propaganda that the British had pumped into its colonies during the war.[16]

By counting, naming, and situating Indians in the Berlin of the nineteen-twenties and thirties, the social life of the community comes into view. Life in the city was marked by transience, frequent moves, and the lack of roots. And yet, there was also a logic and structure to colonial life, by which a sense of community and belonging was created and sustained. Despite the ever-changing composition of the community, the structures of Indian diasporic life remained remarkably consistent, even into the period of National Socialism. Webs took form by the traffic in propaganda and by the circulation of anticolonial agents and political elites, linking the Berlin center with the unfolding events in the Indian colony. The day-to-day news of Indian insurgency and political action, particularly during the high watermarks of 1919 to 1921 and around 1928, reached Berlin almost immediately thanks to news wires.[17] And the trip from Berlin to India, over ports such as Marseilles or Rome, took about two weeks. Since propaganda literature was carried into India by traveling emissaries, the time gap between the printing of materials in Berlin and its arrival in India took less than a month.[18]

The Indian community was concentrated within a five-square-kilometer district around Uhlandstraße in Charlottenburg. Eighty-six of the 140 Indian students on record in the Humboldt University Archive for the period of 1928 to 1932 lived within this region; twenty-one lived within a block of Uhlandstraße itself.[19] The Indian community was characterized by clustering and high demographic density. On Uhlandstraße, Virendranath Chattopadhyaya and Bhupendranath Datta established the Hindustan Haus in 1923. The Indian Students Association stood on the adjacent street, Knesebeckstraße. There were also clusters of Indian students in the cheaper workers' areas of the Berlin districts Moabit and Wedding.

The majority of students aimed to acquire knowledge that would further the political ends of nation-building, as well as the industrialization and modernization of India along lines independent of imperial control.[20] Reminiscent of a large number of American and Japanese student travelers to Germany of an earlier period and also in the twenties, Indians saw Berlin as a laboratory for training in the arts and sciences of modernity, in pursuit of national self-strengthening: chemistry, physics, engineering, statistics, and economic thought.[21]

Leaders of the diasporic community were in charge of creating a sense of belonging by organizing association evenings, festivals, and sports events. Virendranath Chattopadhyaya's house at Georg-Wilhelm-Straße served as a kind of social epicenter.[22] And Zakir Husain, a student of political economy studying with Werner Sombart at the time, was the president of the Indian Students Association; he was later to become chancellor of Aligarh Muslim University and India's Minister for Education after independence. Students participated in a sports club, organized by Bhupendranath Datta, youngest brother of Vivekananda Datta, which met to play cricket and football at a field near Baumschulenweg, and pub nights were held at the Pschorr-Bräu where political discussions often ensued.[23]

[20] Ibid.
[21] "Berlin Pictorial," *Calcutta Review* 3, no. 7 (1923), p. 465.
[22] Daniel T. Rodgers, *Atlantic Crossings: Social Politics in a Progressive Age* (Cambridge, MA, 2001); Hoi-Eun Kim, "Physicians on the Move: German Physicians in Meiji Japan and Japanese Medical Students in Imperial Germany, 1868–1914" (PhD diss., Harvard University, 2006).
[23] Report by I.B., Orientals in Berlin, OIOC, September 3, 1923, L/P&J/12/102. On the use of the back rooms of pubs for political activity, see Werner Abelshauser et. al., eds., *Deutsche Sozialgeschichte 1914–1945* (Munich, 1985), pp. 327–47.
[24] Ida Steiler Sarkar, *My Life with Professor Benoy Kumar Sarkar* (Calcutta, 1977), p. 30.
[25] Letters of the Indian diaspora to their families and friends often spoke of homesickness. See Chattopadhyaya to Jawaharlal Nehru, May 30, 1928, NAI Nehru papers, photocopy in the Krüger Nachlass, Zentrum Moderner Orient, Berlin (henceforth ZMO).
[26] Bomell, Passports of Indians for Germany, OIOC, September 7, 1922, L/PJ/12/98, pp. 4 and 5.
[27] List of Suspect Civilian Indians on the Continent of Europe, OIOC, February 1944, L/PJ/12/659, p. 55.
[28] "Student Life in Germany," *The Modern Review* 33, no. 4 (1923), p. 514.
[29] Statement of Nalini Bhusan Das Gupta, Home Department, Po. 1924, File 21/1, NAI, Horst Krüger Nachlass, item 41, photography.
[30] Willi Münzenberg was called the "red millionaire" because he oversaw the distribution of vast amounts of Soviet funds in setting up front organizations for the Comintern. See "Indische Nationalisten in Deutschland in Verbindung zur Liga," Reichskommissar für Überwachung der öffentlichen Ordnung: Indische Nationalisten in Deutschland in Verbindung zur Liga, May 1927, R1507/R314/212.

There was occasion for celebration in the diasporic community, of course. Ida Steiler Sarkar, an Austrian woman who married Benoy Kumar Sarkar, remembered her wedding celebration within the lively diasporic Indian community in 1921. Friends in Calcutta shipped a tin of Indian sweets, *rasagolla,* to Berlin for the wedding feast. "They had not eaten a *rasagolla* for many years," Steiler recalled, speaking of the Indian guests present, including Virendranath Chattopadhyaya. "So they each got one . . . As they ate they had tears of joy in their eyes."[24] This detail gives an inkling of the nostalgia for home that was a fundamental state typically seen in migrant communities, as embodied by such collective experiences.[25]

Corruption of the Youth

Already in 1922, with the number of Indian students in Germany rising, the British government began raising concerns about the revolutionary leanings of the diasporic community in the city. An intelligence officer in British India reported, "the information recently received regarding the activities of Indian revolutionaries in Germany, and in particular the establishment there of a night school for the manufacture of bombs and explosives, has led the Government of India to consider further the question of the grant of passports for Germany to Indians."[26] In that same year, the Central Intelligence Department of the Government of India began drawing up "blacklists" of Indians suspected of anticolonial activity on the continent, lists they revised yearly and maintained well into the nineteen-forties.[27]

The British, in fact, had good reason to be concerned about Berlin as a crucible for the politicization of Indian students. Far more than an Orientalist fanfare, Rabindranath Tagore's three trips to Germany, and the "Tagore-Rausch" (Tagore frenzy) it created in the twenties, represented an effort to sustain and strengthen the network of Indian nationalists there.[28] Indian students were very openly engaged in anticolonial activities by attending nationalist gatherings, or more directly involved in political intrigue. For example, as a recent physics doctorate recipient, Debendra Mohan Bose, nephew of the world-renowned Indian scientist Jagadish Bose, became associated with Manabendra Nath Roy's communist circle in 1924. He eventually returned to India with anti-British, Soviet literature when he took up his position teaching physics in Calcutta.[29] Gangadhar Adhikari arrived in Berlin to complete a doctorate in chemistry in 1922, but he soon devoted all of his activities to building a communist party in India. He held membership in the KPD (German Communist Party) as of 1928. Kwaja Hamid, also a doctoral student in chemistry, associated with the German communist magnate Willi Münzenberg (the "red millionaire") and became an Indian representative to the 1927 Soviet-sponsored League against Imperialism in Brussels.[30] On the other hand, students like Zakir Husain congregated around anti-Bolshevik nationalists, such as Benoy Kumar Sarkar, Taraknath Das, and M. T. Acharya. The attention of non-communist nationalist leaders in Berlin did not revolve around the labor question and the wave of major strikes in India in the early twentieth century, as was the case with the radical left. They devoted themselves, instead, to more state-centric visions of building national education syllabi, creating an Indian chamber of commerce in Berlin, and to developing theories of state-led scientific industrialization.

By the end of the nineteen-twenties, the number of Indians interested in studying in Berlin, or in other German cities, especially Munich and Heidelberg, was growing significantly. The non-communist nationalists, Taraknath Das and Benoy Kumar Sarkar, both former members of the Swadeshi movement, remained convinced of the need of "national education" to bolster Indian technological know-how, and to speed along the process of industrial modernization. They sought collaborators from within German state institutions. Sarkar and Das established a scholarship program in 1929 at the Deutsche Akademie in Munich, for example. The program ran throughout the Nazi period, up until 1941. This institution of cultural diplomacy (what the Germans called *Kulturpolitik*), headed by the scholar of geopolitics and international relations, Karl Haushofer, aimed at spreading German culture and prestige abroad as a means of redressing the national embarrassment of the First World War.[31] Haushofer, on the prompting of Das and Sarkar, provided funds to twenty Indians per year to study in Germany throughout the thirties.

[31] Eckard Michels, *Von der Deutschen Akademie zum Goethe-Institut: Sprach- und auswärtige Kulturpolitik, 1923–1960* (Munich, 2005).

[32] The Indian Information Bureau in Berlin, run by Virendranath Chattopadhyaya and A. C. N. Nambiar, among others, facilitated the study of Indian students in Berlin. The organization leaders sent monthly reports to Nehru, and they received funds from the coffers of the Indian National Congress beginning in 1928. See letter from A. C. N. Nambiar to Jawaharlal Nehru, March 20, 1929, NAI Nehru Correspondence, photocopy in the Krüger Nachlass, ZMO.

[33] See Nehru to Chattopadhyaya, April 25, 1929, NAI Nehru Correspondence in the NAI Collection, photocopy in the Krüger Nachlass, ZMO, item 47.

[34] Nambiar to Nehru, August 27, 1929, photocopy of Nehru Correspondence in the NAI Collection, photocopy in the Krüger Nachlass, ZMO, item 179.

[35] See report from April 25, 1923, Zentralarchiv der Staatlichen Museen zu Berlin (henceforth ZSMB), I/NG 603, p. 8. After Berlin, the exhibition traveled to the Leipzig Art Association.

[36] See the list of artwork sent, ZSMB, I/NG 603, pp. 12–16.

[37] Benoy Kumar Sarkar, *Economic Development* (Madras, 1926), p. xiii.

[38] Benoy Kumar Sarkar, "The Aesthetics of Young India," *RUPAM* 9 (January 1922), pp. 8–23; Benoy Kumar Sakar, "Social Philosophy in Aesthetics," *RUPAM* 15–16 (July–December 1923), p. 88.

But non-communist nationalists were not the only ones supporting national education as an anticolonial policy. Jawaharlal Nehru, a close friend of Virendranath Chattopadhyaya, supported a student aid organization, begun in Berlin in March 1929, with funds from the Indian National Congress.[32] Nehru wanted Indian students to go to Germany instead of to Britain for education, thereby producing intellectual elites with less dependency on Britain.[33] The Indian Information Bureau, run by Chattopadhyaya and A. C. N. Nambiar, worked to obtain admission for Indian students to Berlin universities. Berlin had the largest number of Indian students studying on the continent at the time.[34]

The Bengal School in Berlin, 1923

Within this crucible of Indian intellectual, cultural, and political life beyond the British empire, a major exhibition of Bengal School artwork was shipped to Berlin for exhibition at the prestigious Crown Prince Palace of the National Gallery in 1923.[35] Only months after an exhibition of Bauhaus paintings went up in Calcutta, under the direction of Stella Kramrisch at Calcutta University, Benoy Kumar Sarkar organized an exhibition of Bengal School paintings for German audiences. Ludwig Justi, director of the Berlin Museum and the individual who collaborated with Benoy Kumar Sarkar on the 1923 exhibition of modern Indian art, greatly admired Tagore's paintings.

In Berlin, from February to March 1923, 113 pieces of Indian modern art from Shantiniketan and Calcutta greeted audiences at the Crown Prince Palace of the Berlin National Gallery. An inspection of the exhibition list shows an extensive selection of pieces by masters of the Bengal School, including Gaganendranath Tagore, Abanindranath Tagore, Nandalal Bose, S. N. Dey, K. N. Mazumdar, and Sunayani Devi.[36]

Benoy Kumar Sarkar organized the Berlin exhibition. As an itinerant nationalist, he once taught at the Bengal National College in Calcutta but now coordinated activities on behalf of the sizeable Indian diaspora in postwar Berlin through the offices of his Indo-European Trading Company and its journal, *Commercial News.*[37] Over the course of 1922, Sarkar was in close contact with O. C. Ganguly, editor of *RUPAM,* and published a series of articles on "futurism" and Indian modern art in that magazine. *RUPAM* editorials from 1922 and 1923 show that Ganguly frequently rehearsed Sarkar's radical arguments about the need for Indian artists to free themselves from tradition and to harness the power of *visva shakti* (world force).

Like Stella Kramrisch's Bauhaus exhibition in Calcutta, Sarkar's Bengal School exhibition in Berlin was the culmination of an intensive period of interpretation and argumentation about the meaning of Indian modern art. Sarkar published his book *Futurism of Young Asia* in 1922, along with the series of essays in *RUPAM.*[38] He even entered into a long-distance dispute with Stella Kramrisch over the role of tradition in Indian modernism.[39] If Kramrisch praised Indian modernists for remaining rooted in what she saw as an Indic tradition, Sarkar hailed Indian modernists for brazenly abandoning concern for tradition. "A certain intellectual unity organically binds the whole modern world of art," Sarkar insisted.[40] Kramrisch emphasized the comparability of Central European and Indian art in terms of "primitivism" and "tradition. Sarkar also emphasized comparability, but in terms of "futurism."[41] In the pages of *RUPAM,* Stella Kramrisch, located in Calcutta, wrote critical rejoinders to Sarkar's essay on futurism, and Sarkar, situated in Berlin, responded with his own critiques of Kramrisch. The transnational dialogue between the two also involved a curious transposition of physical locations and identities. Not only were they arguing, from discrepant perspectives, about the worldliness of Indian art, they were practicing world revelation through their transnational debate.

[39] Both Kramrisch and a scholar with the pen name of Agastya wrote critical rejoinders to Benoy Sarkar's essay on "futurism." Their essays appear in the April, July, and October issues of *RUPAM* in 1922. Sarkar responds in his 1923 essay, "Social Philosophy in Aesthetics," ibid.

[40] Benoy Kumar Sarkar, *Ausstellung Moderner Indischer Aquarelle in der Nationalgalerie* (Berlin, 1923). A copy of this exhibition catalogue is available under call number V-Ind wd 8 at the Ibero-American Institute of the Preußischer Kulturbesitz, Berlin.

[41] See note 39.

[42] Peggy Levitt, *The Transnational Villagers* (Berkeley, 2001), p. 50.

[43] Nadje Al-Ali and Khalid Koser, eds., *New Approaches to Migration? Transnational Communities and the Transformation of Home* (London, 2002); Eva Østergaard-Nielsen, ed., *Transnational Politics: Turks and Kurds in Germany* (London, 2003).

Diasporic Concentrations of Art and Politics

Diaspora is not only a social condition; it is also an intellectual and political one. In recent years, sociologists and anthropologists, in particular, have turned attention to the experiences of diasporic communities, exploring how the group identities of migrants are constructed.[42] In this context, new insight has been gained on how diaspora influences radicalism and nationalist politics, and how the distortions of social dislocation give birth to new, novel forms of cultural production.[43]

There were competing forces at work on Indian travelers in Berlin: the push provided by their own aspirations to escape the imperial axis, but also the pressures of German racism and Orientalism that they encountered in diaspora. But then, of course, there was the pull of their fascination with German technical and scientific learning—especially chemistry, engineering, and physics—and the lure of German cultural and artistic circles. These interfering forces were reflected in the tense and entangled social relations that characterized Indian diasporic life from within, as well as between Indians and the surrounding German social world.

Many scholars have argued that global perspectives and national commitment are not opposed but rather inform each other. It follows that national identity is not only about location in a homeland. While closeness cannot be defined in terms of geographic proximity, it is also true that the study of transnational social interactions and relationships across physical geographies gives us a clearer understanding of how ideas circulate and converge, and how proximate relations emerge among diverse and distant sociopolitical groups. Not just the relations between Indian nationalists at home and abroad, but also the relations between traveling Indians and German-speakers are at issue here. Concentration on intellectual and cultural global horizons goes along with dynamics and their dispersion on the social and geographic planes. The study of the expansion of diasporas over geographic space also allows us to study the concentration and intensification of connections and relays in terms of intellectual, cultural, and artistic life across discontinuous geographies.

Swati Chattopadhyay

Spaces of Conversation: The Avant-Garde in Nineteen-Twenties Calcutta

A 1922 article on Abanindranath Tagore, published in *The Modern Review,* introduced the artist-writer by way of his residence in the northern part of the city: "If you drop into his stately residence on a morning you will find him at work in a spacious verandah, overlooking a small garden, beautifully green and resonant with the song of birds . . . Friends and visitors call frequently while he is at work. He does not seem inconvenienced; on the contrary, he carries on a slow conversation with his eyes fixed on the picture and his fingers moving briskly."[1]

The Modern Review, edited by Ramananda Chatterjee, was the premier English-language monthly magazine published from Calcutta in the first decades of the twentieth century. Reared in the nationalist milieu of post-1905 Bengal, it championed the cause of Indian art by publishing color prints of work by contemporary artists. While some critics decried "these cheap reproductions," Tagore attributed the popularization of Indian art to Chatterjee's pioneering endeavor: "we tried it through the Art Society. It didn't work. Ramanandababu's single-minded dedication to this task and the money he poured into it created the public demand for Indian art."[2]

The perspective on art and politics offered by *The Modern Review* was chosen carefully. The article on Abanindranath reads like an invitation to the artist's open studio to see the master at work and savor the idyllic setting, and it foregrounds the uniqueness of the venue in which a new art

[1] Suresh Chandra Banerji, "Abanindranath Tagore: The Man and His Art," *The Modern Review* (May 1922), p. 583.

[2] Abanindranath Tagore, "Bharatiya Chitrakalar Prachare Ramananda," in *Abanindra Rachanabali,* vol. 1 (Calcutta, 1985), p. 390. The Art Society is a reference to the Indian Society of Oriental Art.

[3] Rathindranath Tagore, "Cousin Gaganendra," in *Gagenendranath Tagore* (1938; repr., Calcutta, 1971); Sumitendranath Tagore, *Thakur Barir Jana Ajana* (Calcutta, 1999), pp. 31 and 37.

[4] Tagore 1999 (see note 3), p. 37.

[5] Ibid., p. 123.

practice and discourse was being shaped. Avant-garde art in Bengal in the first two decades of the twentieth century was a quintessentially urban phenomenon, notwithstanding its exploratory gesture toward the countryside, and was made possible by urban spatial practices that built upon a particular lineage of face-to-face conversation.

The south verandah that Abanindranath shared with his two brothers Gaganendranath and Samarendranath Tagore has become something of a legend in Tagore hagiography: it has been described as the birthplace of the Bengal School.[3] There was a separate dedicated studio and library for the three brothers, adjoining the verandah, but they seemed to have spent a significant part of their daily lives drawing, writing, reading, and conversing in this verandah. From their easy chairs they could glimpse the large mango tree that shaded the inner compartments of the house, and the movement of people in the narrow lane beyond the coconut trees in the garden. The venetian blinds in-between the columns of the verandah and the wrought-iron railing cast crisp shadows on the red floor. A wood partition to the right of Abanindranath's seat shielded the access to the inner compartments from the eyes of the continuous stream of visitors.[4] Tea and refreshments were served in the verandah, and Abanindranath's students often sat on the floor close-by working on their paintings.

We have evocative descriptions of the library, verandah, and garden as a series of spaces unfolding to the public. These recollections emphasize the conviviality of the spaces, connecting them with different networks of sociality that stretched from the immediate familial to the larger urban context. It is evident from Abanindranath's own memoirs that he painted in many different kinds of spaces during his life. When learning European techniques in his youth, he insisted on a studio that received north light. At other times he had worked in the lower-floor verandah; sometimes he sat in a corner of the billiard room painting, while a game was in progress. When he joined the Government School of Art as vice-principal, he occupied a studio that had a sign on the door, restricting access, while later in Shantiniketan he chose the small east-facing corner room in Udayan.[5] The prominence of the second-floor verandah in these recollections thus alerts us to the idealism of open discourse that it exuded, as well as to the limitations of such a space, given the expansion of the social parameters that framed artistic and literary conversations in the city in the nineteen-twenties.

The mansion on 5 Dwarakanath Tagore Lane, which Abanindranath and his brothers called home, was part of a larger property that belonged to the Tagores in the locality of Jorasanko, Calcutta. When the article in *The Modern Review* was published, the house was already a hundred years old, and such spacious verandahs were increasingly becoming obsolete, along with the neoclassicism that the Tagore family residence shared with other colonial mansions of the nineteenth-century city.[6] The Tagore house itself had undergone significant changes in its physical form with corresponding changes in social norms over the nineteenth century, but it retained distinct marks of nineteenth-century elite social arrangement.

The house began its life in 1823 as the *baithak-khana* (salon; literally, meeting-house) of Dwarakanath Tagore, Abanindranath's great-grandfather, a wealthy landlord and entrepreneur. The building was located at a respectable distance from the older main house, now 6 Dwarakanath Tagore Lane. It accommodated Dwarakanath's social gatherings—meetings, soirees, balls, dinners, when he took up Westernized eating and social habits that contravened his family's religious practices and his wife Digambari Debi's wishes.

The two houses differed significantly in design. The older house, begun in 1784, had a spacious outer courtyard for public festivities, and private compartments around inner courtyards.[7] Dwarakanath employed a European architect to design the *baithak-khana bari* on the model of early nineteenth-century colonial houses in Calcutta, with the explicit desire to court European society. Approached through a carriage port on the north, the house was organized around large central halls on each floor, and spacious southern verandahs that stretched across the length of the house to catch the southern breeze. The large room to the east of the hall on the lower floor was designated as a billiard room, while its counterpart on the upper floor was the library. What distinguished this house from the ordinary colonial

[6] Art Deco in the nineteen-twenties and thirties would usurp nineteenth-century neoclassicism as architectural fashion. See Swati Chattopadhyay, "Metro-pattern: Art Deco Residences and Modern Visuality in Calcutta," in *New Cultural Histories of India: Materiality and Practices*, ed. Partha Chatterjee, Tapati Guha-Thakurta, and Bodhisvatta Kar (Delhi, 2013), pp. 373–408.

[7] The initial house was built by Nilmani Tagore, Dwarakanath's grandfather.

[8] Tagore, "Apankatha," in Tagore 1985 (see note 2), p. 30. *Chandimandap* is a roofed gathering space, typically attached to wealthy houses and temples in rural Bengal. A *baradari* is an open-sided pavilion.

[9] Dwarakanath's youngest son, Nagendranath, died at the age of twenty-nine, without children, and his wife Tripurasundari was given property elsewhere in Calcutta.

[10] Tagore, "Jorasankor Dhare," in Tagore 1985 (see note 2), pp. 231–37. The verandah housed some of his father's bird collection and held a large water bath with colorful fish. On special occasions the verandah would be used for dining.

[11] Gaganendranath attended St. Xavier's College, but Abanindranath dropped out of school early and was homeschooled.

[12] Purnima Debi, *Thakurbarir Gaganthakur* (Calcutta, 1999); Tagore 1999 (see note 3); Mohonlal Gangopadhyay, *Dakkhiner Baranda* (1981; repr., Calcutta, 1990).

[13] The venue of the Khamkheyali Sabha, for example, rotated between the houses of the club's members, which included those outside the Tagore family. Rehearsals for plays and musical performances often took place in the second-floor hall in number 5, or in the Birjitalao residence of Satyendranath Tagore and Gnadanandini Debi.

[14] Tagore 1999 (see note 3), p. 53.

[15] Ibid., p. 49.

house of the era was the pavilion-like banquet "hall" on the third floor. It defied nomenclature: not quite the indigenous rural Bengali *chandimandap,* not quite a dining hall, not quite a princely *baroduari/baradari.*[8]

After Dwarakanath's death in 1846, his eldest son, Debendranath (Rabindranath's father), inherited the main house, while the middle son, Girindranath (Abanindranath's grandfather) received the *baithak-khana bari.*[9] The latter had to be significantly reconfigured with the addition of courtyards and rooms to accommodate the needs and privacy of nineteenth-century Bengal domestic arrangement.

Abanindranath described the second-floor verandah as the family's *am-darbar* (open court), where his father, Gunendranath, held his morning meetings and carried on conversations with friends and visitors.[10] As Abanindranath's and Gaganendranath's reputation as artists grew in the first two decades of the twentieth century, the verandah acquired exceptional significance as a social space. The house was the three brothers' primary locale for intellectual and artistic pursuits, only intermittently complemented by attendance at schools/colleges, and service to public institutions of art in the city, namely, the Indian Society of Oriental Art and the Government School of Art.[11] Their domestic attachment may be attributed to the lifestyle changes that occurred in the house after the untimely death of their father. Their mother, Saudamini Debi, widowed in her twenties, took charge of the household and came to see it as a protection against the social dangers and dissipative amusements of the nineteenth-century city.

The memoirs of family members, who recalled the house abuzz with relatives and guests in the early twentieth century, convey the impression that the brothers compensated their domestic orientation with a desire to connect to the outside world through hospitality, publications, and their art collection.[12] The brothers participated in numerous plays and musical performances that took place in one of the two Tagore houses, or in public theaters, and formed clubs that provided a venue for literary, musical, and artistic expositions.[13] These included the Dramatic Club, Khamkheyali Sabha, followed by the Bichitra Club. The latter's proceedings were held in the red brick building adjoining the older house, built by their uncle Rabindranath and named Bichitra. The central halls in these houses served as rehearsal and performance space for experimenting with new plays, and the brothers eagerly supported the art exhibitions at Bichitra. They set up a lithographic press in the lower floor of their house, from which Gaganendranath's caricatures were published between 1915 and 1921.[14]

They expanded their art collection with Rajput and Mughal miniatures and ensured that they received the latest publication or newest edition from the city's booksellers.[15] When the *swadeshi* spirit swept through Bengal and the Tagore household in the wake of the 1905 Partition of Bengal, the brothers abandoned the plush Victorian furnishing of the library and turned it into a studio styled in an Eastern minimalist aesthetic. The carpenter, Dhanashkodi Achari, built a new set of low-height chairs, divans, suited to Indian practices of reading and sleeping, following Gaganendranath's and Abanindranath's designs that blended Indian and Japanese aesthetic conventions.[16] The lower part of the walls of the studio was covered with mats stretched between teak panels. A wooden, twelve-foot-square platform, raised six inches from the floor and fitted with a mattress and cushions, served as a lounging space. A Japanese carpenter, Kasahara, inserted a large circular window in the eastern wall.

Only the studio was given this makeover by being turned into a laboratory for aesthetic experiments. It remained the exceptional space within this sprawling mansion; even the public south verandah remained unchanged architecturally.[17] However, the studio followed the daily rhythms of the household, including the siesta, and much of the new furnishing was devised to facilitate this late-afternoon rest. Sumitendranath Tagore, Abanindranath's grandson, has characterized it as a "siesta gathering" (*dibanidrar ashor*) to convey the relaxed conviviality that the new furniture design was meant to support, recalling the domestic sociality of a bygone era when time was savored, and even the siesta was not an individual activity—it was undertaken in a spirit of togetherness, sprinkled with conversation. It implied a familiarity among peers that verged on the familial, and one that could not be easily accommodated with modern business and livelihood. At the same time, the design itself was intentionally "novel," proposing an aesthetic that deviated from traditional Western taste and was distinct from the ordinary interiors of Indian households. Its originality resided in re-searching cultural origins of habit, art, and taste. In fashioning a "national" cultural identity, it drew its cultural vectors to ancient historic sites and to far-off places. The aesthetic developed here would be applied later to other interiors of the Tagore houses in Jorasanko—in Bichitra, at number 6, and

[16] Tagore, "Jorasankor Dhare," in Tagore 1985 (see note 2), p. 314.

[17] It is important to note that Bichitra, too, followed the pattern of colonial houses. It was not until the experiments in building design of Shantiniketan were begun in the twenties that a new architectural vocabulary would emerge from this milieu of artistic thought.

[18] We find the impact of such spatial conception in the organization of art class in Kala Bhavan, Shantiniketan, where students sat on the floor on mats and worked on low desks.

[19] For example, Abanindranath used the term to refer to his father's coachman, Samsher's *majlish*. Tagore, "Apankatha," in Tagore 1985 (see note 2), p. 21.

[20] See Dipesh Chakarabarty, *Provincializing Europe: Postcolonial Thought and the Colonial World* (Princeton, 2000), Chapter 7; Swati Chattopadhyay, *Representing Calcutta: Modernity, Nationalism, and the Colonial Uncanny* (London, 2006), Chapter 5.

in Shantiniketan. This aesthetic innovation was also an effort to produce a space distinct from the studio conventions of colonial institutions.[18] In so doing, it self-consciously drew upon a range of conversational practices prevalent in the Bengali community at the turn of the century.

Subtle distinctions between different modes of gathering and conversation—*sabha, baithak, ashor, majlish, adda*—were made in the process of middle- and upper-class Bengalis crafting a modern self in the nineteenth century. This was part of the tremendous increase in the number of voluntary associations, and of the expansion of print media and accompanying cultural sphere in the city, which included theater, music, and art. While *sabha* (meeting in a conventional sense) denoted a formal gathering with an agenda, typically of a serious nature, and *ashor* and *adda* carried the connotation of pleasure, and often informality, *baithak* could stand for any meeting that took place in the outer male domain of the house in the *baithak-khana*. *Ashor* assumed someone convening a group around storytelling or music and was the most gender- and space-neutral term, while *majlish* had male, princely connotations of a soiree in a well-dressed setting; even when applied to non-elite gatherings, it presupposed discriminating taste.[19] *Adda,* casual conversation with peers, though typically viewed as a male pursuit, had more flexibility of meaning than *majlish, baithak,* or *sabha. Adda* (often designated *baithaki-adda* or *majlishi adda*) came to be defined by its non-fixity of topic and even of space, suggesting that it cohered around a core group of attendees. *Adda* in the late nineteenth century would typically take place in the *baithak-khana* and was necessarily shaped around the host's interests and resources.[20]

A wide range of intellectual and social activities could be accommodated within the range of *sabha* and *adda,* but a key motivation was to locate a space freed from the regime of salaried labor, one in which cultural aspirations (in the widest sense) could be nurtured. In a colonial context that denied political rights and space to the colonized, Indian (nationalist) political aspirations were nurtured in the sphere of the cultural. As spaces of conversation, *adda/baithak* filled a political vacuum in the city's public sphere and had an ambivalent, if not contradictory, relation with capitalism and the colonial state. This is what made them modern and deeply political.

The theme of relaxed time runs through the descriptions of these venues: "stealing" time to do what one desired as opposed to what one needed for a livelihood. *Ashor* and *adda* were arguments for *abasar*—respite from work—dedicated to creative pursuits and were implicitly or explicitly about denying the time demands placed on individuals and families and the faster pace of life enforced by capitalism. And in many instances, this meant a "clearing," as in the refined simplicity of the Tagore studio. In 1901, Rabindranath expressed this as a yearning for open space (*phanka;* literally, emptiness): "this is not just openness to the sky, breeze, and light—a clearing in life itself—food, clothing, socializing, all uncomplicated, restrained, clean; a calm effortless moderation all around—not a drawing room, not a dining room, not courtliness—*taktaposh* (low platform-bed) and mattress on the floor."[21] A set of themes on body posture, creativity, and spatial imagination flows from these connections made between furnishing, thought processes, sociality, room and spatial configuration—themes that were pervasive in discussions and representations of *adda.*

While there are some extant photographs of the verandah and studio of the Tagore house, the most remarkable is a woodcut print made from a drawing by Nandalal Bose. The drawing produced around the nineteen-twenties is a recollection of the studio space when Nandalal and the critic Ananda Coomaraswamy were regular visitors to the Tagore house. Abanindranath sleeps in the background, while Samarendranath reads in an easy chair, and Gaganendranath lounges on a bed with a book, smoking a hookah. In the foreground, Coomaraswamy, resting on a couch, leans forward toward Nandalal, pointing out something in the painting in Nandalal's hand. Books and artworks populate the shelves in the background, while the railings of the south verandah and trees are visible through the door on the right. The spatial organization suggests the kind of interiority that defined the studio as a social space. The figures of the three brothers are further removed—interiorized—and seemingly oblivious to the rapt conversation between artist and critic in the foreground. The spatial compression expresses the social intimacy of the interior, while its hierarchy signals a social difference: Nandalal, after all, is sitting on the floor, below the other figures; and he is the only one "at work." The figures of Coomaraswamy and Nandalal are also closer to the world outside, marking their status as

[21] Cited in Arunendu Bandopadhyay, "Santiniketan—sthapatya rup, nirmita- paribesh ebong Rabindranath," *Biswabharati Patrika* (New Series, Bengali *Magh-Chaitra,* 1403 [1997]), p. 101.

[22] Jibendra Sinha Roy, *Kalloler Kal* (1973; repr., Calcutta, 1987), p. 80; Tagore 1999 (see note 3), pp. 69–70. Sumitendranath notes that Surendranath Kar made a sketch of this *adda* at Krantik Press, *"betaler baithak."*

[23] Roy 1973 (see note 22), p. 81.

[24] Ibid., p. 9.

[25] Ibid., p. 5.

[26] Ibid., p. 7.

[27] Ibid., p. 9.

guests, even though they were part of the intimate circle. The proxemics and gestures of the figures are also perhaps a commentary on the roles that the hosts, artist, and critic took up in the production of artistic discourse during a period of critical change in Indian art and society.

By the nineteen-twenties, the loci of Bengali speech culture, at least its literary-artistic core, had moved from the confines of the *baithak-khana* to presses, clubs, cafés, and other public spaces. Increasingly, avant-garde literary magazines and their pronounced modern outlook were shifting focus to a younger set of intellectuals, and the venues of conversation were becoming more public and politicized, outside the well-groomed interiors of elite households.

The *addas* formed around printing presses and literary magazines, such as *Bharati, Sabuj Patra, Kallol,* and *Kali Kalam,* were among the most notable intellectual venues in the first two decades. Jibendra Sinha Roy has suggested that as long as *Bharati*'s editorial control remained within the Tagore household, its focus remained narrow, and its gatherings did not acquire the full merits of *adda,* which flourished under Manilal Gangopadhyay's (Abanindranath's son-in-law) aegis (1915–24) in the third-floor room of Krantik Press in Sukia Street.[22] It was, however, an *adda* of select established writers, as was Pramatha Chowdhury's *Sabuj Patra adda.* Chowdhury held center stage in this highbrow gathering in his drawing room, comfortably fitted with couches and sofas, and wall-to-wall bookcases.[23]

In contrast, the origins of Four Arts Club, the precursor of *Kallol,* in a florist shop in New Market provides a better sense of the widening social space of the literary *adda.*[24] The first meeting of the Four Arts Club was an open-air, moonlit event in the Zoological Garden in 1921. Later, club members Sukumar Dasgupta and his wife Nirupama Debi offered the outer room of their house for the club's meetings for a nominal rent. When the gatherings became larger, they met outdoors.[25] The club welcomed novice writers and artists, both men and women, nurtured radical minds, and hosted Gokulchandra's artist friends, Atul Bose, Dhirendranath Gangopadhyay, Jamini Roy, and Debiprasad Roy Chowdhury.[26] The modest club room was dressed with care: a low table in the center with an *alpona* and a vase of tuberoses, an oil lamp, and incense sticks set the atmosphere, while the members sat on the floor on mattresses placed against the walls.[27] The mixed-company gatherings, however, were not well countenanced by contemporaries, and when the club broke up after two years, the literary ambitions of its members resulted in Kallol and its humble abode in 1923. *Kallol* challenged Bengali literary conventions and content, claiming to address real-world conditions of the post-WWI era, as well as the dreams, dissatisfaction, and conflict of youth. What is often overlooked is that *Kallol* also challenged the spatial parameters of the literary *adda.* Unlike the *adda* in the Tagore household or *Sabuj Patra,* or the Monday Club (1915) hosted by Sukumar Ray, no established writer or wealthy patron served as host in *Kallol*'s *adda.* It was held in *Kallol*'s "fist-sized" office on the lower floor of Dineshranjan's brother's small, two-storied house on Patuatola Lane.[28] Situated in an obscure location, the room in Patuatola Lane was architecturally undistinguished: "On one side was a low seat covered with a thin rug, on the other side a half-secretariat table, a few chairs, and a cupboard. And there was a camp-chair. A shabby curtain marked the entry to the private area of the house."[29] What distinguished *Kallol*'s *adda* was its youth—attendees were overwhelmingly young, mostly college students who came to imbibe radical views. Not all among them had literary ambitions; some of them merely desired to partake in the conversation. Often the gathering spilled from the room onto the verandah and the street, and cigarettes were shared over tea in the nearby café: "there was no assurance of comfort." None of these appeared to be impediments to its adherents who spent "the best days of their youth in that tiny room," forging new social and intellectual horizons.[30] *Kallol* "democratized" conversation about literature and art, but its much-debated social realism and claim as the avant-garde owed something to its space on the edge of the street.

[28] Ibid., p. 82. For about a year in 1924, the office was moved to Cornwallis Street.
[29] Ibid., p. 35.
[30] Ibid.

Captions

1 The south verandah, Jorasanko house, n.d., photograph
2 Interior of Rabindranath Tagore's room, 6 Dwarakanath Tagore Lane, n.d., photograph
3 Studio at 5 Dwarakanath Tagore Lane by Nandalal Bose

1

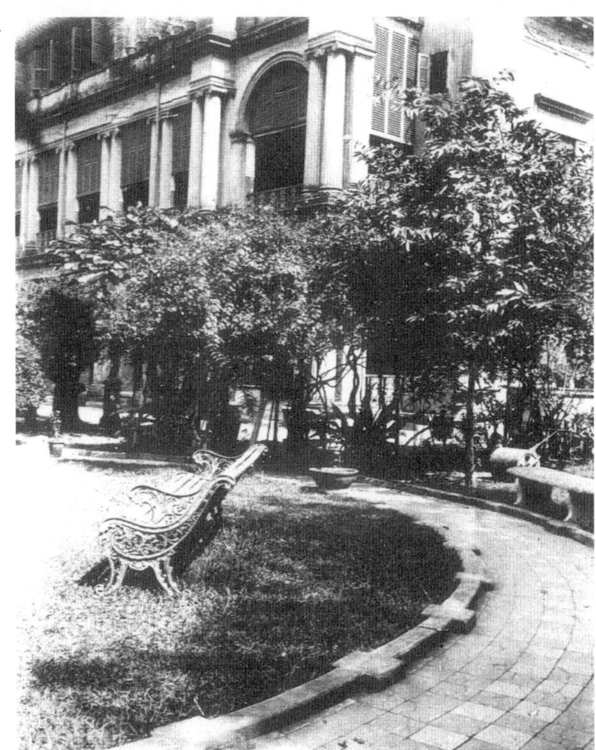

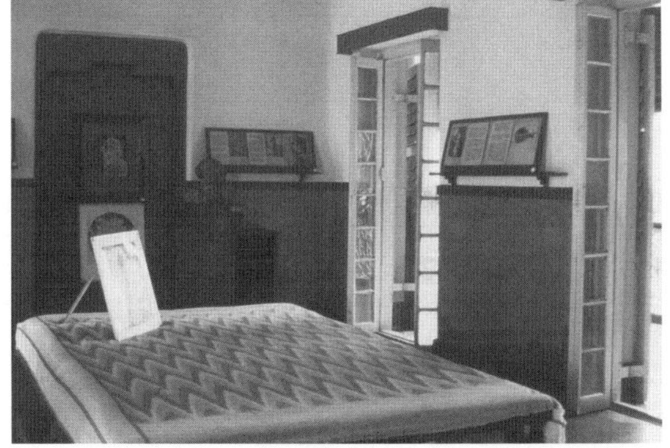

2

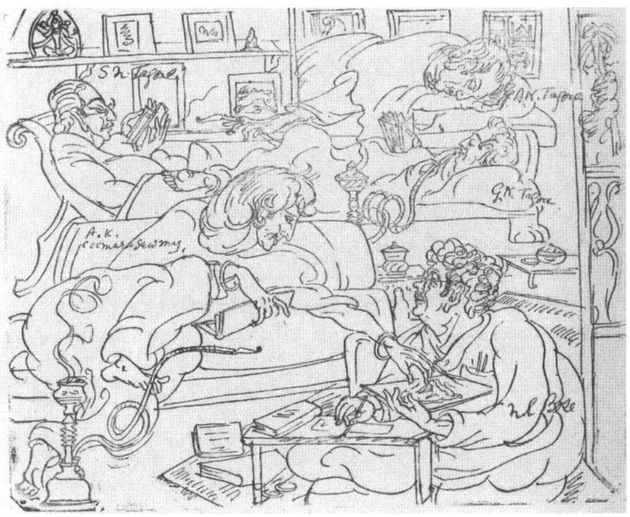

3

Rabindranath Tagore and William Rothenstein

Excerpts from the Correspondence between Rabindranath Tagore and William Rothenstein

TAGORE TO ROTHENSTEIN

Autour du Monde, 9 Quai du 4-Septembre | Boulogne-sur-Seine, April 17, 1921[1]

Dear friend, my short career in the sky was unobscured by clouds and luminous with the April sunshine. The only thing to which I could take objection was the deafening noise which followed me from shore to shore and made me glad to be back to the earth again where one has the choice of diluting all noise with silence as much as it is available.
Let me remind you of our conversation about the International University. It was decided that a committee should be formed in England which would help the committee in India about the selection of teachers and students belonging to Europe and about other matters which would be more convenient for them to deal with. I hope it will be possible for you with the help of Mr Montagu Lord Carmichael and other sympathisers to make a draft of rules and a list of names of those who will be likely to join us.[2] I have reasons to hope that some oriental society in this country can be persuaded to represent us in France and work in our behalf.[3] A considerable number of books have been gathered and sent to our library from here and I feel certain that I can count upon the sympathy and co-operation of some influential persons in this country.[4]
I am afraid I shall have to be extremely busy the few days that I spend in Paris, in fact, all through my tour in the Continent. But I shall be able to bear the strain knowing that my appeal will find response in all countries of Europe. You will be glad to learn that the French translation of my Home and the World has, as I am told, gone through six editions within a very short time.[5]

Affectionately yours
Rabindranath Tagore

ROTHENSTEIN TO TAGORE

Royal College of Art, April 23, 1921

My very dear friend—I was glad to hear news of your arrival & of your journey through the sky. Of this I was a little envious—were this form of transit open to me I would often visit the City of Light.[6]
I went to dine with Lord Carmichael last night, to talk over your great scheme. He fully realizes the importance of it & believes important things will come of it. He feels, as you know, as strongly as I do that a committee of trustees should first be formed. This committee will primarily rid you of much personal responsibility & will give responsible backing to your project. Until you have something of the kind it will be difficult for you to get the people you want,

true scholars, to go out to India, & as things are now, there is the danger of people whom you don't want streaming in. Of all things you have to guard against anything like Adyar.[7]
The young Austrian-Slovakian lady came to see me yesterday to ask if I could help her to get a passport for India. But Lord Carmichael tells me that, however willing Mr Montagu may be, & other people in the India Office, to help you, the Foreign Office, at this particular time, is most unlikely to issue passports to any foreigners, save those having clear reasons for going to India & the backing of their embassies so far as their appropriateness is concerned. When things have settled down in India, there will not be the same difficulty; in this particular case I believe you owe me a cock. For I have saved you from the results of an invitation which the recipient, had she been quite worthy of it, would not have [been] quite so ready to accept. One wants more than a single meeting, on either side, in such important affairs. Perhaps I am unduly suspicious of the softer sex. But when great things have to be carried through, I doubt whether it is wise to encumber yourself with almond eyed ladies, however devoted to stupas & Boddhisatras.[8]
I think you should return, after your European tour, & see Sadler.
Carmichael tells me all sorts of people are coming over regarding Calcutta University & that, if you could put your scheme clearly before people here, such as Sadler, it is precisely the moment for doing so.[9]
I could wish the difficulties less apparent & above all, the presence by your side of someone who would take them on his own shoulders, leaving it to you to inspire men with the strength of your own convictions—some one used to administrative problems, whose vision & judgement would commend themselves to men of affairs.
Until you have found this rare but still obtainable bird, I would venture to counsel caution, so far as actual promises & invitations are concerned. You don't want to entangle yourself. It will take time before a scheme is formulated, buildings equipped, & you are ready to receive scholars. All sorts of questions will have to be threshed out before you can get your ship under weigh [*sic*] & there would be confusion if an attempt were made to start before charts & compasses were provided.
None of your friends wish to see you snowed under by a thousand details best left to less capable minds but more practical heads than yours. To impress caution on others is never an heroic role: but I must play it, seeing that the great parts are more easily filled.
I send you my warmest greetings: it was a great delight to have you back among us for a short time. I could wish you here again, with leisure to talk quietly over many things; but for the minutes we snatched from the many "people of importance" who claimed your time I am grateful. There are few men with whom talk is more peaceful & inspiring than with yourself & we have, you & I, much, I think, in our view of life, in common.

Ever yours affectionately
W. R.

TAGORE TO ROTHENSTEIN

Société Autour du Monde, 9 quai du 4-septembre | Boulogne-sur-Seine, April 24, 1921

My dear friend, when I sent my appeal to Western people for an International Institution in India I made use of the word "University" for the sake of convenience. But that word not merely has an inner meaning but outer associations in minds of those who use it, and that fact tortures my idea into its own rigid shape. It is unfortunate. I should not allow my idea to be pinned to a word like a dead butterfly for a foreign museum. It must be known not by a definition, but by its own life growth. I saved my Santiniketan from being trampled into smoothness by the steam roller of your Education department. It is poor in resources and equipment but it has a wealth of truth that no money can ever buy. I am proud of the fact that it is not a machine-made article perfectly modeled in your workshop—it is our very own. If we must have a university it should spring from our life and be sustained by it. You may say that such freedom is dangerous and that a machine will help to lessen our personal responsibility and make things easy for us. Yes, life has its risks and freedom its responsibility—and yet they are preferable for their own immense value and not for any other ulterior results. Now I am beginning to discover that it was more an ambition than an ideal which dragged me to the gate of the rich West. It must have been the vision of a big undertaking that lured me away from my seclusion in search of big means and big results. And I am being punished deep in my heart. So long I have been able to retain my perfect independence and self respect because I had faith in my own resources and proudly worked within their sovereign limits. This is the

[1] On April 19 and 21, Tagore and Rathindranath called on Romain Rolland, who noted that Rabindranath, despite his charming manner, seemed convinced of the moral and intellectual superiority of the East, and of India in particular, over Europe (see Romain Rolland, *Inde: Journal, 1915–1943*, rev. ed. [Paris, 1960], p. 20). For Tagore's itinerary, October 1920 to April 1921, see Stephen N. Hay, "Rabindranath Tagore in America," *American Quarterly* 14, no. 3 (Fall 1962), pp. 452–56, and Sujit Mukherjee, *Passage to America: The Reception of Rabindranath Tagore in the United States, 1912–1941* (Calcutta, 1964), pp. 85–92 and 214–15.

[2] Edwin Samuel Montagu (1879–1924) was still Secretary of State for India (1917–22). Thomas Gibson-Carmichael, 1st Baron of Skirling (1859–1926), was Governor of Madras, (1911–12) and Governor of Bengal (1912–17). Rothenstein hoped to recruit Herbert Fisher and Michael Sadler as well, altogether a group impressively influential, well-disposed, and well-informed. Tagore had asked James Woods to help start a similar committee in the United Sates (Tagore to Woods, December 14, 1920. David G. Williams.). Neither committee materialized.

[3] Perhaps the Société des Amis d'Oriente, Paris.

[4] The London Macmillans had already given the Santiniketan library a large collection of books (Tagore to Macmillan, April 8, 1921. MP:BM).

[5] Rabindranath Tagore, *La maison et le monde*, trans. F. Roger-Cornaz (Paris, 1921). Originally published as *The Home and the World* (New York, 1916).

[6] At this stage, principally a matter of nerves, but perhaps related to the heart condition diagnosed in 1925.

[7] Theosophical Society ashram and headquarters near Madras.

[8] The lady was Dr. Stella Kramrisch (1898–1993), Professor of Indian Art, Calcutta University (1923–50); Lecturer, Courtauld Institute, London (1937–40); as of 1950 Professor to Emeritus Professor of South Asian Art, University of Pennsylvania; as of 1954 Curator of Indian Art, Philadelphia Museum of Art; editor, *Journal of the Indian Society for Oriental Art* (1932–50).

[9] Those coming to London on behalf of Calcutta University went virtually unrecognized in parliamentary debate. Two years later Herbert Fisher asked what was being done to implement the findings of Michael Sadler's Calcutta University Commission, and the Under Secretary of State of India replied in flawless bureaucratese: "Owing to financial and other difficulties it has not so far been possible to give effect to the proposals of the Commission in regard to the University of Calcutta, but the complex problems involved are receiving most careful consideration by the Government of Bengal." (*The Parliamentary Debates [Official Record]*, series 5 [C], [April 11, 1923], vol. 162, col. 1228.)

[10] Perhaps James Woods, but Tagore's letters to Woods make no mention of this. "British Agency": Criminal Investigation Department. Neither this nor similar subsequent charges are substantiated by evidence in any correspondence examined by the editor.

first time in my life when I have come to the foreign door asking for help and co-operation. But such help has to be bought with a price that is ruinous, and the bird has to accept its cage if it must be fed with comfort and regularity. However, my bird must still retain its freedom of wings and not be turned into a sumptuous nonentity by any controlling agency outside its own living organism.

I know that the idea of an International University is complex, but I must take it simple in my own way. I shall be content if it attracts round it men who have neither name nor worldly means, but who have the mind and faith, who are to create a great future with their dreams. Very likely I shall never be able to work in harmony with a board of trustees, influential and highly respectable, for I am a vagabond at heart. But the powerful people of the world, the lords of the earth, may make it difficult for me to carry out my work. I know it, and I had experience of it in connection with my Santi Niketan and also in my tour in America. But am I afraid of failure? I am only afraid of being tempted away from truth in pursuit of success.

The temptation assaults me occasionally I admit, but it comes from the outside atmosphere—my own abiding faith is in the light and life and freedom, and my prayer is: "Lead me from the unreal to Truth."

This letter of mine is only to let you know that I free myself from the bondage of help and go back to the great Brotherhood of the Tramp, who seem helpless, but who are recruited by God for his own army.

Ever yours
Rabindranath Tagore

ROTHENSTEIN TO TAGORE

18 Sheffield Terrace | London, April 28, 1921

My dear friend—indeed I am neither a believer in machines nor an Inspector of Schools, nor an enemy of freedom; yet you write as though I were all these things. I think you mistake not myself only, but your own self too. For I believe you to be a poet, an inspirer of noble motives, a friend to all the gallant things that man has made & thought, a lover of the common things of life. I do not believe you to be a man of action & of affairs & I foresee many difficulties in your path if you take that dusty road. Your letter does not change my foreboding. To me you should point the way, but others should organize the road making—people who can deal with labourers & contractors better than you or I can do. I felt, when you were here, that some one must stand first of all between you & the quick sympathy of your heart. You say you do not want the learned & powerful; but likewise you do not want the campfollowers—of the arts & of the artists: these last are not the lowly & simple of heart. No, by no means.
Secondly, the life of man is short, but he can build fabrics which endure. And if you build well now, the foundations you are laying should support walls to outlast all of us now quick & strong. I still believe you need men of capacity & integrity to take certain responsibilities from your poet's shoulders. But you need not choose Europeans. Further, unpleasant & humiliating though it may be, the fact has to be envisaged that you cannot approach European scholars & leave English people unconsulted. If these last are not considered, you are making further difficulties for yourself. That is why I suggested you should return here before actually inviting foreign guests to stay with you in India.
But I realize that it is an ignoble thing to be sober when one's fellow guests are intoxicated; it is an attitude above all others hateful to me. You must admit you have taken full advantage of your jug of wine! My prayers will be for your noble venture. I think I know something of the vision that holds you & of the passionate desire to give rather than to take which possesses great hearts. So my blessing on your pilgrimage. No more sensible words shall come from me to irk your spirit. You shall lay the foundations of your city with your desires; these will make good mortar to hold the bricks & stones together.

Ever yours
W. R.

All send affectionate greetings.

TAGORE TO ROTHENSTEIN

Geneva, May 8, 1921

My dear friend, when I was in America the British Agency thwarted me in my appeal to the people for the proposed University. An American friend, who is struggling against obstacles to raise funds for this object has lately informed me that the British Consul in his town is hindering him.[10] I am not trusted. How can I be certain that this mistrust which has nearly killed my mission by its antagonism will not kill it by its help? But possibly your point is that trying to be independent will not further my cause. That is true. It would be presumptuous for me to imagine that my project can thrive against suspicion lurking in the minds of British authorities. At the same time I feel strongly that it is far better to allow it openly to be strangled by that mistrust than to be fettered by its help. I remember your suggesting to me once in course of conversation that exuberant protestation of friendliness towards me on the part of the Continental people of Europe was easy because they had no responsibility with regard to such demonstrations. You are right. For disinterested relationship is the only pure channel through which sympathy and cooperation can have a clear flow. Possibly these very people would also be wisely suspicious in a similar case where they had their own interest to consider. I have often heard that when the French people tried to be hospitable to our Indian soldiers in the late war the British officers in charge of them were alarmed. It was easier for the French to be human and grateful towards those foreigners who had their own anxieties about these soldiers which were not purely human. Similarly when I, who belong to a subject race under British rule, am too warmly received in America or in the Western countries, the British agency may feel uneasy—for their interest in me and my cause is not purely human and simple. Your contention is that the man who is sober in his mind accepts such facts as facts and deals with them accordingly and that it is a sign of moral drunkenness to be able to think that one can ignore them in pride of his self-sufficiency. But of one thing you may be certain that I have a natural power of resistence in me against intoxication produced by praise, and my mind at the present moment is not in a dazed state of drunkenness. I am not in the least oblivious of the fact that the breath of official suspiciousness can blight in a moment my cherished scheme. But I have already told you in my last letter that I try to follow the teaching of Geeta according to which all idealism should spurn to seek their value in success, but only in truth. So long as my motive is true, my method is honest and the process of my work open to the view of all corners from all countries I shall not be afraid, ashamed of the meagerness of result, poorness of appearance, or afraid of an utter failure at the hands of a ruling power which would hesitate to allow us freedom for giving expression to our higher nature. With love to you all

Ever yours
Rabindranath Tagore*

* The original correspondence was published in Mary M. Lago, ed., *Imperfect Encounter: Letters of William Rothenstein and Rabindranath Tagore, 1911–1941* (Cambridge, MA, 1972). Reprinted with the kind permission of Houghton Library, Harvard University, MS Eng 1148 (1475). Stylistic conventions have been adjusted to conform to the publication at hand.

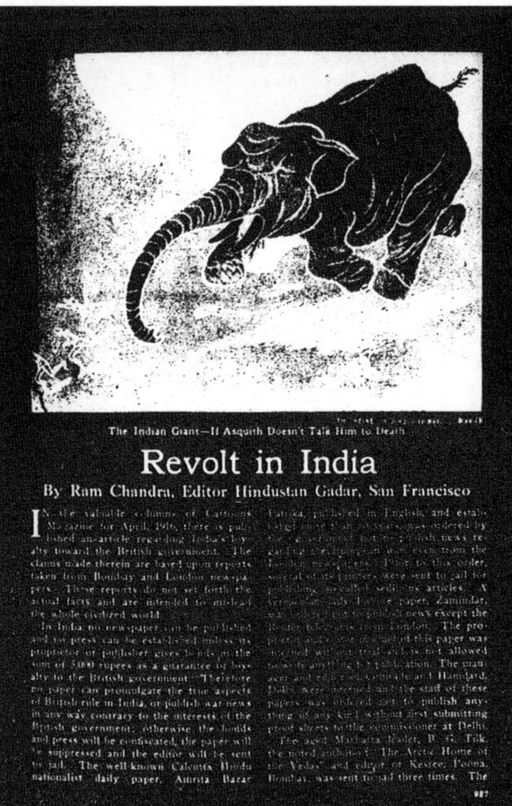

Revolt in India

By Ram Chandra, Editor Hindustan Gadar, San Francisco

Indien unter englischer Herrschaft.

In San Francisco besteht ein Komitee der indischen Revolutionspartei, das von Zeit zu Zeit Flugschriften über die Lage Indiens herausgibt. In einer der letzten heißt es:

„1. Die Engländer erheben in Indien und bringen nach England jährlich 665 Millionen Mark; infolgedessen sind die Eingeborenen so verarmt, daß das durchschnittliche Tageseinkommen eines Indiers 50 ₰ pro Kopf beträgt.

2. Die Grundsteuern belaufen sich auf mehr als 65 Prozent.

3. Für die Erziehung einer Bevölkerung von 200 Millionen gibt die Anglo-Indische Regierung jährlich 100 Millionen Mark aus; für das Gesundheitswesen 24 Millionen Mark; für das Heer jedoch 360 Millionen Mark.

4. Unter der englischen Regierung sind die Hungersnöte im beständigen Zunehmen begriffen, und in den letzten zehn Jahren sind 20 Millionen Menschen an Hunger gestorben.

5. Die Pest hat in den letzten 16 Jahren 8 Millionen Menschen dahingerafft und der Prozentsatz der Todesfälle ist im Laufe der letzten 39 Jahre von 24 auf 34 pro Tausend gestiegen.

6. Mittel aller Art werden angewendet, um Feindschaft und Zwietracht in den Eingeborenenstaaten zu säen, wodurch der englische Einfluß in jenen Staaten gesteigert wird.

7. Die Engländer bleiben straflos, wenn sie eingeborene Indier töten oder wenn sie die Ehre indischer Frauen schänden.

8. Mit dem von den Hindus und Mohammedanern erhobenen Gelde werden die christlichen Missionare subventioniert.

9. Auf alle Arten wird der Streit zwischen den Hindus und den Mohammedanern geschürt.

10. Die Künste, Gewerbe und die einheimische Industrie Indiens werden zugunsten des englischen Handels zerstört.

11. Mit dem Gelde Indiens und mit dem Blutopfer der indischen Soldaten führt und führte England seine Kriege in China, Afghanistan, Burmah, Persien und Aegypten.

12. Seit der letzten großen Revolution in Indien im Jahre 1857 sind 59 Jahre vergangen. Die Bevölkerung Indiens, die in den Eingeborenenstaaten aus 70 Millionen Eingeborenen und in den von den Engländern beherrschten Gebieten aus 240 Millionen Eingeborenen besteht, hat nur eine englische Militärmacht von 79 614 englischen Offizieren und Soldaten und 38 948 Mann eingeborenen Truppen über sich. Wie lange wird es daher dauern, bis sich das indische Riesenvolk zu einer neuen Revolution aufrafft?"

1

2

Captions

1 Ram Chandra, "Revolt in India," report in an American journal, n.d.

2 Author unknown, "Indien unter englischer Herrschaft" (India under English Rule), *Hamburger Echo* (May 1916)

3 Gagonendra Nath Tagore, *Astronomical Scream: First Appearance of a Bengali Governor*

4 Gagonendra Nath Tagore, *Psychical Scream: The Ceremony of Exorcism*

5 Gagonendra Nath Tagore, *Student's Scream: Sold-per-force*

6 Gagonendra Nath Tagore, *Chemical Scream: "Out dammed spot, out I say"*

3–6 In the book Gagonendra Nath Tagore, *Reform Screams: A Pictorial Review at the Close of the Year 1921* (Calcutta, 1921)

খুঁজি খুঁজি নারি, যেপায় তারি।

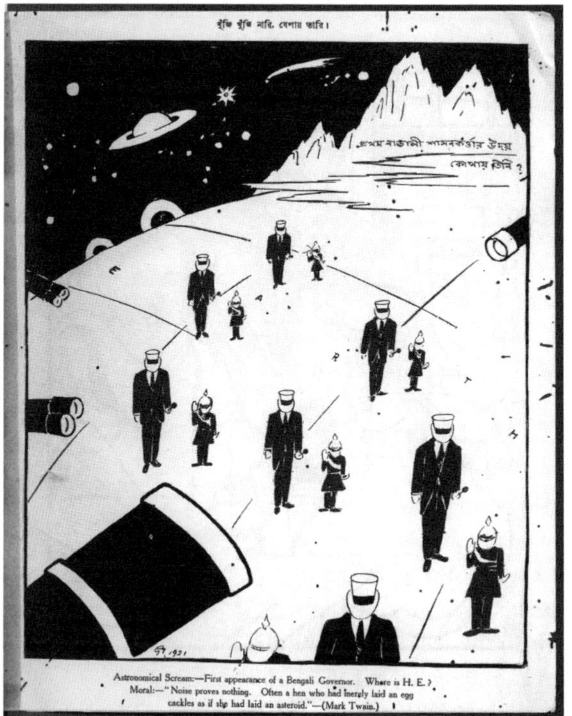

Astronomical Scream:—First appearance of a Bengali Governor. Where is H. E.?
Moral:—"Noise proves nothing. Often a hen who had merely laid an egg cackles as if she had laid an asteroid."—(Mark Twain.)

3

ভুতগত ব্যাপার

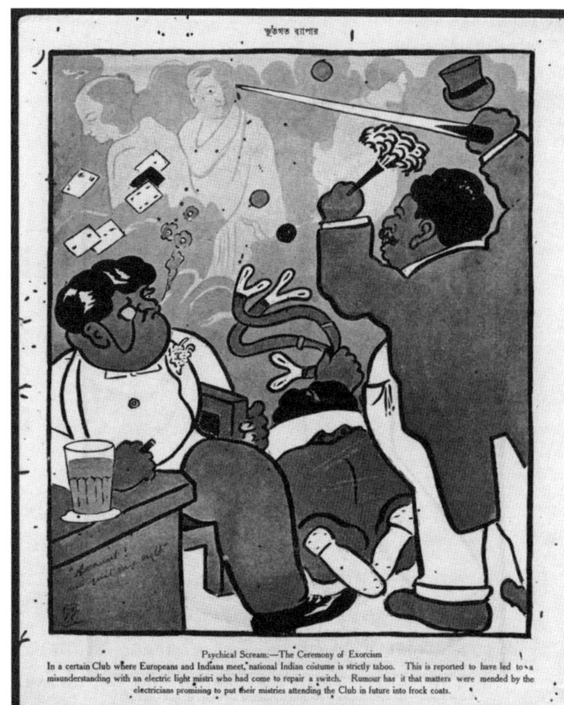

Psychical Scream:—The Ceremony of Exorcism
In a certain Club where Europeans and Indians meet, national Indian costume is strictly taboo. This is reported to have led to a misunderstanding with an electric light mistri who had come to repair a switch. Rumour has it that matters were mended by the electricians promising to put their mistries attending the Club in future into frock coats.

4

প্রজাপতির নির্বন্ধ——ক'নের মা কাঁদে, আর টাকার পুঁটুলি বাঁধে

Student's Scream:—Sold-per-force.
In Bengal the butterfly symbolises marriage. The bridegroom is mourning No. 1, but is not exactly inconsolable, for his mother loses no time in fishing up for him No. 2, together with a dowry. The absorbing character of these repeated transactions stands in the way of Bengal's display of soul force.

5

জাতি গঠনের বাধা——ঘি দিয়ে ভাজো নিমের পাতা,
তবু না যায় তার জাতের যাতা।

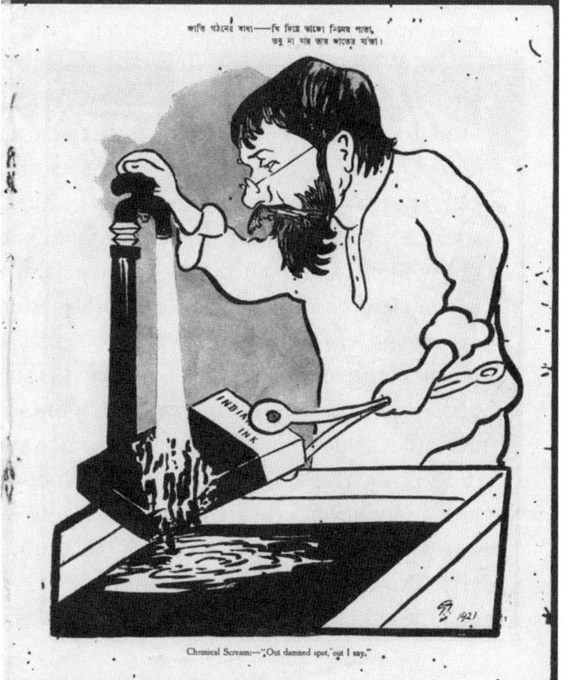

Chemical Scream:—"Out damned spot, out I say."

6

Kobena Mercer

Art History after Globalisation: Formations of the Colonial Modern

The phrasing of the term "colonial modern" is quite promising for it suggests a fresh approach to understanding the interrelationship between modernism and colonialism. In an attempt to tease out what the implications might be for art history, my focus in this contribution is to reflect upon the three cognate terms at the heart of the debate—modernism, modernity and modernisation—in light of what has become known, in the sociology of culture, as the "multiple modernities" thesis. Drawing on examples from the "Annotating Art's Histories" texts which I recently completed as series editor, my aim is to suggest what cross-cultural studies in art history might look like when we carry out archival research "after" globalisation.

While there is the view that globalisation is an intrinsically "new" phenomenon that refers to an increasing sense of worldwide connectedness brought about by new technologies, the alternative perspective of the *longue durée* (literally the "long term") gives us the advantage of a much wider canvas upon which to theorise cross-cultural interactions as a variable in the social production of art. Describing the features of contemporary globalisation which are indeed "new"—transnational corporations, neoliberal economics, the heightened role of information technologies and the culture industries—Stuart Hall nonetheless stresses that it is merely the most recent phase in a long term-process. In his scheme of periodisation, "the fourth phase, then, is the current one, which passes under the title of 'Globalisation' *tout court* (but which, I argue, has to be seen as an epochal phase in a longer historical *durée*)." In the context of discussing "creolisation" as a specific modality of cross-culturality arising out of colonisation and forced migrations, Hall states: "I date globalization from the moment when Western Europe breaks out of its confinement, at the end of the fifteenth century, and the era of exploration and conquest of the non-European world begins."

[1] Stuart Hall, "Creolization, Diaspora and Hybridity in the Context of Globalization," in *Creolité and Creolization* (Documenta XI, Platform 3), ed. Okwui Enwezor et al. (Ostfildern-Ruit, 2003), pp. 193–94.

Adding that, "somewhere around 1492 we begin to see this project as having a global rather than a national or continental character," his account of this first phase of globalisation makes it "coterminous with the onset of the process which Karl Marx identified as the attempt to construct a world market, the result of which was to constitute the rest of the world in a subordinate relationship to Europe and to Western civilization."[1]

To say that globalisation is nothing new, and that it is simply our intellectual understanding of it that has changed in recent years, is to take a critical position with regards to routine orthodoxies in current thinking about cultural difference in the arts. Opting to start with ideas that are deliberately "big" in scale, I want to convey my sense of what is at stake in the paradigm shift which is currently underway in art history, to which the "Annotating Art's Histories" series has contributed some small steps. But the issue of scale also helps put in perspective those obstacles to historical thinking on cross-cultural dynamics which need to be addressed at a metatheoretical level before we can adjust our orientation towards the archive of colonial modernity. Two such obstacles can be characterised in the following terms: inclusionism and presentism.

To the extent that difference is widely addressed today through an ideology of multicultural inclusionism, there is a strong tendency to elevate the horizontal axis, embracing an ever wider capture of identities over and above the vertical axis which would attempt an historical explanation of their mutual entanglement. Across survey exhibitions and anthology textbooks, the pervasive emphasis on the horizontal breadth of coverage tends to de-historicise and flatten out the contradictory relationships among the diverse elements brought together in the name of inclusion. What results is a pluralist illusion of plenitude which assumes each of the parts coexist in a side-by-side relationship with little interaction or dynamism among them. Where the language of multiculturalism is evoked to compensate for past exclusions (as a kind of solution to a legitimation crisis on the part of art world institutions) we not only find the view whereby cultural diversity is seen as a mere "novelty" which belongs to contemporary art alone, but that such presentism also works in insidious ways to preserve earlier canons of modern art whose monocultural authority thus remains intact. The consequences of ahistorical presentism can be seen in a conservative approach to descriptive ekphrasis whereby critics seek to "match" the contemporary theorisation of globalisation with art practices which supposedly embody such concepts. Niru Ratnam's chapter on "Art and Globalisation" in *Themes in Contemporary Art,* 2004—devoted to works shown in Documenta XI in 2002—starts by qualifying the "newness" of globalisation theory by pointing out that it "exhibits continuity with earlier practice and theory exploring the legacy of European colonialism," but then dismisses any relationship to postcolonialism on the basis of Negri and Hardt's view that, because "the post-colonialist perspective remains primarily concerned with colonial sovereignty . . . it may be suitable for analysing history, [but] it is not able to theorise contemporary global structures."[2]

Where theory takes precedence over the concrete actuality of the work of art as an object of study in its own right, we find that art is reduced to a passive illustration of a concept which the theorist has already arrived at, thereby denying it the autonomy of its own aesthetic intelligence. Moreover, traditional historiography remains intact and is unaltered by its encounter with other disciplines. In his edited collection, *Is Art History Global?,* 2007, senior scholar James Elkins assembles an international cast of contributors to debate the epistemological shifts of the past thirty years in which the canonical scholarship of Panofsky, Hauser, Schapiro and others has been displaced by post-structuralism, feminism, visual culture and post-colonial studies. Approaching the debate in such abstract terms, however, we find that no actual works of art are discussed by Elkins at all. Moreover, by merging the topic of globalisation with the category of "world art," the area studies model established in anthropological and archaeological orientations towards non-Western art maintains an essentialist notion of self-contained "cultures" as discretely boundaried totalities. When the non-Western is confined to pre-modern antiquity we face another paradox; namely that modern art, Western or otherwise, has no place within the category of "world art."[3] As I argue in the introduction to the first volume in my series, *Cosmopolitan Modernisms,* 2005, post-colonial theory (which originated in literary scholarship) is itself highly culpable with regards to the tendency towards theoreticism. Having revealed the constitutive rather than reflective role of representation in constructions of colonial reality, the emphasis on the positioning of "self" and "other" has led to an imbalance whereby studies of visual othering in Western art constantly refer back to the imperial ego, as it were, in such a way that overshadows the agency of colonial and diasporic artists as creators and subjects of representations in their own right.

[2] Niru Ratnam, "Art and globalisation," in *Themes in Contemporary Art,* ed. Gill Perry and Paul Wood (New Haven and London, 2004), pp. 293 and 295.

[3] James Elkins, ed., *Is Art History Global?,* vol. 3: *Art Seminar* (New York and London, 2007).

[4] Victor Burgin, "The Absence of Presence: Conceptualism and Postmodernisms," in *The End of Art Theory: Criticism and Postmodernity,* ed. Victor Burgin (London, 1986).

[5] Hal Foster, "The 'Primitive' Unconscious of Modern Art, or White Skins, Black Masks," in *Recodings: Art, Spectacle, Cultural, Politics* (Seattle, 1985); Simon Gikandi, "Picasso, Africa and the Schemata of Difference," *Modernism/modernities* 10, no. 3 (September 2003); James Clifford, *The Predicament of Culture* (Cambridge, MA, and London, 1988).

Standing back for a moment, one might observe that the so-called dominant narrative of modern art has been under attack ever since conceptual art called the optical model of visuality into question, precipitating a crisis for modernism as such.[4] But it is one thing to dismantle an influential way of seeing, quite another to put forward a sustainable alternative. Rather than suggest a fully-fledged model for the study of cross-cultural relations in art, my series drew attention to the gradual and incremental steps needed to both deconstruct the dominance of formalist universalism while exploring methods which similarly refuse the converse tendencies of sociological or contextual reductionism. As a case in point we may consider how the modernism/colonialism relation is mostly addressed within the episteme of art history in the extremely limited purview of primitivism. Considering the amount of ink spilled on the subject of *Picasso's Demoiselles d'Avignon,* 1907, during the 1980s and since—from criticisms of William Rubin's *Primitivism: Affinities of Tribal and Modern,* 1984, to the debates on *Magiciennes de la Terre,* 1989, curated by Jean-Hubert Martin—one might say that the disavowal of primitivism's colonial contexts within the formalist narrative of morphological "borrowings" was held fully intact for the best part of 80 years. The idea of "significant form" proposed in the 1920s by Bloomsbury critics Clive Bell and Roger Fry was only dislodged from epistemological privilege by the psychoanalytic concept of fetishism which informed readings of Picasso by Hall Foster and Simon Gikandi, and by James Clifford's notion of the circulation of tribal artefacts in museum collections and other institutional sites of exchange.[5]

In the 25 years since this breakthrough moment, it is the concept of appropriation, above all, which has played a transformative role in our understanding of subaltern agency and authorship; yet because such concepts have been mostly deployed in relation to contemporary art, it is only in the last ten years or so that its paradigm-shifting potential has been activated in archival and historical research. It strikes me that architecture further contributes to breaking primitivism's interpretative monopoly on our understanding of modernism and colonialism, for *In the Desert of Modernity,* 2008, like my own series, shares a timeline of research which also includes work such as *Modern Architecture and the End of Empire,* 2003, by Mark Crinson.

For my part, starting from the premise that modernity defines a state of being or condition of life in which disparate material elements and social actors are constantly uprooted from their origins and brought into contact by proliferating networks of trade, travel and market exchange, the "Annotating Art's Histories" series set out to demonstrate that, far from being limited to primitivism, cross-cultural dialogue plays a meaningful and ever-present role in the entire story of modernism as a whole. From movements such as Surrealism, through major underlying processes such as abstraction or montage, to the "high" and "low" crossovers of pop which inaugurated the problematic of postmodernism, cultural difference is not aberrant, accidental or "special," but a structural and even normative feature of artistic production und the conditions of modernity which had become global by the late nineteenth century.

Modernism, one might say, has always been multicultural—it is simply our consciousness of it that has changed. Each of the ruptures inaugurated in European modernism c. 1910 made contact with a global system of transnational flows and exchanges—from Malevich's conception of monochrome painting, shaped by his reading of Vedic philosophy and Indian mysticism, to Duchamp's readymades, which mirrored the decontextualised mobility of tribal artefacts. Modernist primitivism may be the generic paradigm in which these (unequal) exchanges are most visible, but a broader understanding of cross-culturality as a consequence of modern globalisation also entails the necessity of questioning the optical model of visuality which determines how cultural differences are rendered legible as "readable" objects of study.

Because current thinking on globalisation breaks the foundational equivalence between modernisation and Westernisation, it interrupts the classical geometry of centre and periphery which was indispensable for earlier approaches in development studies and world-system theory in Marxism. The assumption that becoming modern was at all times identical to the process of becoming Western (and hence giving up one's identity) has been wholly undermined by awareness of the agency of selective appropriation on the part of social actors who were indeed subordinate to the hegemony of the Western centre economically and politically, but who nonetheless exercised choices in what they adapted and what they rejected in the space of the cross-cultural encounter. Whereas previous theories saw imperialist globalisation in the age of empire as a steamroller of dominance, eliminating local, tribal and indigenous differences in total, the agency of adaptation on the part of the colonised made the lived experience of colonialism a contradictory phenomenon on all sides, thereby creating multiple sites of resistance, antagonism and negotiation. This emphasis on the mutual entanglement of contradictory forces is what distinguishes the multiple modernities thesis. With the greater focus given to spatial processes of globalisation in the work of urbanist Anthony King, along with Arjun Appadurai's studies of

[6] See Anthony D. King, ed., *Culture, Globalization and the World-System* (New York, 1991); Arjun Appadurai, *Modernity at Large* (Minneapolis, 1996); Roland Robertson et al., eds., *Global Modernities* (London, 1995); John Tomlinson, *Globalization and Culture* (Chicago, 1999); Jan Nederveen Pieterse, *Globalization and Culture: Global Mélange* (Lanham, MD, 2003).

[7] David Morley, "EurAm, modernity, reason and alterity," in *Stuart Hall: Critical Dialogues in Cultural Studies*, ed. David Morley and Kuan-Hsing Chen (London and New York, 1995), p. 349.

[8] Howard J. Booth and Nigel Rigby, *Modernism and Empire* (Manchester, 2000), p. 28.

localised adaptations of material and symbolic goods in global circulation, and Ulf Hannerz's account of transnational flows, the range of analytical perspectives brought together by Mike Featherstone, Scott Lash and Roland Robertson in *Global Modernities,* 1995, defined a turning point in the sociology of culture which was further developed by John Tomlinson and Jan Nederveen Pieterse.[6] Far from resulting in a pluralist free-for-all in which there are as many modernisms as you like, the attention that the multiple modernities thesis gives to complex dynamics of structure and agency shows that the process of modernisation-as-Westernisation rarely resulted in a fully achieved or "finalised" state of colonial subjectification because it was constantly made ambivalent by the generative agonism of power and resistance.

When told as a narrative which emanates from a unitary "centre," the material processes of modernisation—the application of scientific knowledge to technologies of social infrastructure and wealth creation which act as engines of "progress"—is often conflated with the philosophical condition of modernity. This concerns the lived experience or subjectivity of the atomised individual which is taken to characterise the rationalist self-consciousness associated with secularisation. But by decoupling the equation between modernity and the West, contemporary globalisation theory calls for historical investigation of the *combinatory formations* whereby certain aspects of the objective process of modernisation may be accepted while certain subjective features of modernity are deselected. Although never colonised, imperial Japan accepted modernisation in science and technology but not democracy in politics; Arab nations of the Middle East similarly adopted capitalist infrastructure while retaining religious traditions instead of individualism. Whereas Eurocentric ideology told the story as a linear sequence from the Renaissance and Reformation to the Enlightenment and the Industrial Revolution, the alternative is to conceptually disaggregate the constituent processes, as David Morley explains in the context of cultural studies methodology:

> The association between the Occident and modernity has to be viewed as radically contingent in historical terms. If there is no necessary relation between these terms, then it follows that to oppose either one of them is not necessarily to oppose the other.[7]

Taken up in their literary history of the modernism/colonialism relationship, Booth and Rigby add, "This would mean for instance that modernity could be . . . welcomed in the non-Western world, even as the precise form it takes in the West, or the West's way of promoting or exporting it could be stridently opposed." Hence it is equally important to bear in mind the dis junctions whereby, "rather than thinking of empire as actively involved in the exporting or disseminating of modernism (which . . . might be ideologically or politically suspect in the eyes of imperialists), we could see it as exporting modernity."[8]

Understood as culture's answering response to predicaments and dilemmas thrown up by the lived experience of modernisation, modernism was not only a multi-voiced phenomenon within the West—at times celebrating "progress" in the machine age, at times articulating critique of capitalist alienation—but was further fractured in the "envelope" of colonial modernity where the exported reality of the nation-state constituted a decisive frontier of cultural and political agonism. In the context of anti-colonial struggles in India, Partha Mitter notes that the circulation of modernist ideas following the 1922 exhibition of Bauhaus artists in Calcutta (including Kandinsky and Klee) played a catalytic role for painterly experimentation by Gaganendranath Tagore, Amrita Sher-Gil and Jamimi Roy, who in his view articulated a variant of primitivism which acted as a *counter-discourse of modernity.* Whereas nationalist artists of the 1890s such as Ravi Varma and the Bengal School embraced academic naturalism and inserted indigenous content, the formal break with verisimilitude on the part of Indian modernists combined local and global elements to forge a cosmopolitanism in which the binarist logic of imperialism and nationalism alike was displaced. Because "the very ambiguities of primitivism provided a powerful tool for challenging the values and assumptions of modern industrial civilization, that is the west," Mitter regards its presence in early Indian modernism as a "counter-modern rather than an anti-modern tendency, because it is really the twin sister of modernity, it's [*sic*] alter ego; it's within it and yet continually questioning it."[9] Where indigenous traditions among Bengali intelligentsia created favourable conditions for the reception of modernism, the agency of appropriation produced semiotic transformations of the "primitive." As Mitter adds:

> I think of Mahatma Ghandi, in this sense, as the most profound primitivist critic of western capitalism. He fashioned the philosophy of non-violent resistance, and the self-sufficiency of village life in India, as symbolised by the humble spinning-wheel, out of elements associated with the discourse of primitivism.[10]

Within the same timeline of the 1890s to the 1920s, Ian McLean examines formations of colonial modernism and anti-colonial modernism in

[9] Partha Mitter, "Reflections on Modern Art and National Identity in Colonial India: An Interview," in *Cosmopolitan Modernisms, ed. Kobena Mercer* (Cambridge, MA, and London, 2005), p. 42.

[10] Ibid., p. 42.

[11] Ian McLean, "Aboriginal Modernism in Central Australia," in *Exiles, Diasporas & Strangers,* ed. Kobena Mercer (Cambridge, MA, and London, 2008), p. 92.

[12] Ibid., p. 76.

[13] Stanley Ikem Okoye, "Unmapped Trajectories: Early Sculpture and Architecture of a 'Nigerian' Modernity," and McLean, "Aboriginal Modernism," in Mercer 2008 (see note 11), p. 76.

Aboriginal Australia. Breaking with the standard view that modern art by Aboriginal artists only began with the use of canvas and acrylic paints in the 1970s, McLean argues that an artistic response to Western modernity began at the point of first contact with remote desert communities in the late nineteenth century. Ceremonial dances received European visitors with acts of performative mimicry. Sacred carvings were refashioned for secular purposes in such a way that their "outside designs" sought to educate white foreigners even as they contained "inner secrets" known only to initiates. During the 1930s Albert Namitjira produced watercolour landscapes, but while his technical mastery rendered him "inauthentic" under Eurocentric eyes, McLean reveals how his choices "make a claim for his Aboriginal inheritance, especially for the sacred sites of Arrernte Dreaming."[11] McLean accepts that exported modernisation established a universal condition, but he insists that "far from being a purely western or European construct, modernity is a mode of living that has taken root in many traditions, including ones often considered antithetical to it." Hence rejecting the view that indigenous peoples and cultures were passively "victimised" by modernity as an "alien invader," McLean's emphasis is on the combinatory logics of hybridisation in art's answering response:

> Modernity's apocalyptic effects on all traditional societies, including Aboriginal ones, are undeniable. However, such argument easily slips into a binary logic that flattens the ambiguities of the colonial encounter and silences the historical adaptations of the colonised; thus colonising them all over again. This binary logic is the principal reason why western critics have had such difficulty accepting the modernism of non-western and especially tribal art. In reality, the agents of tradition did what they always had: they adapted and adjusted to the new, even appropriated some of its ideas. Admittedly the adjustment was often bumpy and at times contradictory, but the history of Aboriginal modernism is the story of such adaptation.[12]

In my third example of the colonial modern I would cite the Adinembo House built in the Niger Delta between 1919 and 1924 by the Nigerian architect James Onwudinjo, which is the focus of Stanley Ikem Okoye's contribution to the fourth volume in the series, *Exiles, Diasporas & Strangers.* Observing how the building's flat roof struck a double-sided contrast with both the clay and thatch materials of indigenous dwellings and the brickwork of British colonial architecture, Okoye devotes attention to the use of reinforced concrete as a "foreign" technology which found a receptive environment on the part of the local elite, including the wealthy Igbo trader who had commissioned the house. Where Okoye highlights the decorative and ornamental features on its external walls, by way of contrast to Adolf Loos, the key point is the overlapping timeframe in which modernist architects in Austria and West Africa explored similar concerns.[13]

My own contributions to the series focused on the modern Black diaspora, from Caribbean abstract painters in the New Commonwealth era (Aubrey Williams and Frank Bowling) to the photomontage of Romare Bearden in the African-American scene of the 1960s. In one sense, as products of forced migrations, diasporas are very distinct from colonies—in the latter your land has been taken away from you, whereas in the former you have been taken away from your land. But with methods opened up by Paul Gilroy's concept of the Black Atlantic as a circulatory space of migrant flows, the study of diasporic modernity provides a fresh point of entry into the archive, with sometimes surprising results. We mostly tend to see the Harlem Renaissance as the origins of Black modernism, but with the broader concept of "modernity" we not only see visual mediums such as photography as a key site in which the representation of autonomous selfhood was staged after the abolition of slavery, but we begin to notice that it was also in the 1890s that a distinctive philosophical discourse of self-enquiry was generated among African-American intellectuals such as WEB DuBois.

DuBois took part in the 1900 Exposition Universelle held in Paris, where he travelled to oversee the installation of the American Negro exhibit—a collection of photographs, maps, books, journals and scientific charts documenting his research at Atlanta University. World fairs and international expositions have been widely studied as spectacles of imperial power—and in the Dahomey Village in the French pavilion, Africans were put on display in 1900 as living specimens of otherness—but how much richer would our understanding of these contested sites of global modernity be once we factor in the *simultaneous* presence of Black diaspora subjects? What DuBois exhibited, to be sure, was not art but information; however, the documents of self-improvement he displayed in the American Negro Exhibit were understood by DuBois himself as a manifestation of Black self-modernisation. The nineteenth century networks of travel which paved the way for the Pan-African Congress (whose first meeting, in London in 1900, was attended by DuBois) encourage us to conceptualise the Black Atlantic as a "counter-culture of modernity" not only in music and literature but in the visual arts as well.[14] Dominant discourses of internationalism, designed to harmonise capitalist competition among rival nation-states (which, for Hall, defines the second

[14] Paul Gilroy, *The Black Atlantic: Modernity and Double Consciousness* (Cambridge, MA, and London, 1993).

[15] Hall, "Creolization," in Enwezor et al. 2003 (see note 1), p. 194.

[16] See Jan Nederveen Pieterse, "Hybridity, So What? The Anti-Hybridity Backlash and the Riddles of Recognition," *Theory, Culture & Society* 18, nos. 2–3 (2001).

phase of globalisation up to the imperialist catastrophe of the First World War) were themselves shadowed and antagonised by an internationalism-from-below. The transatlantic journeys African-American artists took to Paris in the 1930s were prefigured in the nineteenth century by sculptor Mary Edmonia Lewis and painter Henry Ossawa Tanner—whose work was not modernist *per se* even though it was engaged with self-conscious reflection on the dilemmas of life under conditions of diasporic modernity.

Revisiting the formative period of the 1890s to the 1920s through the lens of the multiple formations of modernism on a global scale now gives us the opportunity to examine how each of these cross-cultural variants are structured in dominance and subordination. In other words, we can think of the genealogy of modernism not as an "internalist" or self-generating story which begins and ends only in the West but as the narrative of a decisive moment in which the driving contradictions of the modern global conjuncture gave rise to many different forms of artistic production. Having touched upon anti-colonial appropriations which generated a cosmopolitan modernism that rejected neotraditionalism and nationalism, and a diasporic modernity that was shaped by the transnational journeys of Black artists who travelled as world citizens, it must be stressed that art history is only now—extremely belatedly—beginning to arrive at a truly universalist understanding of the "logic of transculturation" in the visual arts.

In periodising the global, Hall characterises "the third phase, culminating in the post-World War II period" as marked by "the decline of the old European-based empires, the era of national independence movements and decolonisation," which "coincides with the break-up of a whole visual, conceptual epistemological framework which we call 'modernism.' Modernism follows the wider index by shifting from its origins in turn-of-the century Europe to the US."[15] In the trauma-based temporality of *Nachträglichkeit*—that is, deferred action or literally "afterwardsness"—the interdependent or co-constitutive imbrication of modernism and colonialism only became visible with the break-up of hegemonic consensus brought about by the "post" in postmodernism and post-colonialism. The critical attention given to hybridity in artistic practices that broke into visibility as a result of this crisis of earlier modes of globalisation indicated a growing awareness of the generative potential of cross-cultural dynamics in cultural production, yet the anti-hybridity backlash that soon followed also revealed the short-term "presentism" by which analytical inquiry was limited to contemporary art alone.[16] But instead of rejecting hybridity on account of its origin in the biological sciences and appealing only to cognate terms from the human sciences, such as syncretism in anthropology or creolisation in linguistics, the broader category of the "cross-cultural" allows us to view each of these concepts—as well as terms such as *métissage* in Francophone colonialism and *mestizaje* in Spanish-speaking regions—as historically situated metaphors for the combinatory dynamics of mixture and assemblage which arise when disparate cultural elements are brought into contact.[17]

Where the "cross-cultural" describes the power relations through which different cultures transform one another during their mutual encounter, it clears the ground for understanding how culture itself is formed as a result of the processes of differentiation that modern thought variously describes as "*différance*" (Derrida), "dialogism" (Bakhtin) or "translation" (Benjamin). The conceptual challenge that the multiple modernities thesis brings to art history, then, is not simply to adapt each of these concepts to a global understanding of modernism in the visual arts, but to show how they reveal a broader logic of visual transculturation under the conditions of modernity. Where transculturation describes "how subordinated . . . groups select and invent from materials transmitted to them by a dominant or metropolitan culture," art historical research starting from a cross-cultural point of view thus promises to demonstrate how such dynamics affect all of the identities involved, including those of the metropolis.[18] By clarifying the differential combinations of modernisation and modernity in specific historical conjunctures of the global we may move towards a more rounded view of modernism as a "world-making" practice of art which was always already driven by cross-culturality.*

* This essay was originally published as *Colonial Modern: Aesthetics of the Past – Rebellions for the Future*, ed. Tom Avermaete, Serhat Karakayali, and Marion von Osten (London, 2010), pp. 233–43. Stylistic conventions have been adjusted to conform to the publication at hand.

[17] Critiques that stress the biological origins of the hybridity concept include Robert JC Young, *Colonial Desire: Hybridity in Theory, Culture and Race* (London and New York, 1995), and in the specific context of art, Jean Fisher, "The Syncretic Turn," in *New Histories*, ed. Malina Kalinovska, exh. cat. (Boston, 1995). Taking the critique on board, but developing the notion of "translation" as a means of conceptualising cross-cultural relations, an alternative view is offered in Stuart Hall and Sarat Maharaj, *Modernity and Difference*, vol. 6: *Annotations* (London, 2001).

[18] Mary Louise Pratt, *Imperial Eyes: Travel Writing and Transculturation* (New York and London, 1992), p. 8.

Saloni Mathur

The Exhibition as "Re-Job"

Reconstructing the Bauhaus in Bengal

The "Re-Job"

The collaborative effort to reconstruct an exhibition that occurred in Calcutta in 1922, that brought together modern Indian painters with artists from the Bauhaus, for the purposes of a contemporary exhibition at the Bauhaus in Dessau is a curatorial and historical exercise with few precedents in our current era. Inevitably, this provocative and ambitious exhibition experiment invites several questions at the outset. What does it mean to restage an exhibition some ninety years after the fact, in a different time and a different place? Could the reconstructed exhibition in Dessau ever approximate, for its viewing subject, the experience of the viewer in Calcutta in 1922? How can we know, given the absence of any visual record of the event, how the art was arranged, displayed, lit or unlit, or how it appeared on the gallery walls? To recreate what viewers saw is one thing, but *how* they saw or *what* they took away—is it ever possible to reconstruct this in full? In other words, how should this determined effort to retrieve these "original" works of art stand in relation to the "original" exhibition and become meaningful as an act of repetition that might also serve the needs of a critical art-historical practice in the present?

Such questions attach themselves to this project, but they have also emerged in other exhibitions in one form or another, where art from the modern era has reentered the display spaces of museums and galleries today. The notion of "reperformance," for example, involving the reenactment of performance art within the institutional structure of the museum, has raised similar kinds of questions and problems for scholars of dance and performance art.[1] What such projects appear to have in common, in spite of the differences raised by media and genre, is the fact that the "re-job"—the reconstruction, restaging, reinstallation, reinvention, reenactment, or re-creation—has forced open the separations made by space and time, rather than the opposite, creating new intellectual and methodological considerations for any act of curatorial revisitation. One important lesson from these contexts is that the value of the "re-job" does not (and should not) rest exclusively on the exactitude of its archival pursuit, or its ability to retrieve with historical precision the "authenticity" of a forgotten past. Instead, the real contribution lies in what any self-conscious act of reinscription has the potential to make possible—the new ideas and communities it can activate, the nature of the discussion it can galvanize, and the new frameworks it can help to construct for viewership and debate in the present. In other words, the current exhibition should not be approached as an insular time capsule from a previous era, or a pristine record that has been dusted off for display, but as a dynamic reassemblage of artists, ideas, histories, and nations, which point to contemporary and future directions in indefinite, and hopefully surprising, ways.

Looking back from the present, the curators of the 2013 *Bauhaus in Calcutta* exhibition in Dessau have posited the 1922 exhibition in Calcutta—curated by Stella Kramrisch, one of Indian art history's most illustrious figures—as a "laboratory of the avant-garde." If laboratory signals a self-consciously experimental platform where specific arguments that run counter to the conventional narrative are tested, then this designation is equally applicable to the current show. However, the real laboratories were undoubtedly the broader experimental contexts of the Bauhaus in Weimar and Shantiniketan in Bengal, two dynamic educational institutions that are central to understanding the artistic sensibilities at stake, and that are inseparable from their moorings in the tumultuous societal conditions of their time.

When the Bauhaus opened in Weimar, Germany, in 1919 under the directorship of Walter Gropius, the first of its three directors, it defined itself first as a pedagogic project—a physical school—rather than as an international modernist style, as the term "Bauhaus" tends to evoke today. And this identity as an experiment in education is what connects it most strongly to Kala Bhavan, the art school established in 1919–20 by Rabindranath Tagore at his university, Visva-Bharati, in Shantiniketan, in a rural setting outside of Calcutta. Kala Bhavan, like the Bauhaus, was conceived in response

[1] Klaus Biesenbach, ed., *Marina Abramović: The Artist Is Present* (New York, 2010); Amelia Jones et. al., "Forum: Performance, Live or Dead," *Art Journal* 70, no. 3 (Fall 2011), pp. 32–63. See also Miwon Kwon and Phillip Kaiser, eds., *Ends of the Earth: Land Art to 1974* (Los Angeles and Munich, 2012); and Britt Salvesen, ed., *New Topographics* (London, 2010).

[2] Martin Kämpchen, "Rabindranath Tagore's Paintings in Germany," in *The Last Harvest: Paintings of Rabindranath Tagore*, ed. R. Siva Kumar (New Delhi, 2011), pp. 30–33; Kris Manjapra, "Stella Kramrisch and the Bauhaus in Calcutta," in Kumar 2011, pp. 34–40; Partha Mitter, *The Triumph of Modernism* (London, 2007) and *Bauhaus in Calcutta* (unpublished manuscript).

[3] Uma Das Gupta, "Rabindranath Tagore: A Biographical Sketch," in Kumar 2011 (see note 2), p. 14.

to the conservative legacy of the nineteenth-century art academy, seeing itself as a creative and unconventional alternative to the existing structures of visual-arts education. Both sought to create a sense of community and purpose within a deeply intellectual framework; both privileged craftsmanship and rejected the separation between fine art and craft; and both were egalitarian in spirit, though less so in practice, given the fraught status of women in the arts. Finally, both sought to carry their utopian ideals outward into society at large. And yet, Shantiniketan's rural setting, with its vast stretches of barren land, earthy groves of palm trees, and scattering of small villages, could not seem further removed from the sleek architectural landscapes of the Bauhaus, with the radiant cube-like buildings designed by Walter Gropius and Ludwig Mies van der Rohe.

Nonetheless, the Bauhaus's modern industrialist sensibility and Shantiniketan's primevalist one would each exert a powerful influence on the successive generations of artists who flocked to their environs. That these aesthetic projects further intersected with intense periods of nationalism, leading to the political events that forced the closure of the Bauhaus by the National Socialists in 1933, on the one hand, and the escalation of the civil disobedience movement and freedom struggle in India throughout the nineteen-thirties, on the other, is a matter of significant historical complexity, suggesting no simple equation between these part educational settings, part aesthetic avant-gardes and the discrepant forms of cultural nationalism in which they were so famously entangled.

The Stage: Early Bauhaus Meets Late Bengal School

Delving into English, Bengali, and German language archives, a handful of scholars have constructed a remarkable portrait of cultural and intellectual interaction between Bengal and Germany in the early decades of the twentieth century as a crucial backdrop to the 1922 Calcutta exhibition.[2] Their accounts present a web of intellectual and social connections, at the intersections of theosophy, literature, art, and aesthetics, that were shaped through exhibitions, lectures, scholarly journals, and the public press, in both India and Europe throughout the nineteen-twenties. At the center of this historical stage was the legendary figure of Rabindranath Tagore, the Bengali intellectual, writer, and artist who had received the Nobel Prize in Literature in 1913 and was well known to the German public by the time he visited the country in 1921. Tagore's vision for releasing India from, in his words, the "hypnotic hold which this gigantic system of cold-blooded repression has taken on the minds of our people"[3] had inspired Germans in their own anguished search for identity following the collapse of the German empire after the First World War. If German audiences had responded to Tagore as something of a messiah in 1919, then his popularity had also peaked by 1930, the year when a major exhibition of his paintings toured Europe and when he made his final trip to Germany. As the writer and historian of the Indo-German encounter, Martin Kampchen, has observed, Germany no longer needed a messiah from India to redeem its people from crisis: by 1930, "other 'messiahs' had emerged."[4]

When Tagore visited Oxford in 1919 and hired Stella Kramrisch to teach art history at Kala Bhavan, she had just completed her doctoral dissertation on early Buddhist art from Sanchi and Barhut but had yet to visit India or see an actual Hindu or Buddhist temple. Kramrisch, an Austrian Jew who grew up in prewar Vienna, developed her interest and affinity for India through a rigorous intellectual framework that included the ideas of thinkers as wide-ranging as Alois Riegl, Bronisław Manislowski, Immanuel Kant, Baruch Spinoza, and Erwin Panofsky, along with the study of Sanskrit, Greek language and culture, German poetry, and training in dance and ballet. Hers was, in other words, a truly complex synthesis of intellectual cultures, according to her distinguished student and biographer, Barbara Stoler Miller. "For Stella," she observed, "Vienna was less the city of Strauss waltzes than of Gustav Klimt's and Egon Schiele's paintings."[5] This environment would thus shape her extraordinary sixty-year career as a scholar, teacher, and curator of folk, ancient, and religious Indian art; but it also instilled in her an ongoing interest in contemporary art of the modern era, especially in art that challenged the status quo in terms of visual languages and societal relationships. Kramrisch viewed the avant-garde movements of modernism in Europe, like Cubism, Expressionism, and Post-Impressionism, as powerful challenges to the conventions of form "developed out of the need of the moment," as she stated in her introduction to the Calcutta exhibition catalogue of 1922, "and no artist in whom the present is alive can escape their formulae."[6]

[4] Kämpchen in Kumar 2011 (see note 2), p. 31.

[5] Barbara Stoler Miller, "Stella Kramrisch: A Biographical Essay," in *Exploring India's Sacred Art: Selected Writings of Stella Kramrisch*, ed. Barbara Stoler Miller (Philadelphia, 1983), p. 6.

[6] Stella Kramrisch, *Catalogue of the Fourteenth Annual Exhibition* (Calcutta, 1922), p. 21.

[7] Klaus Weber, "Lothar Schreyer: Death House for a Woman, c. 1920," in *Bauhaus 1919–1933: Workshops for Modernity*, ed. Barry Bergdoll and Leah Dickerman (New York, 2009), p. 78.

[8] Tut Schlemmer, ed., *The Letters and Diaries of Oskar Schlemmer*, trans. Krishna Winston (Middletown, CT, 1972), p. 115, cited in Peg DeLamater, "Some Indian Sources in the Art of Paul Klee," *Art Bulletin* 66, no. 4 (December 1984), p. 657.

[9] Magdalena Droste, *Bauhaus 1919–1933* (Berlin, 2012), p. 58. See also Rose-Carol Washton Long, "From Metaphysics to Material Culture: Painting and Photography at the Bauhaus," in *Bauhaus Culture from Weimar to the Cold War*, ed. Kathleen James-Chakraborty (Minneapolis, 2006), p. 45.

[10] Charles W. Haxthausen, "Walter Gropius and Lyonel Feininger: Bauhaus Manifesto, 1919," in Bergdoll and Dickerman 2009 (see note 7), p. 64.

[11] Jean-Paul Sartre, preface to *The Wretched of the Earth*, by Frantz Fanon (New York, 2004), p. xlviii.

The Bauhaus works included in her show represent the early years of the Bauhaus, when it was still closely associated with Expressionism and preoccupied with medieval architecture and experiments in mysticism in the form of "wide-eyed reformist schemes and esoteric teachings."[7] The exhibition embodied the still-developing vision of Gropius and his first three faculty hires: the painters and art theorists Johannes Itten and Lyonel Feininger and the sculptor Gerhard Marcks. (They would be joined by Georg Muche and Paul Klee in 1920, Lothar Schreyer and Oskar Schlemmer in 1921, and Wassily Kandinsky in 1922, all of whom also contributed works to the show.) Itten was undoubtedly the most influential of the initial cohort: he had developed the *Vorkurs,* or preliminary course, that quickly became the core of the Bauhaus program. But Itten had also famously incorporated meditation exercises into his teaching and converted the student cafeteria to vegetarianism, leading Schlemmer to comment by 1921 on the "cult of India" that prevailed at the Bauhaus.[8]

Ultimately, Itten would resign in the months following the Calcutta exhibition because of his escalating differences with Gropius. The latter had already begun to move the school away from these self-consciously spiritual or metaphysical orientations and toward a more rigorous engagement with industrial society, that which he had defined by 1922 as "a new unity" between art and technology.[9] The art brought from Germany for Kramrisch's show thus makes visible the negotiations with the radical formalism that was to eventually become the hallmark of the Bauhaus, but at a time of transition rather than arrival, when the direction of each artist's embrace of abstraction remained to be seen. Significantly, the Bauhaus works included in her show are *not* the increasingly rationalist forms that we see emerging from the workshops in Weimar, and then Dessau, as the decade progressed. There is no experimental collage; no film, photography, found objects, or three-dimensional works; no ceramics, crafts, or metal sculptures; no furniture made with tubular steel. Instead, Feininger's woodcut prints, with their sharp diagonals and intersecting shafts of light, recall his iconic image, *Kathedrale* (Cathedral), adopted for the cover of Gropius's Bauhaus manifesto of 1919. This image, with its strange blend of Gothic-meets-Cubism, was the perfect embodiment of Gropius's utopian call in the manifesto for the creation of a "new guild of craftsmen" who could end the "arrogant class division between artisans and artists," even as it turned for architectural inspiration to a romantic and idealized medieval past.[10]

Stella Kramrisch's appeal to the Indian public to "study this exhibition," so as to learn more about European art and the lessons it can hold for India, recalls, to my mind, Jean-Paul Sartre's 1961 preface to Frantz Fanon's *The Wretched of the Earth:* "Europeans, open this book, look inside . . . Take advantage of it to discover your true self . . ."[11] This is not because the young female art historian can be seen as standing in alignment with the French philosopher's anticolonial politics or his radical leftist positions in any way. On the contrary, Kramrisch's intellectual life seems oddly detached from the revolutionary social movements that rocked the three decades she spent in India, from 1921 to 1950, which saw the freedom struggle, the attainment of independence, and the violent crises of partition. Nonetheless, her short introduction to the exhibition catalogue shares with Sartre's preface an investment in the possibility of humanist knowledge forged through the self–other relation across the cultural divide. Kramrisch's plea to Indians to "study this exhibition" does not have the moralizing ring-tone of colonial pedagogy in India. It betrays instead the ethical project of humanism in the twentieth century, and it captures something of the vanguard character—and dialectical spirit—of her larger curatorial intervention. The exhibition was also a platform upon which Tagore and Kramrisch could advance their progressive views in favor of internationalism in the visual arts to an Indian audience who, above all, reflected Indian nationalism's ambivalent, and often contradictory, stance toward all manner of ideas emerging from the West. These views were hotly debated in *RUPAM,* the journal of the Indian Society of Oriental Art, and in various outlets of the German press; and it stood in stark contrast to the outright rejection of Europe that characterized the earlier positions of the Bengal School painters and their supporters. It was a pioneering moment, in other words, of the *exhibition as argument.* This model, which unites the role of curator and scholar and also invests in exhibition-making as a socially responsible, partisan practice, has emerged, significantly, in the past few decades within the contestatory field of contemporary art's "global turn" as more politically relevant than ever before.[12]

Stagings and Restagings: Exhibitionary Dialectics

It is additionally significant that works by many of the Bauhaus artists in the present exhibition—namely, Feininger, Itten, Kandinsky, Klee, Marcks, Muche, and Schreyer—were featured in an earlier exhibition "re-job" curated by Stephanie Barron, at the Los Angeles County Museum of Art in

[12] See, for example, Ranjit Hoskote, "Biennials of Resistance: Reflections on the Seventh Gwangju Biennial," in *The Biennial Reader,* ed. Elena Filipovic et. al. (Ostfildern, 2010), pp. 306–12; Geeta Kapur, "Curating in the Public Sphere," in *Cautionary Tales: Critical Curating,* ed. Steven Rand and Heather Kouris (New York, 2007), pp. 56–68; Carolee Thea, ed., *On Curating: Interviews with Ten International Curators* (New York, 2010).

[13] Stephanie Barron, ed., *"Degenerate Art": The Fate of the Avant-Garde in Nazi Germany* (Los Angeles and New York, 1991).

[14] Kampchen in Kumar 2011 (see note 2), p. 32.

1991.[13] Barron and her team had reconstructed the infamous show mounted by the National Socialists in Germany in 1937, titled *Entartete Kunst* (or "Degenerate Art"), which featured over 650 examples of modernist artworks deemed unacceptable and "un-German" by Nazi authorities. The original exhibition, which traveled for four years throughout Germany and Austria and was viewed by an estimated three million visitors, exemplified the larger politicization of aesthetics by Hitler and his Third Reich in Germany. The Nazis had condemned all contemporary artists who worked in a modernist style, regardless of their politics (or their status as Jews, for that matter, as only six of the 112 artists in the show were Jewish). Thus was the fate of the entire faculty of the Bauhaus, who were placed alongside Cubists, Expressionists, Surrealists, and so on, and cast as degenerate, debased, and outside the law. Ironically, it was also the fate of five drawings by Rabindranath Tagore, gifted by the artist to the Nationalgalerie in Berlin, where they, too, were labeled "*entartet*" in 1937, leading to questions about their whereabouts today.[14] If the purpose of the Nazi exhibition was to condemn, defame, denounce, and obliterate, then the act of reconstructing the show in 1991 was to ensure that, in the end, the National Socialists had failed in their bid to erase the modernist vision that so threatened their own. Barron's exhibition, which painstakingly restaged the sequence of the installation room-by-room and wall-by-wall, and which included extensive documentation in the form of photographs, press clippings, exhibition pamphlets, and eyewitness accounts, was thus offered as an ambitious counter-argument, poetically and polemically conceived, to the ruinous premises of the original show.

These earlier displays of the Bauhaus artists included in the current exhibition highlight the dialectics of staging and restaging, inscription and reinscription, through which the meaning-making practices of art history acquire shape. The story of the Bauhaus is also a story of how its formal innovations dispersed and proliferated beyond the forced closure of the school in 1933; how its ideas and theories about art traveled and spread through its famous émigrés (with the arrival, for instance, of Walter Gropius at Harvard, László Moholy-Nagy and Mies van der Rohe at Chicago, and Joseph Albers at Black Mountain College and then Yale); and how its forms became uniquely inscribed in the specific conditions of postwar America, entangled as they were in that country's rise to superpower status during the Cold War era. It is a story about the relationship between art and politics in the modern era, one that—like its counterpart in colonial Bengal—throws into relief the complicated interface between nationalist agendas and the sphere of aesthetics. Whether the austere designs, rationalized forms, and later embrace of technology, advertising, and mass culture that we tend to shorthand as "the Bauhaus style" were seen as democratic—as Alfred Barr, the pioneering director of the Museum of Modern Art in New

York, had argued in his 1938 catalogue introduction to the exhibition that first introduced the Bauhaus to America—or as more authoritarian, even protofascist, because of the way its artists' embraced the mounting mechanization of Weimar Germany, is surely part of the great complexity and world-historical significance of the Bauhaus.[15] Its meanings have remained, in other words, "perfectly ambiguous,"[16] always irreducible, and entangled in the multiple strands of reception, reinscription, and reinterpretation by successive generations across the global stage.

A striking parallel emerged in India during the nineteen-twenties with the diffusion and proliferation of Bengal School painting, the similarly diverse formal project that nonetheless represented the "art of modern India" in Kramrisch's show. Spearheaded by Abanindranath Tagore and his circle in Calcutta, the Bengal School was bred in the atmosphere of the anti-colonial Swadeshi movement and had announced itself as the "new Indian art" soon after the turn of the century, in 1905. The question of national regeneration and the recovery of tradition was equally pressing for this group of painters in colonial Bengal, and they ushered in a powerful shift in the self-image of the Indian artist within the broader transformations to the middle class occurring in Bengali society. The period was wracked by a paradox, however, that both echoes and departs from the specific experience of the Bauhaus in Weimar—the paradox of a self-consciously nationalist, yet firmly depoliticized art movement, one that perceives itself as avant-garde but stands also at a distance (or at a loss) next to the revolutionary politics surrounding it. Moreover, by the twenties, the time of Kramrisch's show in Calcutta, "the new Indian art" had become part of the establishment itself, expanding outward through teaching and patronage into that of an all-India movement, resulting in a somewhat fixed aesthetic, a predominantly Hindu iconography, and patterns of conformity to the "Indian style."[17] There is no doubt that the 1922 show was, for its key protagonists, Stella Kramrisch and Rabindranath Tagore, an argument *against* the narrow historicism of the increasingly orthodox Bengal School model. The two of them were in pursuit of broader, more universal, modern values, embodied by the freewheeling

[15] Barry Bergdoll, "Bauhaus Multiplied: Paradoxes of Architecture and Design in and after the Bauhaus," in Bergdoll and Dickerman 2009 (see note 7), pp. 41–61; James-Chakraborty 2006 (see note 9); Rosalind Krauss, "Jump over the Bauhaus: Avant-Garde Photography in Germany, 1919–1939," *October* 14 (Winter 1980).

[16] Krauss 1980 (see note 15), p. 110.

[17] Tapati Guha-Thakurta, *The Making of a New "Indian" Art: Artists, Aesthetics and Nationalism in Bengal 1850–1920* (Cambridge, 1992); Partha Mitter, *Art and Nationalism in Colonial India, 1850–1922: Occidental Orientations* (Cambridge, 1994).

[18] Mitter 2007 (see note 2), p. 23.

[19] See Geeti Sen, "Iconising the Nation: Political Agendas," in *India: A National Culture?*, ed. Geeti Sen (New Delhi, 2003), pp. 155–75.

experimentation of the painter Gaganendranath Tagore, who seized the new technique of Cubism as a "wonderful stimulant," as he commented to a journalist in 1926.[18] This is a far cry, regrettably, from certain trends witnessed in the India of today, where the gendered icon of the motherland, which received its first expression in Abanindranath Tagore's luminous 1905 painting, *Bharat Mata,* has been politicized in startling and effective ways by a militant and aggressive Hindu nationalism united by a set of xenophobic values that represent the opposite of those envisioned by the Tagores. In other words, the essential ambiguity and continued power of the oddly-secular-yet-wholly-Hindu aesthetic of the Bengal School painters suggests, at the very least, that—like the Bauhaus—its relationship to the social imaginary of democracy cannot be taken for granted.[19]

The Bauhaus and colonial Bengal: in the end, these are two dramatic—indeed explosive—historical constellations that do not stand still for a viewer, and that can only be grasped through the dynamic unfolding of their ideas, and the radical diffusion of their aesthetic forms. The current exhibition in Dessau reconstructs, and allows us to *see* for the first time, a single point of contact in these histories, which opens onto larger circuits of visual, historical, and sociocultural understanding. It galvanizes two powerful moments of convergence between art and politics at the beginning of the twentieth century, inviting us to consider them seriously through a dialectical and comparative frame. It would be a disservice to dissolve the difficulties and paradoxes into a picture of coherence labeled the "cross-cultural avant-garde," if such a notion presumes a uniform collective impetus or seeks to recuperate a simple fable of rapport. Fortunately, the artworks by the Indian and European artists collected, or rather re-collected, here do not resolve the formal, cultural, or philosophical differences they encountered in one another at the threshold of modernism in the previous century. Instead, they invite a view of our collective experience through the cracks and collisions of the twentieth century, and they demand from us a critical re-engagement with the stories that art history has told. This project bears all the promising signs, then, of a "re-job" well done.

The Authors

REGINA BITTNER

studied cultural sciences and art history at the Universität Leipzig and received her PhD from the Humboldt Universität zu Berlin. Head of the Bauhaus Kolleg of the Bauhaus Dessau Foundation since 2003, she has also been its Deputy Director since 2009. For this institution and others she has curated numerous exhibitions on modern culture and urban history. Her research and publications cover fields ranging from international architectural and urban research to heritage studies.

TORSTEN BLUME

studied art history and is a research and arts associate at the Bauhaus Dessau Foundation. He works as an art historian, scenographer, and curator, and his publications focus on the history and theory of modern art and design. Since 2007 he has worked with diverse partners on performative projects dedicated to the history of avant-garde dance and theater in the context of the modern "body culture movement." He is currently organizing the exhibition *Human-Space-Machine: Stage Experiments* at the Bauhaus in collaboration with Christian Hiller (opening December 2013).

SRIA CHATTERJEE

is a PhD candidate as the Frank J. Mather fellow at Princeton University and, from the fall semester 2013–14, a fellow at the Max Planck Kunsthistorisches Institut (KHI) in Florence. She studied English literature in Jadavpur University and history of art at the University of Oxford. Her research interests lie in South Asian art, architecture, and historiography with a focus on the late nineteenth and early twentieth centuries. She has edited, with Jennie Renton, an anthology of essays titled *Kolkata, Book City: Readings, Fragments, Images* (2009), and her essay "People of Clay: Portrait Objects in the Peabody Essex Museum" will soon be published in *Museum History Journal*, vol. 6.2 (forthcoming, 2013).

SWATI CHATTOPADHYAY

is professor and chair of the Department of History of Art and Architecture at the University of California, Santa Barbara. She received her B.Arch. from Jadavpur University, Kolkata, her M.Arch. from the University of Arizona, Tucson, and her Ph.D. in architecture from the University of California, Berkeley. She is the author of *Unlearning the City: Infrastructure in a New Optical Field* (2012) and *Representing Calcutta: Modernity, Nationalism, and the Colonial Uncanny* (2005, paperback 2006) and is the current editor of the *Journal of the Society of Architectural Historians.*

BORIS FRIEDEWALD

studied art history, education, and theater studies in Bochum and Berlin. He works as a freelance art historian, author, and dramaturge and has published numerous books on the Bauhaus and on modern art and cultural history, including *Living Art: Bauhaus* (2009) and *Die Engel von Paul Klee* (2011).

TAPATI GUHA-THAKURTA

studied art history at the University of Calcutta and at the University of Oxford. She is a professor of history and director of the Centre for Studies in Social Sciences in Calcutta. Her extensive research and publication activities focus on the art and cultural history of modern India, the history of art institutions, and art historiography in colonial and postcolonial India. She places a further emphasis on research into contemporary popular culture.

KRIS MANJAPRA

is a historian and a graduate of Harvard University. He was a fellow of the Alexander von Humboldt Foundation in 2010–11 and has taught history at the Tufts University in Medford since 2008. His international research and publication activities focus on South Asian and German intellectual history.

SALONI MATHUR

is an associate professor of art history at the University of California, Los Angeles. She is the author of *India by Design: Colonial History and Cultural Display* (2007), editor of *The Migrant's Time: Rethinking Art History and Diaspora* (2011), and co-editor (with Kavita Singh) of *No Touching, No Spitting, No Praying: Modalities of the Museum in South Asia* (forthcoming).

KOBENA MERCER

studied art history and diaspora studies at Middlesex University London and graduated from Goldsmiths College in London. He is a professor of art history and African American studies at Yale University and has also taught at New York University and the University of California in Santa Cruz. In 2006 he was one of the first recipients of the Clark Prize for Excellence in Arts Writing. His extensive teaching, research, and publication activities take a cultural-studies approach to the art of the "Black Atlantic." With publications such as *Cosmopolitan Modernisms* (2005) or *Exiles, Diasporas & Strangers* (2008) he has opened up new scientific perspectives on art historiography.

PARTHA MITTER

is an emeritus professor at the University of Sussex and a member of Wolfson College, Oxford. He has accepted numerous international fellowships, e.g., at Clare Hall, the University of Cambridge, the Institute for Advanced Study, Princeton, the Getty Research Institute, Los Angeles, and the Clark Art Institute, Williamstown, MA. His publications on the history of Indian modernism, such as *Much Maligned Monsters: A History of European Reactions to Indian Art* (1977), *Art and Nationalism in Colonial India 1850–1922* (1994), and *The Triumph of Modernism: India's Artists and the Avant-Garde 1922–1947* (2007) are standard works of international art history.

KATHRIN RHOMBERG

studied art history and classical archaeology in Salzburg. She was curator and head of the exhibition office of the Secession, Vienna (1990–2001) and managing director of the Kölnischer Kunstverein (2002–07). Rhomberg is presently co-curator of the project *Former West* in the Haus der Kulturen der Welt, Berlin, and a lecturer at the Academy of Fine Arts Vienna. She has curated numerous exhibitions, including *Manifesta 3*, Ljubljana (2000, with Francesco Bonami, Ole Bouman, and Maria Hlavajova), *Projekt Migration*, Cologne (2002–06, with Marion von Osten), the Slovakian and Czech Pavilion for the 53rd Venice Biennial (2009), and the 6th Berlin Biennale for Contemporary Art (2010).

R. SIVA KUMAR

is an art historian and curator. He studied at the University of Kerala and Shantiniketan and is a professor of art history at Visva-Bharati in Shantiniketan. He has published numerous works on the history of modern Indian art and curated various exhibitions, including the exhibition of Rabindranath Tagore paintings that was shown at nine international museums.

SANJUKTA SUNDERASON

studied history and art history at the University of Calcutta and the Jawaharlal Nehru University, New Delhi, and graduated from University College London. She teaches modern South Asian culture at the Institute for Area Studies, Leiden University. In her research and publications, Sunderason focuses on the aesthetics, politics, and ideology of the twentieth-century art of South Asia. Since completing her dissertation on the nationalist and left-wing art movements of India, she has been researching the aesthetics of decolonialization in South Asia in the nineteen-fifties and sixties.

CHRISTOPH WAGNER

has been professor and chair of the Department of Art History at the University of Regensburg since 2007. He has been visiting professor at the École pratique des hautes études at the Sorbonne, Paris (2008), the Institute of Advanced Study in Bern (2010), and the Univerisdad Nacional Autónoma de México (2012–13). Wagner's main areas of focus lie in art, art theory, and the aesthetics of the twentieth century. He has authored various books, including *Das Bauhaus und die Esoterik: Johannes Itten, Paul Klee, Wassily Kandinsky* (2005), *Esoterik am Bauhaus: Eine Revision der Moderne?* (2009), and his most recently completed book *Itten, Gropius, Klee am Bauhaus in Weimar: Utopie und historischer Kontext* (forthcoming).

List of Illustrated Works

17 * Wassily Kandinsky, untitled, 1915, watercolor and ink on paper, 13.9 × 20.9 cm, Centre Pompidou, Paris

18 Paul Klee, *Maske* (Mask), 1922, 61, watercolor and pencil on paper on cardboard, 27 × 13 cm, private collection, Germany

19 Paul Klee, *Herzdame* (Queen of the Hearts), 1922, watercolor and pencil on paper, watercolor, and pen, 29.5 × 16.4 cm, Museum Sammlung Rosengart, Lucerne

20 Paul Klee, *rot / violett x gelb / grün gestuft* (Rose, Violet & Yellowish Green), 1922, 64, watercolor and pencil on paper on cardboard, 21.1/21.4 × 29.2/28.7 cm, private collection, Switzerland, on loan at the Zentrum Paul Klee, Bern

21 Paul Klee, *Schleusen* (Sluices), 1922, watercolor and pencil on paper on cardboard, 20.3 × 30.7 cm, Staatliche Museen zu Berlin, Museum Berggruen

22 ** Gerhard Marcks, *Die Mäusejagd [Mäusejagd]* (The Mouse Chase), 1921, woodcut on Japan paper, 25 × 23 cm, Gerhard Marcks Foundation, Bremen

23 Gerhard Marcks, *Holzhacker* (The Wood Cutter), 1920, woodcut on laid paper, 27 × 17 cm, Gerhard Marcks Foundation, Bremen

24 ** Gerhard Marcks, *Der Pfingstkuchen [Der Osterkuchen]* (The Easter Cake), 1922, woodcut, 31.3 × 22.3 cm, Kunsthalle Bremen – Der Kunstverein in Bremen

25 ** Gerhard Marcks, *Raucher [Mann mit Pfeife]* (The Man with a Pipe in his Mouth), 1922, woodcut on laid paper, exemplar 14/50a, 31.2 × 21.7 cm, Gerhard Marcks Foundation, Bremen

26 ** Gerhard Marcks, *Ferkelkauf [Die Ferkel]* (The Young Pig), 1921, woodcut on Japan paper, 14.3 × 19.7 cm, Gerhard Marcks Foundation, Bremen

27 Gerhard Marcks, *Der Schäfer* (The Shepherd), 1921, woodcut on Japan paper, 23.9 × 14.6 cm, Gerhard Marcks Foundation, Bremen

28 Georg Muche, *Der Mond* (The Moon), n.d. [1922], copperplate etching, 26.8 × 20.1 cm, Bauhaus Archive Berlin

29 Georg Muche, *Im Anfang war das Wort [cogito ergo credo]*, 1922, copperplate etching, 16.7 × 11.8 cm, Bauhaus Archive Berlin

30 Lyonel Feininger, *Mellingen*, 1919, woodcut on Japan paper, 30.4 × 25.5 cm, Bauhaus Archive Berlin

31 Lyonel Feininger, *Gelmeroda*, 1920, woodcut on Japan paper, 33.1 × 24.5 cm, Bauhaus Archive Berlin

32 Lyonel Feininger, *Werder I*, 1916, watercolor and tempera on paper, 24.5 × 32 cm, MART 930, Mart, Museo di arte moderna e contemporanea di Trento e Rovereto

33 Lyonel Feininger, *The Anglers [Die Angler]*, 1915, watercolor and ink on paper, 24.3 × 31.4 cm, private collection, courtesy Moeller Fine Art, New York – Berlin

34 ** Johannes Itten, *Linienrhythmus [Komposition IV]* (Composition IV), page 10 from the portfolio *10 Originallithographien*, 1919, lithograph on glossy art paper, 60 × 45 cm, Bauhaus Archive Berlin

35 Johannes Itten, *Komposition (Komposition III)* (Composition III), page 9 from the portfolio *10 Originallithographien*, 1919, lithograph on glossy art paper, 60 × 45 cm, Bauhaus Archive Berlin

36 ** Johannes Itten, *Waldrandblumen* (Flowers on the edge of the Forest), page 2 from the portfolio *10 Originallithographien*, 1919, lithograph on glossy art paper, 60 × 45 cm, Bauhaus Archive Berlin

37 Johannes Itten, *Mädchen* (Maiden), page 5 from the portfolio *10 Originallithographien*, 1919, lithograph on glossy art paper, 60 × 45 cm, Bauhaus Archive Berlin

38 * Lothar Schreyer, *Farbklang* (Colour tone), 1922, watercolor on paper, 36.7 × 26 cm, Bauhaus Dessau Foundation

39 Margit Téry-Adler, cover of *Utopia: Dokumente der Wirklichkeit* (Weimar, 1921), color lithograph, 33 × 24.5 cm, Bauhaus Archive Berlin

40 * Margit Téry-Adler, *Portrait (Frauenkopf)*, ca. 1919–20, charcoal on paper with white highlights, mounted on cardboard, 50.3 × 33.8 cm, Bauhaus Archive Berlin

41 * Margit Téry-Adler, *Blumen in Vase* (Flowers), ca. 1919–20, charcoal on paper, 36.7 × 47 cm, Bauhaus Archive Berlin
42 * Gaganendranath Tagore, *Nocturne in Blue and Gold: The River Padma,* 1912–15, gouache on paper, 32.1 × 44.5 cm, The Savara Foundation for the Arts, New Delhi
43 * Gaganendranath Tagore, untitled, n.d., ink and gray wash on paper, 35.6 × 27.9 cm, The Savara Foundation for the Arts, New Delhi
44 * Gaganendranath Tagore, untitled, 1920–25, pencil on postcard, 14.3 × 9.5 cm, Victoria and Albert Museum, London
45 Gaganendranath Tagore, *Artist at Jorasanko House,* n.d., ink and wash on paper, 11.2 × 14 cm, National Gallery of Modern Art, New Delhi
46 * Gaganendranath Tagore, *Cluster of Puri Temples,* n.d., watercolor on paper, 13 × 21.5 cm, National Gallery of Modern Art, New Delhi
47 * Gaganendranath Tagore, *Composition,* n.d., watercolor on paper, 32.7 × 24.4 cm, National Gallery of Modern Art, New Delhi
48 * Abdur Rahman Chughtai, untitled, n.d., 56 × 42 cm, Art Konsult Gallery, New Delhi, courtesy Mr. Suresh Jindal, New Delhi
49 * Abdur Rahman Chughtai, untitled, 1938, 49 × 33.6 cm, Art Konsult Gallery, New Delhi, courtesy Mr. Suresh Jindal, New Delhi
50 * Abdur Rahman Chughtai, untitled, n.d., watercolor on wood, 53 × 71 cm, Vijay Aggarwal Collection, New Delhi
51 * Deviprasad Roychowdhury, untitled, n.d., watercolor on paper, 23 × 29 cm, Chitrakoot Art Gallery, Calcutta
52 * Abanindranath Tagore, *Buddha,* 1918, watercolor and wash on paper, 25.4 × 17.8 cm, The Savara Foundation for the Arts, New Delhi
53 * Abanindranath Tagore, *Song Birds Amongst Bamboo,* ca. 1920, watercolor on paper, 20 × 14.5 cm, The Savara Foundation for the Arts, New Delhi
54 * Abanindranath Tagore, *Black Girl,* ca. 1920, wash on paper, 32.1 × 22.8 cm, The Savara Foundation for the Arts, New Delhi
55 * Abanindranath Tagore, *At The Ganges,* ca. 1920, watercolor on paper, 26.7 × 16.5 cm, The Savara Foundation for the Arts, New Delhi
56 * Abanindranath Tagore, *Journey's End,* n.d., tempera on paper, 15 × 21 cm, National Gallery of Modern Art, New Delhi
57 * Kali Pada Ghoshal, untitled, 1938, watercolor on paper, 26 × 26 cm, Vijay Aggarwal Collection, New Delhi
58 * Bireshwar Sen, untitled, n.d., watercolor on paper, 55.5 × 34.5 cm, Vijay Aggarwal Collection, New Delhi
59 * Sunayani Devi, untitled (Lady with parrot), n.d., watercolor and tempera on paper, 27 × 19 cm, Collection Nirmalya Kumar
60 * Sunayani Devi, untitled (Portrait), back of page, figure 53, n.d., watercolor and tempera on paper, 23.5 × 19 cm / 22.5 × 19 cm, Collection Nirmalya Kumar
61 * Sunayani Devi, untitled (Shiva & Parvati), front of page, figure 52, n.d., watercolor and tempera on paper, 23.5 × 19 cm / 22.5 × 19 cm, Collection Nirmalya Kumar, New Delhi
62 * Sunayani Devi, *Milkmaid,* ca. 1920, gouache and watercolor on paper, 39.9 × 32.2 cm, Delhi Art Gallery Collection, New Delhi
63 * Sunayani Devi, untitled (Woman), n.d., watercolor and tempera on paper, 30 × 24.5 cm, Collection Nirmalya Kumar
64 * Nandalal Bose, *Krishna,* before 1920, watercolor on silk, 76 × 51 cm, Vijay Aggarwal Collection, New Delhi

Cover illustration: Unknown artist, painting class, n.d., photograph

* Denotes reference works.
** The titles in square brackets are the original titles for

Picture Credits

P. 13, fig. 1: *Catalogue of the Fourteenth Annual Exhibition Indian Society of Oriental Art Samavaya Mansions Calcutta,* December 1922, title page; pp. 14–16, figs. 2–4: *Catalogue of the Fourteenth Annual Exhibition Indian Society of Oriental Art Samavaya Mansions Calcutta,* December 1922, pp. 21–23; p. 17: © VG Bild-Kunst, Bonn, 2013, photo: bpk/CNAC-MNAM/Paris, Centre Pompidou-CNAC-MNAM/RMN-GP (00100982); pp. 18, 20: photo: Zentrum Paul Klee, Bern; p. 19: photo: Museum Sammlung Rosengart, Lucerne; p. 21: photo: bpk/Nationalgalerie, Museum Berggruen, SMB/Jens Ziehe (00022489); pp. 22–23, 25–27: © Gerhard-Marcks-Stiftung, Bremen, photo: Gerhard-Marcks-Stiftung, Bremen; p. 24: © Gerhard-Marcks-Stiftung, Bremen, photo: Kunsthalle Bremen – Der Kunstverein in Bremen / Karen Blindow; pp. 28–29: © Bauhaus-Archiv Berlin, photo: Bauhaus-Archiv Berlin; pp. 30–31, 34–37: © VG Bild-Kunst, Bonn, 2013, photo: Bauhaus-Archiv Berlin; p. 32: © VG Bild-Kunst, Bonn, 2013, photo: MART, Museo di arte moderna e contemporanea di Trento e Rovereto; p. 33: © VG Bild-Kunst, Bonn, 2013, courtesy of Moeller Fine Art, New York – Berlin, photo: Moeller Fine Art, New York – Berlin; p. 38: © Schreyer, Hamburg, photo: Stiftung Bauhaus Dessau / Kelly Kellerhoff; pp. 39–41: © Judith Adler, photo: Bauhaus-Archiv Berlin; pp. 42–43, 52–55: photo: The Savara Foundation for the Arts, New Delhi; p. 44: photo: Victoria and Albert Museum, London; p. 45: photo: National Gallery of Modern Art, New Delhi; pp. 46–47, 56: photo: National Gallery of Modern Art, New Delhi; pp. 48–49: courtesy of Mr. Suresh Jindal, New Delhi, photo: Art Konsult Gallery, New Delhi; pp. 50, 57–58, 64: photo: Vijay Aggarwal Collection, New Delhi; p. 51: © Chitrakoot Art Gallery, Calcutta, photo: Chitrakoot Art Gallery, Calcutta; pp. 59–61, 63: photo: Collection Nirmalya Kumar; p. 62: photo: Delhi Art Gallery Collection; p. 67, fig. 1.1: © Bauhaus-Archiv Berlin, photo: Bauhaus-Archiv Berlin; fig. 1.2: Ananda K. Coomaraswamy, *Coomaraswamy: Selected Papers,* © 1977 Princeton University Press, 2205 renewed PUP reprinted by permission of Princeton University Press; fig. 1.3: © Deutsches Literaturarchiv Marbach; fig. 1.4: © Rabindra-Bhavan-Archiv, Shantiniketan; figs. 1.5, 1.7: © 2013 Curatorial Assistance, Inc. / E.O. Hoppé Estate Collection; fig. 1.6: Mary Lago, ed., *Imperfect Encounter* (Cambridge, MA, 1972), p. 3; fig. 1.8: Mary Lago, ed., *Imperfect Encounter* (Cambridge, MA, 1972), n.p.; fig. 1.9: © Archiv der Universität Wien; fig. 1.10: © Klassik Stiftung Weimar, Goethe- und Schiller-Archiv, Bestand Nietzsche-Ikonographie, GSA 101/245, photo: Klassik Stiftung Weimar; fig. 1.11: © Itten-Archiv Zürich, fig. 1.12: © Philadelphia Museum of Art, Archives; p. 69, fig. 2: Indian Society of Oriental Art, Calcutta 2012; fig. 3: Thüringisches Hauptstaatsarchiv Weimar, Staatliches Bauhaus Weimar Nr. 57, Bl. 1r; fig. 4: Thüringisches Hauptstaatsarchiv Weimar, Staatliches Bauhaus Weimar Nr. 57, Bl. 2r–4r; p. 71, fig. 5: Thüringisches Hauptstaatsarchiv Weimar, Staatliches Bauhaus Weimar Nr. 57, Bl. 64r/v; fig. 6: Thüringisches Hauptstaatsarchiv Weimar, Staatliches Bauhaus Weimar Nr. 57, Bl. 67r; fig. 7: © Rabindra-Bhavan-Archiv, Shantiniketan; p. 75, fig. 10: Wienbibliothek im Rathaus, manuscript collection, estate Josef Strzygowski, item no. 69; p. 77, fig. 11: Wienbibliothek im Rathaus, manuscript collection, estate Josef Strzygowski, item no. 69; p. 79, fig. 11.1: Wienbibliothek im Rathaus, manuscript collection, estate Josef Strzygowski, item no. 69; p. 81, fig. 12: photo: © MAK/Georg Mayer; fig. 13: Thüringisches Hauptstaatsarchiv Weimar, Staatliches Bauhaus Weimar Nr. 1, Bl. 76r; figs. 14–15: photo: Bauhaus-Archiv Berlin; p. 92, fig. 1: © Samiran Nandy, source: Deutsches Literaturarchiv Marbach, D20130114-140, photo: Deutsches Literaturarchiv Marbach; p. 100, fig. 1: photo: Staatsbibliothek zu Berlin – Preußischer Kulturbesitz; p. 103, fig. 2: photo: Staatsbibliothek zu Berlin – Preußischer Kulturbesitz; p. 108, fig. 1: © Samiran Nandy, photo: Deutsches Literaturarchiv Marbach; p. 115, figs. 2–5: © Rabindra-Bhavan-Archiv, Shantiniketan; fig. 6: © Samiran Nandy, photo: Deutsches Literaturarchiv Marbach; p. 116, fig. 1: © VG Bild-Kunst, Bonn, 2013, photo: Stiftung Bauhaus Dessau / Kelly Kellerhoff; p. 121, fig. 2: photo: Bauhaus-Archiv Berlin; fig. 3: photo: © Musée Albert-Kahn – Département des Hauts-de-Seine 4: Thüringisches Hauptstaatsarchiv Weimar, Generalintendanz des Deutschen Nationaltheaters und der Staatskapelle, Weimar, Nr. 1891, Bl. 279; p. 125, fig. 5: © VG Bild-Kunst, Bonn, 2013, photo: Itten-Archiv Zürich; fig. 6: © The Nekbakht Foundation www.nekbakhtfoundation.org; fig. 7: Thüringisches Hauptstaatsarchiv Weimar, Staatliches Bauhaus Weimar Nr. 14, Bl. 144r; p. 127, fig. 8: © The Nekbakht Foundation www.nekbakhtfoundation. org; fig. 9: © VG Bild-Kunst, Bonn, 2013, photo: Stiftung Bauhaus Dessau / Kelly Kellerhoff; p. 132, fig. 1: © VG Bild-Kunst, Bonn, 2013, photo: Bauhaus-Archiv Berlin; fig. 2: photo: Bauhaus-Universität Weimar, Archiv der Moderne; fig. 3: © akg-images; fig. 4: Thüringisches Hauptstaatsarchiv Weimar, Staatliches Bauhaus Weimar, file no. 6, p. 143; p. 133, figs. 5, 7–8: photo: Bauhaus-Archiv Berlin; fig. 6: photo: Bauhaus-Universität Weimar, Archiv der Moderne; pp. 147–49, figs. 1–5, 10: Itten-Archiv Zürich; figs. 6–7: Itten-Archiv Zürich, © VG Bild-Kunst 2013; figs. 8–9: © VG Bild-Kunst, Bonn, 2013, photo: Bauhaus-Archiv Berlin; p. 150, fig. 1: *The Modern Review* (August 1921), p. 258; p. 171, fig. 1: photo: Sumitendranath Tagore, Thakur Barir Jana Ajana, 1999 ; fig. 2: photo: Swati Chattopadhyay, fig. 3: Boston Museum of Art; p. 178, fig. 1: Zentrum moderner Orient, Berlin, Krüger Files/Ram Chandra Papers 684/Box 5; fig. 2: Zentrum moderner Orient, Berlin, Krüger Files 6044/Box 39; p. 179, figs. 3–6: Gagonendra Nath Tagore, Reform Screams (Calcutta, 1921); pp. 210–11, photos: © Nicole Six & Paul Petritsch, VBK, Wien 2013; pp. 210–12, fig. 1: Thüringisches Hauptstaatsarchiv Weimar, Staatliches Bauhaus Weimar Nr. 57, Bl. 79r.

Cover illustration: © Rabindra Bhavan Archive, Shantiniketan

B
A
U
H
A
U
S EDITION

SELECTION OF AVAILABLE PUBLICATIONS FROM THE EDITION BAUHAUS SERIES

EDITION BAUHAUS 11
Bauhausstil: Zwischen International Style und Lifestyle, ed. Regina Bittner (Berlin, 2003).

EDITION BAUHAUS 21
Bauhaus. Bühne. Dessau: Szenenwechsel / Bauhaus. Theatre. Dessau: Change of Scene, ed. Torsten Blume and Burghard Duhm (Berlin, 2008).

EDITION BAUHAUS 23
Archäologie der Moderne: Sanierung Bauhaus Dessau / Archaeology of Modernism: Renovation Bauhaus Dessau, ed. Monika Markgraf (Berlin, 2006).

EDITION BAUHAUS 24
Ikone der Moderne: Das Bauhausgebäude in Dessau / Icons of Modernism: The Bauhaus Building Dessau, ed. Walter Prigge (Berlin, 2006).

EDITION BAUHAUS 25
Transnationale Räume / Transnational Spaces, ed. Regina Bittner et al. (Berlin, 2007).

EDITION BAUHAUS 32
Bauhaus Streit: 1919–2009, Kontroversen und Kontrahenten, ed. Philipp Oswalt (Berlin and Ostfildern, 2009).

EDITION BAUHAUS 33
Internationale Bauausstellung Stadtumbau Sachsen-Anhalt 2010: Weniger ist Zukunft, 19 Städte – 19 Themen, ed. Ministry of Regional Development and Transport of the State of Saxony-Anhalt, exh. cat. Stiftung Bauhaus Dessau (Berlin, 2010).

EDITION BAUHAUS 34
Kurt Kranz, Schwarz. Weiß / Weiß. Schwarz (Leipzig, 2011).

EDITION BAUHAUS 35
Raumpioniere in ländlichen Regionen: Neue Wege der Daseinsvorsorge, ed. Kerstin Faber and Philipp Oswalt (Leipzig, 2013).

The Bauhaus Dessau Foundation also publishes the *Bauhaus Taschenbuch* series and *Bauhaus* magazine.

More information is available at
www.spectorbooks.com
and www.bauhaus-dessau.de

B
A
U
H
A
U
S

D
E
S
S
A
U

PUBLICATION

This book is published in conjunction with the exhibition *The Bauhaus in Calcutta: An Encounter of Cosmopolitan Avant-Gardes*
March 27 – June 30, 2013
Bauhaus Dessau

Editors: Regina Bittner and Kathrin Rhomberg for the Bauhaus Dessau Foundation, www.bauhaus-dessau.de
Managing editor: Katja Szymczak
Translation: Rebecca Philipps Williams
Copyediting: Dawn Michelle d'Atri
Graphic design: Nicole Six & Paul Petritsch
Typesetting: Anne Meyer
Production: Julia Günther, Hatje Cantz
Reproductions: Pixelstorm, Vienna
Typeface: Korpus, Theinhardt
Paper: Hello Silk, 115 g/m^2; Munken Lynx, 100 g/m^2
Printing and binding: DZA Druckerei zu Altenburg GmbH, Altenburg

Edition Bauhaus 36

Published by
Hatje Cantz Verlag
Zeppelinstrasse 32
73760 Ostfildern
Germany
Tel. +49 711 4405-200
Fax +49 711 4405-220
www.hatjecantz.com

Hatje Cantz books are available internationally at selected bookstores. For more information about our distribution partners, please visit our website at www.hatjecantz.com.

ISBN 978-3-7757-3657-2 (English)
ISBN 978-3-7757-3656-5 (German)

Printed in Germany

Cover illustration © Rabindra-Bhavan-Archiv, Shantiniketan

EXHIBITION

Curatorial team: Regina Bittner and Kathrin Rhomberg with Sria Chatterjee, Boris Friedewald, and Partha Mitter
Exhibition coordination: Katja Szymczak
Conceptual advising: Ranjit Hoskote
Scholarly advising: Sanjukta Sunderason, Tapati Guha-Thakurta, Kris Manjapra, and R. Shiva Kumar
Intern: Tim Leik
Film and photography: Thomas Lehner
Exhibition design: Nicole Six & Paul Petritsch
Exhibition setup: Rüdiger Messerschmidt, Holger Ziolkowski, and Henning Seilkopf
Editorial support: Lutz Schöbe
Communications and public relations: Ingolf Kern and Gesine Bahr
Head of administration: Florian Bolenius
Financial administration: Monika Lieweke
Director and executive board: Philipp Oswalt

LENDERS

Art Konsult Gallery, New Delhi
Bauhaus-Archiv Museum für Gestaltung, Berlin
Walter Feilchenfeldt, Zurich
Boris Friedewald, Berlin
Centre Pompidou, Museé national d'art moderne / Centre de creation industrielle, Paris
Chitrakoot Art Gallery, Kolkata
Delhi Art Gallery, New Delhi
E. W. K., Bern
Gerhard-Marcks-Stiftung, Bremen
Ibero-Amerikanisches Institut Berlin – Stiftung Preußischer Kulturbesitz
Kulturhistorisches Museum Rostock
MART, Museo d'arte moderna e contemporanea di Trento e Rovereto
Partha Mitter, Oxford
Museum Folkwang, Essen
Museum für Asiatische Kunst – Staatliche Museen zu Berlin
National Gallery of Modern Art, New Delhi
Nirmalya Kumar, London
Private collection, Courtesy Moeller Fine Art, New York – Berlin
Sprengel Museum Hannover
Staatsbibliothek zu Berlin – Stiftung Preußischer Kulturbesitz
Stiftung Bauhaus Dessau
The Savara Foundation for the Arts, New Delhi
Universitätsbibliothek Tübingen
Vijay Aggarwal Collection, New Delhi

ACKNOWLEDGMENTS

We would like to extend our thanks to all of the institutions and individuals who have supported us in the preparation of this catalogue and exhibition:

Rajeev Lochan, Director of the National Gallery of Modern Art, New Delhi; Heiko Sievers, Director of the Goethe-Institut, Max Mueller Bhavan, New Delhi; Martin Wälde, Director of the Goethe-Institut, Max Mueller Bhavan, Kolkata; Jutta Jain-Neubauer, Cultural Department of the German Embassy, New Delhi; Martin Kämpchen, Shantiniketan; Nirmalaya Kumar, London School of Economics and Political Science; Tejendra Kumar Roy, Indian Society of Oriental Art, Kolkata; Reba Som, Indian Council for Cultural Relations, Kolkata; Raju Raman, Kolkata; Georg Lechner, Board Member at the Indien-Institut, Munich; Marion von Osten, Berlin

This exhibition and accompanying publication have been generously funded by the German Federal Cultural Foundation, the Ernst von Siemens Art Foundation, the Lotto-Toto GmbH Saxony-Anhalt, and the Institute for Foreign Cultural Relations (ifa).

The Bauhaus Dessau Foundation is a nonprofit organization under German law. It is supported by the German State of Saxony-Anhalt, the German Federal Commissioner for Culture and the Media, and the City of Dessau-Roßlau.

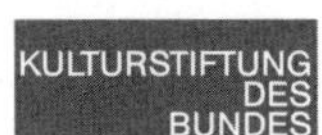

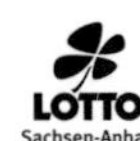

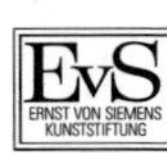

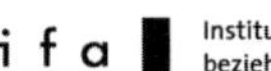

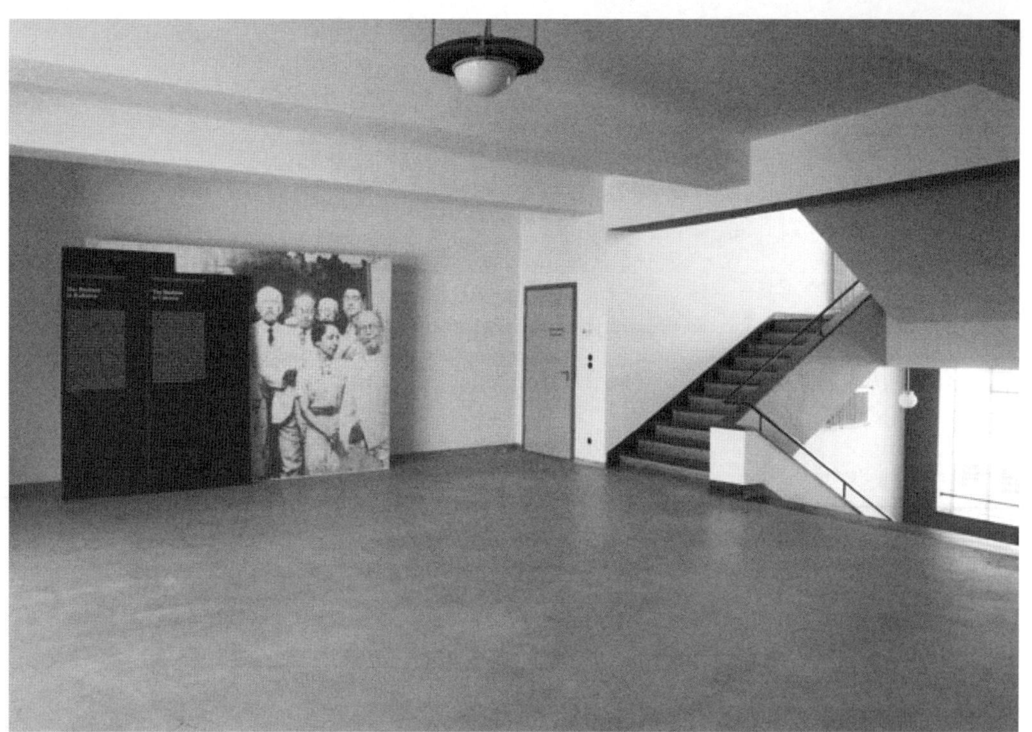

1

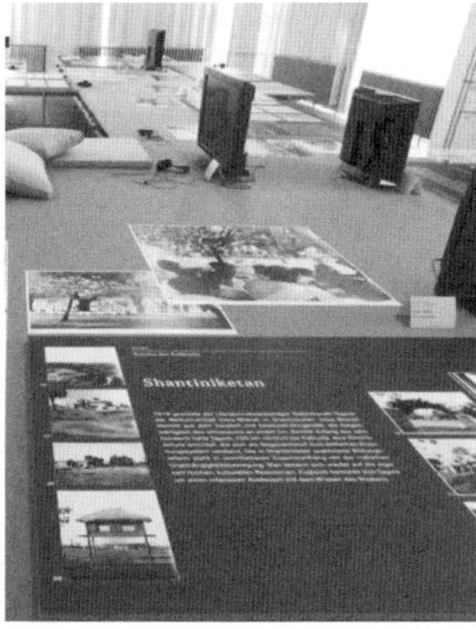

2

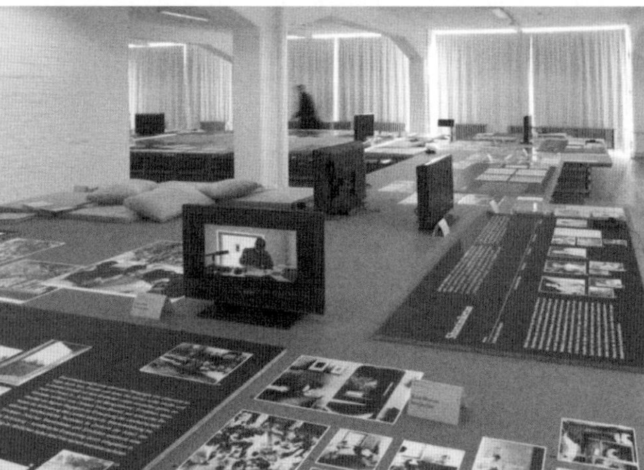

3

Captions

1–3 Installation views: documentation space
4–5 Installation views: gallery space

4

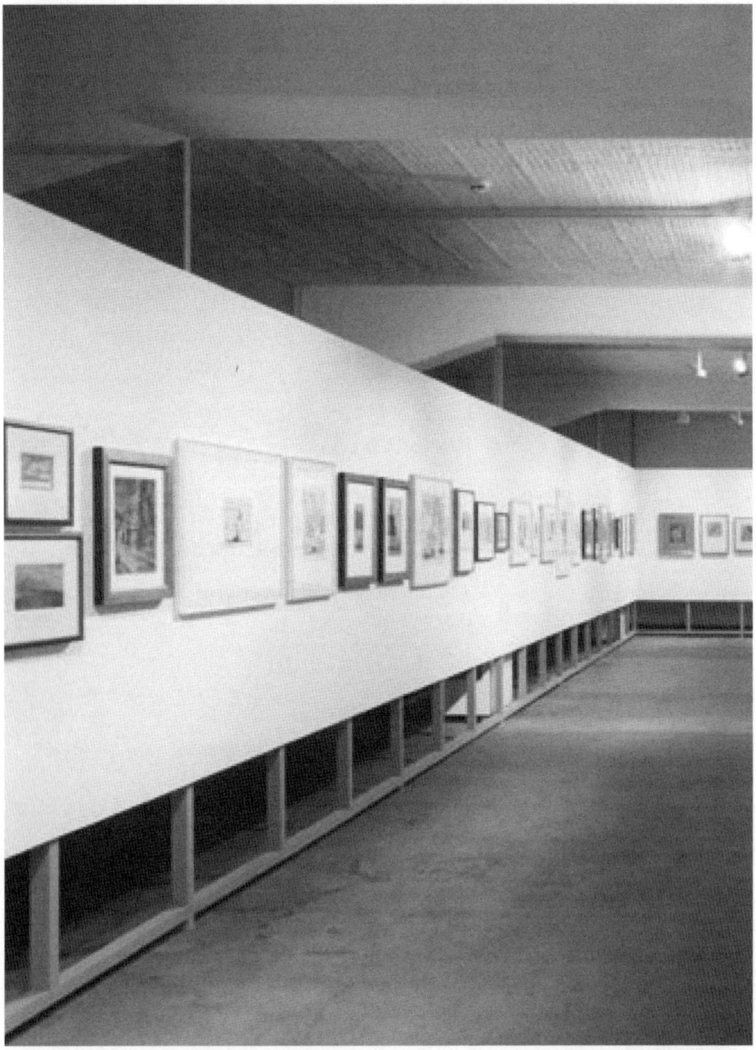

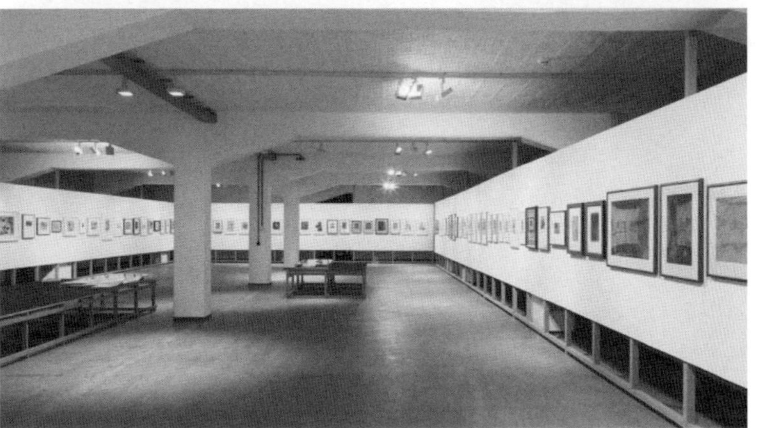

5

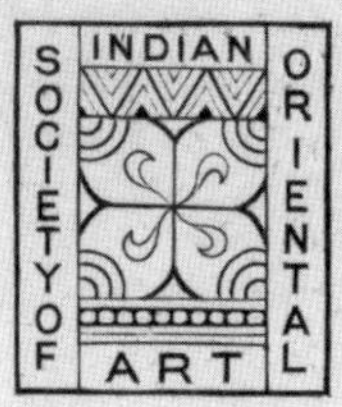

000079

SUITE NO.12.
SAMAVAYA MANSIONS.
CALCUTTA 21.3. 1923.

12.4.1923

To

Herr Lotte Husenfeld.

Adminstration Secretary.

Staatliches Bauhaus.

W E I M A R .

Dear Sir,

I am directed to inform you that pictures sent here for Exhibition have this day been sent to your address per postal parcel, which please acknowledge when received. The one by Sofie korner (no 125) is sold for £3/- which will be sent to you by next mail. The list of the pictures is sent in a different cover.

ZUR KENNTNIS
VORZULEGEN

Yours faithfully,

P. K. Chatterji

for Assistant Secretary.

Caption

Letter from the Assistant Secretary of the Indian Society of Oriental Art, P. Zhatteiger, to Lotte Husenfeld, Calcutta, March 21, 1923